The Complete B

USING A DI

for the First Time

For a complete list of Management Books 2000 titles,
visit our web-site on http://www.mb2000.com

The Complete Beginner's Guide to USING A DIGITAL CAMERA for the First Time

Bill Hall

Author of:
The Complete Beginner's Guide to
Using a Computer for the First Time
and
The Complete Beginner's Guide to
Using Email for the First Time

2000

First published in 2003 by Management Books 2000 Ltd
Forge House, Limes Road
Kemble, Cirencester
Gloucestershire, GL7 6AD, UK
Tel: 0044 (0) 1285 771441/2
Fax: 0044 (0) 1285 771055
E-mail: m.b.2000@virgin.net
Web: mb2000.com

Printed and bound in Great Britain by Biddles, Guildford

British Library Cataloguing in Publication Data is available
ISBN 1-85252-430-8

Contents

Exercises:

Contents

In Ch 9:

In Ch10:

Introduction
– the Scope of this Book

This book is the third in the 'First Time' series of computer guides and its aim is to provide instructions on using a digital camera, the accompanying software and a photo-quality inkjet printer. It will be of particular value to people who may have no expert on hand to teach them, or those who prefer to learn by themselves at their own pace.

Like the two in the same series before it, this book has a narrative style that is easy to read. It teaches by example using a number of practical exercises for you to follow, and each step is carefully explained and illustrated so that you always know what to do next. I am a firm believer in the principle of learning technology by yourself and at your own speed. By doing things in this way, you are not dependant on others, and you can build your own confidence and knowledge slowly, in such a manner that what you learn is much more likely to be remembered. Even if you do forget one item or another, you will know that you have done it before, and you know where to go to refresh your memory. That is the real advantage of a book over a live tutor – the book can be with you for twenty-four hours in the day, and is always there ready, waiting and willing to help!

When an old hand begins to write a beginner's guide, it is all too easy to forget what it was like when starting out. Knowledge and skills are very difficult things to remove, and often the old hand will miss out writing some very simple and seemingly obvious comments that a beginner would really appreciate. I recognise this fact only too well, and that is the reason why I like to use a team of two or three people to independently work through my writing and tell me when I am committing the same cardinal sin. I leave them much to their own devices, and they report back to me if I haven't explained something that I should have, or in a manner to their liking. This principle was used to great effect in writing this book, just as it was to the other books in the series. I am much indebted to the team and I thank them for all their hard work. You, the reader, are the beneficiary of this approach.

Skimming quickly through the topics covered, the first half of the book begins with a quick overview in Chapter 1 explaining how the digital camera works. It then moves on in Chapter 2 to examine the first use of the camera and taking pictures. This chapter ends with how to show these pictures on an ordinary TV set, so even if you don't possess a computer, you can still see the pictures on a big screen. Chapter 3 demonstrates how pictures can be transferred to a personal computer via cable, and provides some good advice on the connections. Chapter 4 will then show you how to first view them on the computer and how you might want to adjust them in software to make an even better picture than the one you first took. Chapter 5 talks about photo-quality inkjet printers, and how you can install such a printer for yourself. This chapters ends with printing out your very first quality digital photograph, and shows you how you use a personal trimmer to cut your pictures out and trim them, from large sheets of paper.

The second half of the book covers the process of producing digital photographs in much more detail. Chapter 6 tells you in depth all about the features you will find on a good digital camera and provides more exercises to understand them fully. Chapter 7 has more to say about using software to enhance your pictures, to add text captions and speech bubbles. This chapter ends with laying out several pictures onto one large sheet, so that you can print them out in one go. Chapter 8 then tells you more about photo-quality printers and how to get the best quality photographs.

The final two chapters take you beyond photographs. Chapter 9 covers the use of email to send your pictures to relatives and friends, and it solves a problem experienced by many of the picture being too large to see properly, when it is received at the distant end.

Chapter 10 shows you how you can use your digital camera to have video link ups with your family and friends over the Internet. This is so simple to do, yet so very effective. When I first wrote the exercises in this chapter, I tested them out and I could not believe what I was really seeing! This chapter is magic!

Finally, to show you what a digital camera has in store for you, here is an example of what you can expect to produce ...

May your first ugly duckling attempts grow into beautiful ones just like this – enjoy yourself!

Bin Ham.

Acknowledgements

I would very much like to thank the following people for their valued contributions in making this book a reality ... Eileen and Gordon Gowthorpe, and Vic Reading, who were my three test team members for this third book. They have read each chapter as it was produced, and worked through all the exercises. It was hard work for them but their feedback has been excellent. Ana Tarazona, Andy Ford and Cameron Macsween, of Digital Dream Co. Europe Ltd, for their very valuable help and support with camera queries. Annette Bontke and Jody Haskayne, of Tiscali UK Ltd, for their help and patience in receiving my emails and responding so promptly. Jill Wardropper and Lindsay Baldwin, of the Hewlett Packard Company, for help and support in respect of printer queries. Mark Taylor, of Dahle UK Ltd, for his help with personal trimmer queries. James Alexander, of Management Books 2000 Ltd, for his guidance in steering this book to its finished form, and for his patience too. And finally once more, I must thank my wife Norma, who greatly deserves credit for her faith and sharing the burdens of producing it.

Conventions used in this book

Throughout this book, there are a number of practical exercises for readers to perform using their own computer systems. During these exercises, readers are asked to carry out certain actions with their mouse or keyboard. The following conventions have been adopted in describing these actions:

click   This means swiftly press and release the normal left mouse button.

right-click   This means swiftly press and release the right mouse button.

drag   This means press the left mouse button and keep it pressed as you move the mouse pointer to a new position. Only release the left mouse button when you have reached the new position.

press   Unless the text specifically refers to a keyboard key, this means position the mouse pointer over an 'on-screen' button and then press and release the left mouse button.

select   This refers to a menu and means position the mouse pointer over the item to be selected, then press and release the normal left mouse button.

1

How Digital Pictures Are Made

1.1 Opening remarks

Welcome to the amazing world of digital cameras. In this book I hope to show you that digital pictures are worth a lot more than a thousand words! To help you learn about digital cameras in a very simple way, I am going to use the same method in the forthcoming chapters that I have with other books in the 'First Time' series. This is to guide you by providing illustrated step-by-step exercises that you can study and copy for yourself. The digital camera I will be using is a low cost but fully featured model that you can readily purchase from most high street stores. If you have not yet bought a camera, you may choose to buy this same model – then following my worked exercises will be easier than 'falling off a log'. If you already possess a digital camera, you may have some interpretation to do to match up my instructions with the controls of your particular model, but these same exercises will still be able to guide you along and achieve the desired end results.

The specific camera I have chosen for this book is called the **epsilon 1.3** made by the Digital Dream company, and I will be using the 'gift pack' version, which has an additional higher capacity memory card and tripod stand included. A very interesting characteristic of this camera is that it has a TV output connection for connecting the camera directly to a television set by a simple cable. You can therefore view all of the pictures that you take with it on an ordinary television set, providing that either the TV set itself or your video recorder has a 'video signal' input connection. Most modern appliances have these input connections, and this is a very handy way to see your digital pictures on a large screen without showing them on a personal computer. If your family or friends come to visit then you can show them your pictures in the comfort of the living room, instead of huddling around a computer screen in a small study or bedroom!

To get the real benefits of digital photography, you will need the use a personal computer, and you may choose to use a colour printer too. For a number of the worked exercises in this book, I shall be using a low-cost photo quality inkjet printer. As before with the camera, if you decide to purchase the same specific model then you will find it very easy to follow and you can print out your pictures to get some very stunning results. The printer model is called the **HP Photosmart 7150** from the Hewlett Packard company, and, like the camera, it is an excellent product. If you don't want to use your own colour printer, then you can still obtain colour prints by employing the services of various third party companies that offer to print your pictures for you. Many high street stores now provide this facility and you can also find companies on the Internet.

Let us now begin our journey into this world of digital cameras with an overview of how to produce your own photographs. We will commence at the point of picking up a camera and clicking the shutter, and work our way through to printing out the resultant picture and holding it in our hands. After reading the overview, you then will understand and appreciate the various stages involved.

1.2   The digital camera

To create a digital photograph, you start by taking a picture with the digital camera in a very similar fashion to using an ordinary film camera. The digital camera has a glass lens system and shutter button, just the same as an ordinary camera, but the process of capturing and storing images is where things begin to differ.

Because digital cameras are 'all-electronic' devices, you must always first switch them on so that battery power is applied to the internal electronics. Some conventional film cameras also use electronics and they too have an on/off battery power switch.

Whereas with a conventional camera the image for the picture is captured and stored internally on a photographic film, with a digital camera the image is captured by a special electronic 'chip' that has a very clever and very detailed surface layer covered in a myriad of tiny light sensitive areas.

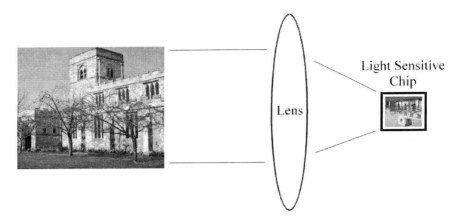

Light Sensitive
Chip

Lens

These tiny areas are arranged in a rectangular grid of rows and columns. When the chip is switched on, the image from the camera lens falls upon the surface of the chip, and each tiny area receives a different amount of light. If we could take a closer look at the surface of the chip with the picture focussed upon it (and appearing the right way up!), it might appear something like this...

The light that is falling upon every tiny area is converted into its own individual digital signals, defining both the colour and the intensity of light that the area is receiving. The collection of all such signals coming from each and every area is what makes the complete digital picture. These areas are technically referred to as pixels, being a new jargon word derived from two ordinary words – 'picture elements'.

It is because these tiny areas (the pixels) are arranged very regularly in their rows and columns that we are able to reconstruct the picture at a later time – for example in a photograph – just from the complete collection of all their signals. We know where every area is in the matrix of rows and columns, and its digital signals tell us the colour and intensity of each tiny piece of light that has to be reproduced there in the reconstructed picture. This effectively is 'painting by numbers' on a very grand scale!

The final quality of the digital picture that we take is very much dependent on the size and total number of these pixels. The smaller their size, and the greater their number, then the finer the detail our picture will contain. In real life cameras, the actual total runs to a very large number so we use the prefix word 'mega' to refer to each million. We talk about digital cameras having so many megapixels, and now you can appreciate that this is referring to the number of millions of picture element areas on the surface of the light sensitive chip. Generally speaking, the higher the megapixel number the better the quality of the camera (and the more expensive it becomes!). However, a very high number of megapixels can prove to be a mixed blessing. There are occasions when too many can be a bit of a handicap and we shall see why later in the book.

To take the digital picture, we now press the shutter button, just as we would do for an ordinary camera. What this does is to 'freeze' the state of the electronic signals coming from each pixel at that very instant when the shutter button is pressed. Once frozen, further electronic circuitry inside the camera then rapidly scans through the signals coming from each area in turn, measuring them as a pure number and transferring these numbers to the electronic memory of the camera. When they have all been measured and transferred then the picture has been 'taken'.

Now here is a very important point to understand and remember. If there are 'millions' of signals to measure and transfer, then even at the speed of electronic circuitry (which is microseconds) it takes a good second or two to complete the lot. As you might imagine, there is a great deal of work to do! So when you come to press the shutter button of a digital camera, you will discover that quite markedly it seems to be much, much slower to 'take the picture' than it does for a conventional film camera. This is one of the small drawbacks with digital cameras. However, there are plenty of serious advantages to compensate, as we shall discover.

We may now appreciate that the **memory** inside the camera – being the place where the digital numbers for our pictures are transferred to and stored – is the equivalent of the 'film' in a conventional camera. As each digital picture is taken, so this memory begins to fill up. The memory starts out life being completely empty (before any pictures have been taken) and eventually will become full. Once it is full up, then you cannot take any more pictures until either ...

    a.   You have transferred them out of the camera into a computer (or other form of electronic storage),

or ...

    b.   You have deleted them (effectively throwing the pictures away).

This is one of the practical advantages of a digital camera. When you remove the pictures from the **memory**, it becomes empty and you can use it again. Over and over again! This is really the equivalent of a re-usable 'film'. Thank heavens at last, you may say. No more fiddling about trying to rewind an old exposed film and threading a new one!

Another big advantage with this digital technology is that you can also transfer a picture out of a digital camera before you have completely filled up the memory. Now this is a major step forward from the old conventional cameras. No longer do you have to wait several weeks for the 'film' to be used up! You can get to see your pictures (and print them out if you want to) literally minutes after you have taken them. Furthermore, if you don't like them, you may be able to go back and take them again!

These are just a few of the benefits of a digital camera.

Okay. So much for an overview of what happens inside the camera. Now how do we transfer digital pictures out of the camera? This we discuss in the next section.

1.3 Transferring pictures to a PC

There are several methods by which pictures can be transferred from a digital camera to a personal computer (a PC). Probably the most common method is by using a special cable. One end of the cable is plugged into a small socket located on the side of the camera, and the other end is plugged into the computer.

To perform the transfer, you need to run a particular program on the computer that sends command signals to the camera. The camera responds automatically to these commands by returning copies of its pictures back down the cable and into the computer. The technical term for this process is known as 'downloading' and when they arrive within the computer, the pictures can be stored on the hard drive for safe keeping. What is actually travelling down the cable is simply a mass of numbers. This is the digital signal information previously stored in the camera's memory.

This term 'downloading' that I have mentioned here is going to get me into trouble with a few purists. It is a debatable point as to whether it should really be called 'uploading' instead. It is all about which end of the cable should be considered as 'up' and which end considered as 'down'. Either way, the essential point is that we are 'loading' from the camera into the computer. Many big name camera companies also call it downloading so I'm in good company even if not strictly correct!

Note

The term 'downloading' should normally be used for transferring or 'loading' information from a **major or larger** computer storage device to a **minor or smaller** one, and the term 'uploading' should be used for transferring in the opposite direction (Oxford English Reference Dictionary, revised second edition 2002).

At the end of the transfer process, the computer may or may not send signals to the camera to tell it to erase the picture information from the camera's memory. This usually depends on how you use the controlling program. It is possible to simply copy this information without erasing it from the camera. Obviously to empty the memory, you need to make sure that the 'delete camera pictures' option or command is chosen following the transfer.

With some cameras, you must first turn a switch to the 'transfer position' before it will accept the computer's command signals. With the camera that we shall be describing in this book this is not the case. It instantly realises that you want to transfer pictures as soon as the cable is plugged into both itself and the computer, and it prepares itself accordingly.

Another common feature that you may experience with quite a number of the latest types of digital camera (and it is true for the one I shall be illustrating) is that when the connecting cable is attached, then the camera 'behaves' as though it was a new 'removable disk drive' for the computer with its own 'drive letter'. If you are familiar with disk drives and drive letters, then the meaning of this statement will be obvious to you so you may skip over the next paragraph.

If you are not so familiar, then what I'm getting at is that the camera behaves like a new form of memory disk, similar to a hard disk, floppy disk, or CD-ROM disk. Each of these three disk types has its own mechanics inside the computer's central processor box, where you insert these disks. These mechanics are generally described in computer jargon as 'drives' and each one has an alphabetic letter together with the colon symbol to refer to it. For example, the floppy disk is known as the A: drive, the hard disk is the C: drive, and maybe the CD-ROM disk becomes the D: drive. Well, when the camera is connected by the cable to the computer, then its own memory can appear to the computer as though it was a new E: drive or possibly an F: drive. This makes life a lot simpler when you wish to transfer or delete pictures inside the camera because you can use the regular computer commands such as **'Cut'**, **'Copy'**, **'Paste'** or **'Delete'**, which are available in many programs and also available from the desktop folder known as 'My Computer'.

 If you want to learn more about drives and drive letters, read section 8.3 of the first book in the series titled *'Using a Computer for the First Time'*, which Note goes into this business in much further detail.

There are alternative methods of transferring the pictures from a camera to a computer other than by using a connecting cable. The camera's memory often takes the form of a small removable component that you can physically take out of the camera body. When you do so, the pictures will still be safely held inside it. Memory like this which retains information, even after it has been disconnected form the source of electrical power, is called **non-volatile memory**.

You will see various designs of removable non-volatile memory in high street camera shops with names such as 'CompactFlash' 'SmartMedia' or the very latest form is called 'SD' (short for Secure Digital). The term 'CompactFlash' by the way has nothing whatsoever to do with the flash bulb of a normal camera, it is an unfortunate term that has emerged independently from the world of electronics ('flash' memory is electronic memory that can be reprogrammed very quickly, yet retains its information long term) The picture on the left below shows a 'CompactFlash' card, and the picture of the right shows a 'SmartMedia' one.

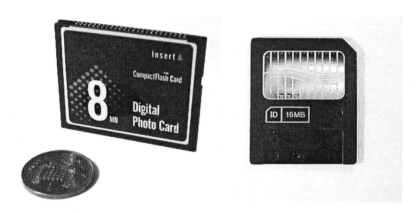

If you purchase the epsilon 1.3 camera as featured in this book, then the basic model has some 8 Megabytes worth of memory permanently built into the camera's electronics and this is not removable. If you purchase the camera in the gift pack box, then you receive the same basic camera plus an additional 16 Megabyte 'SmartMedia' card, which is removable, just like the one in the picture shown on the right above. For those readers who don't buy the gift pack, you can still purchase a 'SmartMedia' card separately to insert inside your camera in order to have removable memory. These cards come in different memory capacity sizes and you should think about buying the largest one that you can reasonably afford, so that you can store more pictures before it becomes full. However, be aware at the time of writing that

128 Megabytes is the largest size that is compatible with the camera.

Because you are able to physically remove the memory component, and because it is non-volatile, you may take it out of the camera and fit it into an adapter that connects directly into the computer hardware. There are various designs of adapter ranging from the 'floppy disk look-alike' (which allows the memory to pretend it is a floppy disk and you can then slot it into the floppy disk drive) to the USB (Universal Serial Bus) adapter that allows you to plug it into one of the USB sockets at the rear of the computer. If you are new to USB sockets, we talk about them more in section 3.2 and you will find a picture there too.

Okay, we have discussed the transfer of pictures from the camera into a PC. Let us now investigate what we can do to manipulate these once they are in there, before attempting to print them out as a digital photograph.

1.4   Adjusting the pictures with software

With your digital pictures now stored inside the computer, the next stage is to prepare them ready for printing out on a printer. Before you go ahead and start your print, you might like to view them first on the computer monitor screen and maybe make a few adjustments.

Up until a few years ago, the type of program that you would use for the task of viewing and manipulation was generally referred to as a 'graphics-editing program'. These are very powerful programs handling all manner of graphic images, not just those pictures from digital cameras. They are packed with many different features and require a high level of skill to use them properly. Nowadays, with the rapid growth and development of digital cameras, a number of much simpler programs have come onto the market dedicated to handling photographic style pictures. These are much easier to use and are generally referred to as 'photo-editing programs'. The one we shall be using later in this book is a special edition of a program known as MGI PhotoSuite 4. This comes free with the epsilon 1.3 camera but is also available as a stand-alone product that you can buy from software suppliers. The camera also comes with some other free programs for you to use, but more of these later in the book.

One of the beauties of digital photography is that you have much more personal control over the exact form of the final picture. You can, if you want to, simply print the picture exactly as it appeared when you took it, or you can make some changes.

22

In the next illustration, we can see a typical scene of a churchyard. If I wish to only show the church building in my final image, I can reduce the whole picture content to just the part outlined inside the black rectangular line. This type of operation is known as 'cropping' the picture, and it is a very useful way of quickly rearranging the central focus of the final image. It is also a useful way for excluding unwanted parts of a picture, such as the shadows cast over on the left-hand side. You can see the full effect of the cropping operation by comparing this illustration with the very first one in this chapter demonstrating the lens and the light sensitive chip.

There are many other ways that you can adjust the picture before you actually print it. For example, you can enlarge the whole image or make it smaller – you can change the colours or 'touch up' areas where a blemish is spoiling the look of it – you can even add other things to it such as text labels and 'speech bubbles' (the sort of thing that you find in comic strips!) to add information or a touch of humour to the final photos. When you get really clever, you can merge parts of one picture onto the main image of another picture to create a 'merged' image. The old adage of 'the camera never lies'

is even further from the truth now than it has ever been! (Was it ever true?). You should definitely never believe what you see in a photograph these days!

When you have finished with the preparation work, you are then ready to make the final print on photographic quality printer paper.

1.5   Printing on the printer

The fourth and final stage is the use of the computer program to send the image for printing to the printer. In making a printed photograph from the image that we have created, we shall use a type of printer that is known as a colour inkjet printer. This is a very common type of printer in use these days and can print in a wide range of colours. The specific model used in the exercises of this book – the **HP Photosmart 7150** – has a recommended retail price at the time of writing of around £149, and if you shop around you may be able to purchase it at a lower price.

Inkjet printers have come a long way in terms of performance in a very short space of time. When I first started my own experiments with digital pictures, I used a general-purpose inkjet and produced some reasonably good results. However, the 'photo' type of inkjet printers available today are even better and the quality of digital photographs you can now make for yourself these days is just fantastic.

To achieve photographic quality prints, we don't use the ordinary type of printer paper. We use a special photographic paper (readily available in the high street) that can be bought with a matt, a satin, or a high gloss 'finish' to it. This paper is much thicker than the standard type of printer paper and is designed to dry the ink very quickly so that there is less risk of smudging it when it comes out of the printer. It is also designed to give high-fidelity colour reproduction.

This photographic paper comes in different sizes. You can purchase the exact size of paper for your photographs, such as the standard 150mm x 100mm (6in by 4in). In this case you have no cutting to do. Or you can buy full size sheets such as the standard European A4 size, and print several different pictures on the same sheet. With this larger size paper, you will have to cut the paper in order to separate out the photographs. Later in this book, I will show you how you can use the **Dahle Personal Trimmer** to cut the paper evenly and squarely, in order to get a good edge and a nice rectangular photograph. If you are going to make even a moderate number of your own photographs, this trimmer is a sound investment.

And there we have it. This quick overview of the whole process has taken us from end to end. To summarise, the four stages are:

✓   1. Take the picture with the camera.

✓   2. Transfer the picture from the camera to a computer.

✓   3. Make any adjustments that you wish to the picture.

✓   4. Print it out on a photo quality colour printer

There are many variations to these four stages that you may practically come across with different digital cameras and different colour printers, but these are the basic steps in the overall process of producing a digital photograph. We are now ready to get into the practical exercises and start taking some pictures with the camera, which we do in the next chapter.

2

About the Camera

2.1 Unpacking and fitting the batteries

The epsilon 1.3 camera from Digital Dream is available at the time of writing in two versions. The picture here shows the 'Gift Pack' version, which includes a 16 Megabyte 'SmartMedia' memory card and a small silver tripod. The standard pack does not include these two items, but you can purchase SmartMedia memory cards from many high street stores. The fitting on the base of the camera for the tripod is also a universal standard fitting so you can purchase your own tripod as well if you want to. Throughout this book, I will be describing and using the 'Gift Pack' version. If you have the standard version then there will be a few items mentioned in the text that are not included.

Should you decide to purchase a SmartMedia memory card separately, the compatible sizes are from 16 Megabytes to 128 Megabytes. Obviously, the larger the capacity, then the more pictures you can take and store in the camera before you are forced to transfer them. Choosing a large capacity can be an important consideration in some circumstances. For example, I always take my digital camera on holiday, and I use a very large capacity memory card so that I don't have to worry about transferring pictures while I am away.

Note

Before we proceed, let me just mention a little word of caution about all forms of memory cards. For those where the contacts are exposed – as with the SmartMedia cards – do try and avoid touching these contacts with your fingers. Hold them only by the plastic body. There are two reasons for this. One is that static electricity from your hand can damage the sensitive internal card electronics; the other is that natural oils from your fingers will be deposited on the contact surface.

Now we begin the first of our practical exercises ...

Exercise 1 – Preparing the camera for use and switching on and off

Remove all items from the presentation box and identify the following:

1. The camera itself.
2. A black camera case.
3. Four AAA size batteries (inside the case).
4. A small safety strap to attach to the camera body and a larger black shoulder strap (also inside the case).
5. The SmartMedia memory card (gift pack only).
6. The silver tripod (gift pack only).

Also included in the underside of the box are:

7. A small clear plastic case containing labels and silver 'write protect' dots for the SmartMedia card (gift pack only).
8. A quick reference guide booklet.
9. A sample colour digital photograph.
10. A 5-year guarantee slip with an offer for 6 free glossy photo prints from the favourite pictures of your choice. To get these prints sent to you, log on to the Digital Dream website at www.digitaldreamco.com and follow some simple instructions to transfer your pictures.
11. A video cable to connect your camera to a TV set.
12. A USB cable to transfer pictures from the camera to a computer.
13. A CD-ROM in a white paper envelope containing computer software.

Note   The silver 'write protect' dots in item 7 are similar in action to the write protect tab for floppy disks. They should not be used when performing exercises in this book. This is because we will want to delete digital pictures after transferring them to the PC, in order to free up the memory in the card.

Our first task after unpacking is to fit the SmartMedia memory card and batteries into the camera. Turn the camera upside down with the lens facing towards you, as shown in the pictures below.

With your right thumb in the dimple of the battery compartment lid, press it down slightly and slide it to the right to open up a gap, as seen in the left picture. Then flip up the lid to open the compartment.

If you have the gift pack version, you should now fit the memory card. If you haven't, don't worry because the camera itself has 8 Megabytes of memory permanently built in to it for you to take pictures with.

Take the SmartMedia memory card and turn it upside down so that the 'cut-away' corner is bottom left and the gold contacts are facing you. Insert it into the thin narrow slot furthest away from you, as shown in the middle of the previous pictures. The label marked 'IN' is a little confusing. The arrow on the label is not pointing to the slot where it should go, but is simply trying to show you which way around the gold contacts should be facing (the arrow is actually pointing at the battery slot!). Now push it fully home into the slot, as shown in the right-hand picture. You may feel the contacts engaging as you slide it in.

Next we fit the batteries, and we must take great care here to make sure that these are inserted into the four battery slots the right way round. If you look carefully, there is a small diagram visible just on the inside of the battery slots, but this too may be a bit confusing. The diagram is actually showing you how the 'tops' of the batteries should look like after they have been inserted, not which end to insert first!

Remove the AAA batteries from inside the black camera case and take off the plastic wrapping. Pick up the first battery and hold it with the little metal 'pip' end (the positive end) nearest your fingers. Pop the opposite end into the first slot on the left, and let the battery fall into place, as shown in this next picture...

Now pick up the second battery and hold it with the 'flattened' end (the negative end) nearest your fingers. Pop the opposite end with the little metal 'pip' into the slot second from the left and let it fall into place.

The third battery is just like the first, and the fourth battery is like the second. When you have all the batteries correctly inserted, just check that they appear like this...

Okay, the next operation of closing the battery compartment lid can be a little tricky! When the first cameras were manufactured, the battery springs were a little strong and it required quite a bit of pressure to press the lid down on top of all four batteries to get it close properly and engage. On later models

these springs were made weaker. Go ahead now and close the lid, remembering it needs to overhang a bit on the right hand side. When you have it flush with the main body then you slide it to the left to complete the task. I find this easier to do this as a two handed job, with both my thumbs on the underside of the camera, and both index fingers pressing down on top of the lid. The secret of success is shown in the next picture!

 Tip – If you have a problem closing the lid, lift it up again and press down on each battery in turn to collapse the springs a little more. Then close the lid using two hands to press it flush to the camera body and slide it to the left, to engage the hooks that hold it shut.

With the lid closed, we are ready to switch the camera on for the first time. The picture below shows the Battery Power On/Off button and the rotary Function switch...

Function Switch

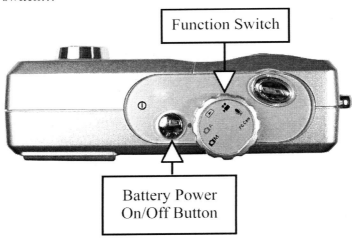

Battery Power On/Off Button

Turn the Function switch such as to make sure that the green symbol marked 'A' is next to the red dot (this red dot tells you which function is currently selected). You should notice in rotating the switch that each function position has a definite 'feel' to it, where it 'clicks' into place when you have it rotated sufficiently. The 'A' here means 'Automatic' and whenever you use this function, all of the settings for the camera – that is the shutter speed and other variable adjustments – are monitored and adjusted 'fully automatically' for the prevailing light conditions. As those conditions change, then the settings will change accordingly.

Now press and hold down the Battery Power On/Off button for about two seconds. This will switch the camera on. (Notice that you must keep this button pressed just a little longer than you might at first expect). You will then see a little red light appear on the back panel, to the right of the viewfinder, to show you that power is on. At that moment you can take your finger off the button. Wait for another six or seven seconds and you will see the light change colour to orange and flicker once or twice, eventually changing its colour to a steady green. You will also see that the 'Monitor Screen' on the back panel lights up and shows a picture. This picture is a 'live' picture of whatever the camera lens happens to be pointing at, at the time. If you move the camera left and right, you will notice the picture changing sympathetically!

Be aware that there is a 'power-saving' feature built in to the camera, which we will describe in a moment. If this catches you out and switches the camera off, you will need to press the Power On/Off button once again to switch it back on!

Okay. Move the camera around now and point it at different things, keeping a watch on the picture displayed on the Monitor Screen. You should see the 'automatic' feature start to operate. If you point the camera towards a very bright subject, for example the light from a window or a light bulb, then at first the picture becomes too bright. After a second or two, the automatic adjustments begin to work and the picture improves such that contrast and brightness alter to give you a much clearer image. Now move the camera to point to a darker subject, for example the floor, and see the opposite effect happen.

This 'Automatic' function that we have selected on the Function switch is probably the one that you are going to use most with the camera. It is the second function position on the switch, the first being a 'Manual' mode of operation. We shall say more about the 'Manual' mode in chapter 6.

I would now like to demonstrate the power saving features. Don't press any buttons but simply watch the picture on the Monitor Screen. After the camera has been switch on for one minute, you will hear two rapid beeps sound from the internal speaker inside the camera, the Monitor Screen display will no longer show any picture, and the green light flickers to an orange colour momentarily and then goes back to green. This is the 'power saving' feature operating. If you leave the camera switched on indefinitely without taking any pictures, then the power in the batteries would be consumed unnecessarily. To help save battery life, the power saver feature shuts down all of the heavy current consuming features (the Monitor Screen in particular is a very 'thirsty' device).

The camera is not switched off at this point, and the green light stays on to show you that the camera is still powered up. However, if you leave the camera in this condition for a further minute without pressing any buttons, then the power saver feature will switch the camera off altogether. Let us now witness this second action working by leaving the camera alone for a while longer. Eventually, you will hear a single' beep' from the speaker and the green light goes out completely. The camera is now completely switched off and if you wanted to put it back into its case and put it away, then you could do so.

Before we finish this first exercise, I would like to demonstrate how to get the camera operating again when the green light is still on but the Monitor Screen has gone blank.

Turn the camera back on by pressing the Power On/Off button again and holding it down for two seconds (this still catches me out! I don't know why but my brain keeps forgetting the two seconds!). Wait for the red light to come on, flicker orange and then turn to steady green. Okay. Now wait for the next minute to hear the two beeps and the Monitor Screen to go blank. When this has happened, just press the Power On/Off button again, but this time very quickly (don't wait two seconds). Almost instantaneously, the Monitor Screen picture comes back on again.

So, there you have it. If the Monitor Screen 'goes to sleep' then providing you click on a camera button, it will immediately wake up. Though we demonstrated this with the Power On/Off button just now, it is also true of the Shutter button too.

Well, the camera is operating now so we will complete this exercise by learning how to turn the camera off without waiting for the power saver feature to activate. With the green light showing AND the Monitor Screen working, simply press the Power On/Off button for two seconds to switch the camera off quickly and completely. By the way, if you attempt to do this when the Monitor Screen is blank, it doesn't work because the camera thinks you are trying to wake it up from power saving! Do it for a second time – when the screen is lit up again – and it will.

This concludes Exercise 1.

2.2   Taking your first digital picture

Now here is where the fun really starts!

Exercise 2 – Taking your first digital picture

At this point, we notice yet another advantage of a digital camera over a conventional camera. There are two ways you can go about taking your picture. You can use the normal viewfinder and hold it up to your eye in the time-honoured fashion, then press the Shutter button and 'bingo' … your picture has been taken. Or you can use the Monitor Screen (as we experienced it in the first exercise) to frame your picture, holding the camera a comfortable distance in front of your face so that your eyes can focus upon the screen before you press the Shutter button. We will do the latter.

If you are a person who normally wears glasses, the digital camera has mixed blessings for you. I am shortsighted, and fortunately by taking my glasses off completely, I can focus quite comfortably on pictures displayed on the Monitor Screen. You will need to find a comfortable way to operate for yourself. If you are long-sighted, or cannot otherwise focus on near objects as a result of the effects of the years rolling by, then you may need to use your reading glasses.

The Shutter button is shown in this next picture.

The Shutter button has two positions. The first is half-pressed, where you press it down until it 'clicks' and then stop when it comes up against further 'resistance'. The second is fully pressed, where you press it down to the first position, and then press it even beyond that point against the resistance.

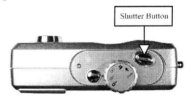

Precisely why there are two positions, we will talk about shortly, when we come to take the picture.

To get a feel for these two Shutter button positions, try out this next experiment while the camera is switched off. Stand the camera upright on a firm surface and use your index finger just to press and release the button gently several times, listening and feeling for the 'click' of the first position with each occasion that you press. When you are confident that you know what reaching this first position feels like, press once again to the first position and hold it there – and then press even further down to the second position. Notice how much more force is required to reach the second position. Slowly release back to the first position and then slowly release it altogether. Repeat this latter action (going to the first position and then on to the second) a number of times. Very soon you begin to get full appreciation of the both the point where the first position exists and the point where the second position exists. Quite importantly, if you are to avoid camera shake on your pictures, you appreciate how much more force is required to get to the second position – and it is this one that will actually take the picture.

Understanding and being able to control the Shutter Button at these two positions is not just an academic exercise, but will be of real benefit to you in a moments time.

Okay. We are almost ready to take the first picture. Turn the camera on as we did for the first exercise, and check that the Function Switch is again in the 'A' position (the green symbol is adjacent to the red dot). Wait for the Monitor Screen to power up and for the green light at the rear of the camera to come on.

In this next bit, I am going to talk about how to hold the camera. If the power saver feature should operate before you get to actually take the picture, remember to briefly click either the Power button, or the Shutter button to the first position, to wake the Monitor Screen up again!

Now exactly how you should hold the camera to take the picture depends to some extent on your eyesight! My first recommendation is shown in the left-hand picture, where the camera is fairly close up and the battery compartment lid is resting on that chunky area of your palm just below your thumb. If you can comfortably view the Monitor Screen at this close distance, then the advantage of resting against your palm is to reduce 'camera shake' when you are pressing the Shutter Button. The button is pressed by the second finger as shown in the picture, which probably has more freedom of movement than your index finger, but you can use either – whichever you feel most comfortable with.

If you find that the camera is too close for you in that position, then the alternative method of holding the camera is shown in the right-hand picture, where you hold it at arms' length more or less equally in both hands, with both of your thumbs on the underside of the camera, and using either your second or your index finger to press the Shutter button (again, whichever you are most comfortable with).

The disadvantage of this latter position is that you are more likely to get 'camera shake' on your pictures, but practically this really depends on how much light is in the scene of the picture you are trying to take. I'll explain why this is so later on in the book.

Okay. Now the moment we have been waiting for! Select a suitable person, object or view to be the 'guinea pig' for your first picture. Choose a subject that is at least a few feet away from the camera lens. Move the camera around a bit until the subject is either central to your view on the Monitor, or you have otherwise decided that you have 'framed' the picture nicely. Squeeze the Shutter button slowly down to the first position. This does not take the picture, but will then 'freeze' those fully automatic adjustments inside the camera, whose settings may have been bobbing up and down to compensate as you swung the camera around.

Now 'squeeze' the button down to the second position and hold it there until you hear a single 'beep' from the internal speaker, after which you can let it go completely. This is the action that actually takes the picture!

After you have heard the beep, you will see the green light begin to flash red and green alternately and quite rapidly, and the Monitor Screen goes blank at this time. This indicates that the camera is scanning all of those millions of tiny picture elements – the pixels – for the photograph, and measuring their independent light values as numbers, then storing this digital information away to the Memory Card. While this is going on, you cannot take another picture. You must wait for the light to stop flashing, for the Monitor Screen to change first to blue and then to start showing a picture again. Only when the Monitor screen is back displaying a picture can you then use the camera again for the next picture.

 Later in chapter 6, we will see that there is a way for you to take several pictures very quickly, 'rapid fire' as it were, one after the other. But for now, Note we have the camera settings such that we are taking single pictures.

Having taken our first picture, now you are no doubt anxious to have a look at it to see how it has turned out. We can review the pictures held within the memory of the camera at any time that we wish to, providing the camera is switched on. We do this by displaying them on the Monitor Screen, and that is the subject for the next exercise.

We are now at the end of Exercise 2. If you want to turn your camera off at this point you can do so, or you can leave it on and be ready to continue straight into Exercise 3.

2.3   Viewing the picture on the monitor screen

Exercise 3 – Viewing the first picture

If the camera is switched off, then turn it on again so that you see the green light at the rear.

Now turn the Function Switch to select the position where the 'small black arrowhead in a rectangle' is next to the red dot, as shown in the next picture.

First you will see the Monitor Screen turn blue, then an 'hourglass' will appear (telling you to wait) together with the words 'Playback Mode' written on the blue screen. After a few seconds, the picture that you took will show itself on the Monitor Screen. This next picture shows you an example of what you might see.

Well, now you can see your first picture, what do you think of it? Does it look interesting? Or did you make a mistake? If it looks good, then you are probably feeling rather pleased with yourself. If you have made a mistake, then don't be concerned. When we have taken a few more pictures, I will show you how you can delete the ones you don't wish to keep.

In the bottom left-hand corner of the screen, you will see some numbers saying '1/1' (if you were impatient and took two pictures it will show '2/2' instead). What these numbers are indicating is this...

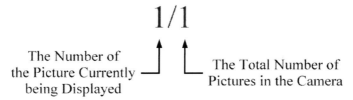

As you take more pictures then these numbers will change and increase. They will also help you to find your way backwards and forwards through the pictures stored inside the camera.

In the bottom right-hand corner you should see something like '100V1310' (or it may say 'epsilon' instead). These numbers or letters are a reference that we will meet again when we come to transferring the pictures from the camera to a computer (section 3.2).

This brings us to the end of Exercise 3.

2.4   Taking some more pictures

Having taken the first picture with the camera and viewed it, we are ready to take some more and chat a little bit about technique. We will also discuss a few tips and tricks along the way.

Exercise 4 – Taking more pictures

To become familiar with the camera generally, we shall in this exercise take nine more pictures of scenes around your house. If it is daylight outside, you can take a few inside the house first and then some more out in the garden or even out in the street. If it isn't then you will have to make do with taking them all inside. Don't worry too much about the subject matter. When we are ready, just simply point the camera towards anything that catches your eye and click away.

Note   This is the great thing about a digital camera! You can take pictures of anything and everything, and not have to worry about wasting film. If you don't like the pictures afterwards you just throw them away! How you throw them away is the subject of Exercise 6.

37

Before we get started, I want to make a few comments that you may find useful ...

While you are taking these pictures, you will begin to realise how often the power saving feature operates. Remember that when it first changes from the normal 'fully on' condition, it will beep at you twice and the Monitor Screen will go blank but the green light will stay on. If you press either the Power On/Off Button momentarily, or the Shutter Button to the first position, then it will quickly switch back out of power saving mode. Now you may be tempted to keep turning it on for all of the time, but you have to resist this temptation because when it is fully on then the battery consumption is high. If you don't resist then you will flatten the batteries much sooner than you expect to. A small icon in the bottom left-hand corner of the Monitor Screen displays the battery charge state when you are taking pictures. It shows all white when fully charged and the white changes to black as the charge runs down.

When taking these new pictures, you will also get more experience at pressing the Shutter Button fully down to the second position, to actually take the picture. Remember that you should hear a single beep from the internal speaker when you have done so. This gives you the first confirmation that the 'picture taking instant' has actually happened. If you don't hear it then chances are that you have not pressed the Shutter Button down far enough.

The 'beep' sound is meant to represent the 'clickety-clack' of a traditional camera's shutter mechanism.

Now the action of pressing the Shutter Button fully down can cause you to move the camera at that very instant when the picture is being taken. Watch out for this and try and remember that it is likely to happen. Forewarned is forearmed, as they say, and taking that extra second of care to keep the camera perfectly still – just at the right moment – will result in much better quality pictures.

Prepare the camera to take the pictures by turning the Function Switch back to the Automatic position (the one where the green camera symbol  labelled 'A' is adjacent to the red dot) as we did in Exercise 2 (for the future, I will simply refer to this as the Automatic position)...

Switch the camera on.

At this point, go ahead and take your pictures. Then come back and read the rest of this exercise where we shall review them when you have a few 'under your belt'. Don't be too fussy about the subject matter or making it your greatest work of art. We are going to delete some of them in any case!

Okay, you now have the pictures. With this little bit of experience, you probably have much more of a feel for the camera and how it works. You should have ten pictures in total inside the camera. The precise number is not important so don't worry if you have been a little too enthusiastic. The next exercise is to see how to review each of these in turn using the Monitor Screen.

This concludes Exercise 4.

Exercise 5 – Viewing all the pictures

Switch the camera on, and hold it so that the back panel is facing you. Turn the Function Switch to select the position where the 'small black arrowhead in a rectangle' is next to the red dot, as shown in the next picture. Again, to avoid describing this again in the future, I will from now on refer to this as the Viewing position …

 On the Monitor Screen, you will see it turn blue and an 'hourglass' symbol briefly displayed with the words 'Playback Mode'. A few seconds later, you will then see one of the pictures that you took. The first picture to be shown on switching to the Viewing position is always the last one taken. This is why you should now see '10/10' in the lower left-hand corner of the screen. Remember that the left number indicates the picture currently being displayed on the screen; the right one tells you the total number of pictures held in memory in the camera.

Now hold the camera with both hands as shown in this following picture, and use the 'spare' index finger (the 'pointing finger'!) to press down on the left-hand edge of the large circular button with the four triangular pointing symbols upon it (this button looks a bit like the four points of the compass that you occasionally see on old maps!).

The large circular button has four different operating switches inside it, which are activated independently, depending on which side of the 'rim' of the circle that you press down upon. It is a type of button that is becoming quite common these days on new electronic gadgets, and has more of a 'rocker' type of action to it than anything I have experienced previously. If you accidentally press on, say, the top edge (the 'North') of the circle, then something strange happens that we are not yet ready to discuss. Simple press down on the bottom edge (the 'South') to undo the accident. In viewing our pictures, we are only going to use the left and the right edges of the button's circular 'rim' (that is, for all you sailors, girl-guides and boy-scouts, the 'West' and the 'East' respectively!).

When you pressed down upon the left-hand edge of the circular button, you should have heard a high-pitched 'pip' sound (rather than a low-pitched 'beep'!). For a brief moment an 'hourglass' symbol reappears, and then the previous picture in memory becomes visible on the Monitor Screen. Witness also that the numbers in the lower left-hand corner of the screen have changed accordingly to '9/10'.

Okay, one at a time, carefully view each of the pictures that you have taken by pressing successively on the left-hand edge of the large circular button. When you examine your pictures, I think you may agree that the technology that we have at our fingertips today is truly amazing! And digital cameras have to be one of the most interesting gadgets now at our service. At each press of the left edge you go backwards in time to display your pictures successively.

When you have reached the very first picture that you took at number '1/10', press the button's left edge just one more time. Notice that the display now 'wraps-around' back to the picture numbered '10/10'. Keep on going to get to picture '7/10'. Fine, now go the other way through each picture by pressing on the right-hand edge of the large circular button. I don't think you will be too surprised to see that when you reach '10/10' and press yet again, it also wraps-around the other way as well.

Remember that you may review your pictures inside the camera at any time that you feel like it. However, the camera is in the 'fully-on' state when you do so, consuming the maximum amount of power from the internal batteries. Don't be too surprised one day if you discover that you have to replace the batteries.

When you see the message 'Low Power' appearing on the Monitor Screen, then all four the batteries will need replacing. I recommend that you use rechargeable AAA batteries instead of alkaline ones because it works out much cheaper in the long run. You might want to purchase two or three sets and a charger, so that you always have a charged set of batteries on hand to use in the camera.

This brings us to the conclusion of Exercise 5, concerning viewing pictures.

2.5   Deleting pictures from the camera

Now that you have a number of pictures taken, there are probably some that you don't want to keep. In this section we will demonstrate how to remove pictures completely from the camera. Rather than explaining the controls you need to use and all about them, I am simply going to give you a procedure for how to do it. The full explanation behind these controls is left for chapter 6.

Before you begin the exercise, use the viewing technique of the last exercise to decide which, if any, you want to delete. If you don't wish to delete any of them, then you may skip this exercise and come back to it when you do. After the exercise, I will explain another similar procedure for deleting ALL of the pictures in one go. This is not part of any exercise that I want you to do, but only something that may be of use if you make a complete mess of things!

Exercise 6 – Deleting one particular picture

1.   Switch the camera on. The Function Switch must be in the Viewing position…

2.   Use either the left or right edges of the Circular button and press a number of times in order to select and view the particular picture you wish to delete. Note the total number of pictures (the second of the two numbers in the bottom left corner).

41

3. Now press the Menu button. You should hear a 'pip' sound. A vertical menu will now appear on the screen consisting of four icon symbols. The top one will be highlighted yellow (the symbol shows a waste bin with many sheets of paper in it).

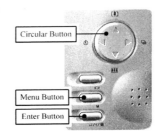

4. Press the bottom edge of the Circular button once. You should hear a 'pip'. The menu will now show the second icon symbol highlighted yellow (the symbol shows a waste bin with a single sheet of paper in it).

5. Press the Enter button. You should hear a 'pip' sound. This is the ACTION button that carries out your choice from the menu. After a second or two, you should see the picture disappear. Your picture has now been deleted. The picture numbering will readjust itself and you should notice that the total number of pictures has now decreased by one.

Can you undo the deletion? No. It has gone for good.

6. Press the Menu button once again to remove the menu from the display. This concludes exercise 6.

Now if you have made a complete mess of the whole business so far, I will now give you a procedure to delete ALL of the pictures stored in the camera. ONLY do this procedure if you want to start all over again. You will need some pictures for the next and subsequent exercises, so only delete them all if you are absolutely sure. You will then have to retake some more.

To delete ALL of your pictures:

A. Switch the camera on. The Function Switch must be in the Viewing position.

B. Press the Menu button (the middle one).

C. Press the Enter button (the bottom one). The screen now shows you a warning message 'Delete All? (OK)'. The next step will delete them all!

D. Press the Enter button again (the bottom one).

E. The screen now turns blue and says 'No Image'. All of the pictures have now been deleted!

Let me end with a final word of caution. The two procedures for deleting only one picture and deleting all pictures are only slightly different. They differ essentially in which icon from the menu is highlighted yellow when you then press the Enter button. The first icon is the wastebasket with many sheets of paper in it – this is the delete ALL icon. The second icon is the wastebasket with a single sheet of paper in it – this is the delete ONE picture only icon. Don't get them mixed up!

2.6   Viewing the pictures on TV

If you have ever fancied seeing yourself, your spouse or your partner on the telly, then this is your opportunity!

Amongst the accessories that came with your camera is a video cable (it was item 11 in Exercise 1). This is a black cable with a yellow 'phono' type plug on one end and a black miniature jack plug at the other. The cable is shown in this next picture with the miniature jack on the left, and the phono plug on the right ...

The first job is to find a suitable Video 'Phono' socket style connector on either the TV set or (possibly more convenient sited) on a Video Recorder that you can use in conjunction with the TV set, to be able to attached it electrically with the camera. You don't have to use a Video Recorder, but if you don't then you may need to have a special type of connector on your telly called a SCART connector, which I discuss later on. Now I am going to  apologise unreservedly for the rest of the text in this section if it gets a bit complicated. Do bear with me because I can guide you through the complexity, but I must take care to carry the whole readership with me, and that means I have to described a few 'ifs' and 'if nots'. My task becomes a little tricky because the variation in design of TVs and Video Recorders is prolific. However, if you take care to search for the connectors that I shall now describe, then you should be successful.

Some words of wisdom to start with – Do not attempt to use the Aerial socket of the TV set or the Video Recorder to plug the video cable into. It won't fit, and even if it did, it is the wrong function for the camera. Aerial sockets carry 'radio frequency' signals not 'video frequency' signals, which are very different signal types.

If you are lucky enough to have a fairly new Video Recorder (and I write these words in March 2003) then you may see a Video 'Phono' socket located on the front of it. In fact you may see three 'phono' sockets as shown in the following picture.

The video 'phono' socket is the one on the left with the yellow-coloured plastic insulation between the inner and outer metal parts of the socket (the one coloured white is a Left-Sound or Mono channel, and the one coloured red is a Right-Sound channel).

If you cannot see a Video 'Phono' socket on the front, then you might find it on the rear panel of the Recorder. Failing that, you might see it on the TV set itself. If you cannot find a Video 'Phono' socket at all then an alternative is to purchase a special type of SCART plug that converts from SCART to PHONO. If, like most folk, you are a stranger to SCART connectors, then a SCART socket on either your TV or your Video Recorder is a strange looking socket that looks like this…

Now SCART sockets are usually marked as 'AV1' or 'AV2' or some other 'AV' number. The 'A' stands for 'Auxiliary' and the 'V' stands for Video, so these sockets are nominating themselves as 'Auxiliary Video 1' or 'Auxiliary Video 2' and so forth. You get the picture (excuse the pun!).

Auxiliary video really means 'alternative video' so they are a way of getting video signals other than those from TV station channels 'in and out' of the Video Recorder or TV set.

This is precisely what we need to do for our next exercise. We need to get video signals out of the camera and into the TV or Video Recorder. Once we have done so, then, in order to view the cameras pictures, you need to select the correct video channel see to the pictures on TV, but we'll come on to that later.

If you are forced into using a SCART socket as an alternative, then the SCART to PHONO adapter that you will need to use is shown from different angles in the next two pictures, and it can be purchased from most high street stores that deal with TV and Video appliances.

The one shown in this picture has a switched marked 'IN' and 'OUT' upon it. This is referring to direction that the video signal is travelling through the SCART connection. If you plug the adapter into the TV's SCART sockets, then you need to have it switched to 'IN', because this means that the video signal will come 'IN' on the 'phono' sockets and go 'IN' on the SCART connector, hence 'in' to the TV.

If you decide to plug your adapter into the Video Recorder instead of the TV, then you still need to switch to 'IN' for the same reason above. You might choose to do this because your TV set does not have a spare SCART socket to use, but the Video Recorder does.

Okay. Let us stop and review the situation. Whether you use an existing PHONO socket directly, or you use a SCART socket together with an adapter, the good news is that we have now the required Video 'Phono' socket that we started searching for at the beginning of this section.

The next task is to connect the camera to the TV set/Video Recorder via the camera's video cable. With the camera switched off, lift up the small grey rubber flap on the camera's side to reveal the two auxiliary sockets shown in this picture ...

Insert the video cable's jack plug into the lower circular socket and push it fully home as far as it will go. The black plug cover should now be butting up against the camera case. Now plug the cable's yellow plug into the Video 'Phono' socket than we have already identified.

With no more ado, we are now ready to commence the next exercise.

Exercise 7 – Viewing the pictures on TV

Switch on the TV and the Video Recorder (if you are using a recorder) and switch on the camera. Turn the camera's Function switch to the Viewing position (see the last exercise if you have forgotten which this is). This time however, because the video cable is plugged into the camera, you won't see anything displayed on the camera's own Monitor Screen but you should see the green light come on as usual. The Monitor Screen is always turned off automatically when the video cable's miniature jack plug is inserted (much like the way the speaker for a radio is turned off when you insert the jack plug for personal headphones).

Do be aware though that the power saving feature for the camera will still operate as normal. So if you leave the camera alone for one minute without pressing any of its button's then the camera's picture output will disappear, as it normally does. However, because the Monitor Screen is turned off when you have the video lead plugged in, you may not realise this has happened. The double beep should still warn you, if you are listening carefully.

Using the remote control[s] (affectionately known in our household as the 'doofer[s]') or the buttons directly on the appliances themselves if you wish to, tune in the viewing channel to the appropriate 'AV' channel to receive the video signal from the camera. Be careful here. This in itself can be a little tricky. If the camera is plugged into a Video Recorder, then it is the remote control for the Video Recorder that will find the appropriate AV channel, not the remote for the TV! The TV in this case should be tuned for the Video Recorder signal as it normally is. On my own Video Recorder, this is marked as 'AV3'. When you have the right one selected, lo and behold you should see the very last of the digital pictures that you took in Exercise 4.

Note

If you cannot see the camera's picture on TV, then there are several reasons why this may be so. It could simply be that it took you more than a minute to find the right TV channel, and that the power saving function has activated itself. In which case, press any of the camera's buttons to bring it out of the power saving state, and check again that you are tuned to the correct AV channel on the TV.

If you can see the camera's picture then ...

Congratulations and welcome to the Armchair Theatre!

Okay. The rest is simple. You just browse through your pictures one by one, using the left-hand and right-hand rim edges of the circular Rocker button on the camera's back panel. What you see now on the TV screen is exactly what you saw before in Exercise 5 on the Monitor Screen.

The first time that I saw my pictures on the TV screen, I have to say that I was very impressed. This is a great way to see them, and you can do it so that the rest of the family can see them easily too. TV screens these days are often substantially bigger than the Monitor Screens for personal computers and much easier to get the family sat around them in comfort.

Now if you think about it, this arrangement for viewing your pictures on TV can be put to some very interesting uses. If you like to give talks to groups of people, maybe at a club, or a day/night class, then you can prepare yourself a presentation, and stand up in front of an audience to do so! What better way to share your digital pictures and be creative with your digital camera! I hope you have some fun!

This concludes Exercise 7, and this chapter about the camera.

3

Transferring Pictures to a PC

3.1 Preparing the computer software

Having viewed your pictures on TV, in this chapter we are going to discuss how you can transfer them from the camera and view them on a personal computer. In order to do so, you will need to install the computer software that came with the camera on to the computer. This software is contained on the Digital Dream CD-ROM, which is item No. 13 identified in the list from Exercise 1.

Note

If you are new to CD-ROMs, they are similar to ordinary audio CDs, but they contain computer data instead. The 'ROM' bit stands for 'Read Only Memory' meaning that the computer can read information from them but cannot store information on to them. In other words, they are factory preset.

Exercise 8 – Installing the camera software

Note

Throughout this exercise, the instructions and pictures presented are based on a computer using the Windows XP system (Home Edition version 5.1.2600). Although these are in general applicable to earlier (or later) versions of the Windows system, you may experience minor variations in the way that your particular computer behaves.

We start this exercise with the computer switched on and showing the normal Windows 'desktop' display on the monitor screen. If any other programs are running then close them now.

Begin the installation process by first removing the Digital Dream CD-ROM from its paper envelope, taking care to avoid fingerprints on the shiny side surface. To manipulate it, you can safely grip the outside edges of the

CD-ROM between your fingers and thumb, or poke a finger through the central hole. Open the CD drive on your computer's processor unit with the drive pushbutton, and place the CD-ROM in the drive tray (printed side uppermost). Press the drive button to close the drive door. Wait and you should see the CD drive light illuminate then begin flashing erratically as the 'Autoplay' feature of the computer starts to read information from it. The **Autoplay** feature will now automatically start the installation procedure.

Note

If the Autoplay feature doesn't operate for some reason then remove the CD-ROM and close the drive tray. Wait for the drive light to go out and pause for about twenty seconds. Now try inserting the CD-ROM for a second time. If it still refuses to operate, you can activate it manually by double-clicking on the 'My Computer' icon on the desktop, then double-clicking on the icon for the CD drive, and finally double-clicking on 'CDSETUP'.

The first screen that you will see is shown in the next picture on the left.

Using the mouse pointer, click on the top menu button labelled 'English' (notice that the pointer symbol changes from an 'arrow' to a 'hand' when you are over the button). You then see the second screen shown in the picture on the right. Click on the top button labelled '**Camera Driver**' (a 'driver' is a piece of computer software specifically designed to allow the computer to work with new hardware).

A short message now invites you to 'Choose Setup Language'. With 'English' showing in the box, click on the **OK button**. This is followed by a set-up 'progress bar' indicator and shortly afterwards a warning message appears saying 'Your system must be USB enabled'. We need to briefly pause here and discuss the implications of this message.

49

If you are familiar with the jargon term 'USB', then you will know this refers to the 'Universal Serial Bus' connectors at the rear of the computer's processor unit, and you will probably know if your computer system is USB enabled or not (enabled here simply means the connectors are present and working). For readers who know their system is 'USB enabled' you can happily continue with a click on the OK button. However, if this business of USB is very new to you then you might want to suspend the exercise at this point and jump ahead to read the next section (section 3.2), where we talk about USB in further detail. If you are then persuaded that your computer system is USB enabled you can return and also click on the OK button. If your system is not USB enabled, then you need to bring the installation procedure to a halt. Unfortunately you cannot stop it at this point. You must continue for a few more messages until you get to see a **Cancel button** (on the '1.3M Digital CAM' window that is coming up shortly).

Following the 'USB enabled' message, a second warning message will now ask you to remove the camera's cable from the USB socket on the processor unit. If it is plugged in then disconnect it. This is important because we need to have the software installed first, and you will run into trouble if it is connected before we are ready. Click once more on the OK button when you are confident that the camera is *not* connected.

A third warning message will now advise you that you may need the original 'Windows Installation CD' to complete the current installation procedure (they mean here the original Windows 98 CD-ROM disk or a later Windows version). If you are using Windows XP then this should not be necessary, otherwise have it handy (but see the next note). Click again on the OK button.

Note

Some computers are sold without ever giving you a Windows 98 CD-ROM disk. What they do instead is copy all of the files from the disk to a folder (often named 'CABS', but it may have some other name) somewhere on your hard drive. If this is the case, then when asked for the CD disk, you must instead change any reference to the CD drive (that may appear in messages on the monitor) to refer instead to this 'CABS' folder on the hard drive.

A window titled '1.3M Digital CAM' will now appear, ready for you to start installation of the actual 'driver' software, and you will see the welcome message shown here in the following picture on the left.

Note For those readers whose system is not USB enabled, then it is here where you exit the installation routine by clicking the Cancel button. You then press 'Exit Setup' and finally 'Exit' on the Digital Dream main menu screen to return to the desktop display.

Continue the installation with a click on the **Next button**. Then the picture on the above right appears. As individual files are copied from the CD-ROM to your hard drive, so the progress bars displayed will alter their appearance. This continues for a few minutes.

After some time, you may see the next picture on the left pop up. This only happens if you are running Windows XP. It is a 'Windows' message warning you that the software has not been specifically tested in an approved laboratory for compatibility with the Windows XP system. Don't be surprised by this. A number of companies choose not to subject their software for such approval because it is an expensive and time-consuming process, and adds nothing to the functionality of the software. If you do see it then click on **Continue Anyway**.

A short while later, the screen shown on the following right will appear to tell you that the copying process has ended. Now before you click on the **Finish button**, you should click on the little circle for 'No, I will restart my computer later'. This will allow us to install other programs from the CD-ROM before we go through the lengthy task of closing the computer down and restarting it again. Now click the Finish button.

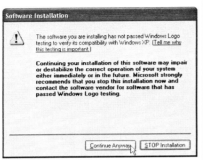

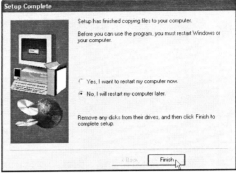

The '1.3M Digital CAM' window will now close and you see the 'Digital Dream' main menu screen once more...

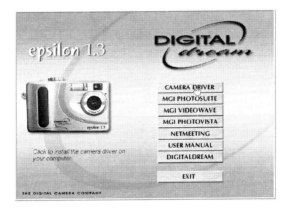

At this point, the 'Camera Driver' software has been installed on the computer but it is not yet active. To make it active, the computer has to be restarted (which we will do later) and it is during the starting phase that the software will become an integral part of the Windows system software. The driver software is not a program in the ordinary sense and you will not see it listed in the 'Programs' menu even after you have restarted the computer. Driver software is for the most part 'invisible' to you the user, but it is essential for the computer to be able to manipulate new gadgets attached to the processor unit – in this case the digital camera. Every manufacturer of a gadget must write their own driver software specifically for their own product, and this is the technique (the installation of such driver software) that extends the Windows system so that it can operate with any and every new bit of computer peripheral hardware produced.

Now we are ready to install some of the user programs. The first one is **MGI PhotoSuite** (the second button in the list on the Digital Dream main menu screen) and this is the program that we shall use to manipulate our digital 'still' pictures. Rather than take you through every screen, it is very straightforward so I will let you 'navigate' your own way and simply advise you as we go along. Click now on the second menu button labelled 'MGI PHOTOSUITE' and the installation procedure will commence.

The first message that you will see is titled '**Choose Setup Language**' and has 'English' shown as the default. Click the **OK button**. As the installation program begins to further load and run, you will then see two very intriguing eyes staring at you! Eventually you will see the '**Welcome**' message – click on the **Next button**. The message following that is titled '**Software License Agreement**' – click on the **Yes button**. Then up pops the '**User Information**' message. Now here you only need enter something in the '**Name' textbox**, which can be as simple as your initials; you may leave the 'Company' textbox blank. Click on the **Next button**. The next message to appear is titled '**Choose Destination Location**' – simply click the **Next button**. Then up pops the '**Select Components**' message – click the **Next button**. The message following that is the '**File Association**' message – click the **Next button**. The next message is titled '**Start Copying Files**' – click the **Next button**.

Now this is where the installation program gets into its stride. In the lower right-hand corner of the screen you will see a 'progress bar' indicating the percentage of the copying task that has been completed as things progress. During this phase, a number of information screens tell you different things about the program and it is interesting to read them while you are waiting. Eventually the copying task progress reaches 100% and this is followed by a '**Setup Complete**' message – click the **Finish button**. At this point, the installation program will automatically run your Internet 'browser' program, which more often than not will be Microsoft's Internet Explorer program. In the browser window will be a 'page' showing a title 'Welcome to the world of PC Photography: MGI Photosuite 4 SE'. MGI, by the way, is the name of the company that owns the PhotoSuite program, and the version you are now installing is a special edition of version 4 provided free with the camera. You can read as much of this page as you wish to but there is a lot of information that may not make a great deal of sense. I suggest that you close the browser window by clicking on the **'X' button** in the top right-hand corner. The next message you will see is the **'Online Registration'** message – click the **Continue button**. Following this, the **'Online Registration Utility'** message will show. Now because I don't want to interrupt the procedure and connect to the Internet at this point, I want you to click the **Cancel button**. This then takes you back to the **'Setup Complete'** message. *Be careful now*. Click on the centre of the little circle labelled 'No, I will restart my computer later' to put a dot in it. Then click on the **Finish button** once more. This action takes you back to the Digital Dream main menu screen.

If you have managed to follow this whole procedure smoothly and without a hiccup, then the MGI Photosuite program is now installed on your computer. As with the camera driver software, this program will not be operational until you have shut down your computer and restarted it again.

Note

Should things have not gone smoothly, then it is difficult to describe all the issues that could arise, however, one suggestion I will make (if you have a problem) is to try and install the program for a second time, starting from the Digital Dream main menu. For a second attempt, click again on the 'MGI PHOTOSUITE' button. It begins in much the same way as before but after you see the 'pair of intriguing eyes' then the next message will be different and titled 'MGI Photosuite 4'. This message will offer you three options to either 'Install additional components', 'Reinstall MGI PhotoSuite 4' or to 'Uninstall MGI PhotoSuite 4' completely. Try the 'Reinstall' option. If you get stuck and cannot proceed, then that is the time when you should telephone the manufacturer's **Support Desk Staff** for professional advice. The various contact phone numbers are listed at the end of the **User Manual** (the sixth button on the Digital Dream main menu).

The next user program on the main menu is **MGI VideoWave**. Unfortunately, space within this book does not permit us to describe how to use this program, so it is really up to you whether you want to install it or not. If you do choose to proceed, however, I want to give you a little warning first...

Installation of MGI VideoWave requires that your computer monitor screen has been previously set up to use a <u>minimum</u> screen resolution of 1024 by 768 pixels. If your screen resolution is less than this then the installation procedure will begin but quickly advise you that it cannot continue and cancel itself.

Note

If you are not sure what your current screen resolution is set to, you can check very simply by clicking on the **Start button** and then selecting **Control Panel** (this is for Win XP users, Win 98 users click **Settings** and then **Control Panel**). When the Control Panel window opens up, double-click on the **Display icon,** and then click the **Settings tab.** The current screen resolution will be shown on this tab.

Changing the resolution of your computer screen is beyond the scope of this book and can run into tricky issues, depending on your equipment. If you are not sure how to go about it then you should get help from someone more expert. If you decide that you would rather not change your screen resolution to the 1024 by 768 setting (it does make your desktop icons appear a lot smaller) then you should miss the installation of MGI VideoWave altogether and skip forward over the next two paragraphs to the third user program MGI PhotoVista. Deciding not to install the program won't affect any of the exercises that we do in this book. You will still be able to create video clips with the camera and play them back on its Monitor Screen. You can also play them on the computer once they have been transferred, or email such clips to friends over the Internet. The only thing you won't be able to do is to manipulate them by editing them. If you wish, you can always return to install the program from the CD-ROM at a later time.

For those readers whose computer monitor screen is set to the required minimum standard, we will now describe how to install MGI VideoWave. From the Digital Dream main menu screen, click on the 'MGI VIDEOWAVE' button and the installation program will begin.

The first items you will see are a few preliminary messages about the installer program. These are automatically followed by the first interactive screen titled '**MGI VideoWave 4 – InstallShield Wizard**' and you now see an intriguing face with blue lipstick staring at you! Click the **Next button.** Then you see the '**License Agreement**' message – click on the **Next button.** Following this, up pops the '**Customer Information**' message. Again, you only need enter something in the 'User Name' textbox, which can be as simple as your initials; you may leave the 'Organisation' textbox blank. Click on the **Next button.** The next message is about the '**Destination Folder**' – click the **Next button.** Then you will see a '**Ready to Install the Program**' message – click the **Install button.** Now this is where the installation program gets into its stride. There are a couple of progress bars again displayed while files are copied from the CD-ROM to your computer's hard drive. This takes several minutes. When the progress bars are ended, you will see the '**Online Registration**' message – click the **Continue button**. Following this, the '**Online Registration Utility**' message will show. Now because I don't want to interrupt the procedure and connect to the Internet at this point, I want you to click the **Cancel button**. You will then see the final message telling you that the '**InstallShield Wizard Completed**'. Click on the **Finish button**. You then are taken back to the Digital Dream main menu screen.

The third user program on the main menu (fourth button) is **MGI PhotoVista**. Again, we have do not have space in this book to describe how to use this program, so it is up to you whether you want to install it or not. However, unlike MGI VideoWave, it is not essential that you have your screen resolution set to the 1024 x 768 setting in order to install it, so you may want to put it onto your computer system anyway.

The **MGI PhotoVista** is a program used for stitching together two or more digital pictures in order to create a single wide panoramic type of picture. For example, if you would like to have one picture that gives you a complete 360 degree view from a landscape beauty spot, or maybe a group photograph where you can't fit everybody in from just the one camera shot, then you can take a series of still pictures each from a slightly different angle, and join them together electronically so that they appear as one single picture. To start the installation routine for this user program, click on the 'MGI PHOTOVISTA' button on the Digital Dream main menu screen, or if you decide not to install then skip forward over this next paragraph.

The first message that you will see is titled '**Choose Setup Language**' and has 'English' shown as the default. Click on the **OK button**. As the installation program begins to run, the next interactive message is the '**Welcome**' message – click on the **Next button**. You will then see the '**Software License Agreement**' – click on the **Yes button**. Following that is the '**Choose Destination Location**' message – click the **Next button**. You then see the '**Select Program Folder**' message – click the **Next button**. Following that is the '**Start Copying Files**' message – click the **Next button**. At this point the installation program gets into its stride. In the lower right-hand corner of the screen you will see a progress bar indicating the percentage of the copying task that has been completed as things progress. This doesn't take long in comparison with the other installation programs. When the progress bars are ended, you will see the '**Online Registration**' message – click the **Continue button**. Following this, the '**Online Registration Utility**' message will show. Now because I don't want to interrupt the procedure and connect to the Internet at this point, I want you to click the **Cancel button**. You will then see the '**Setup is complete**' message – click the **Finish button**. As before, at this point, the installation program will automatically run your Internet 'browser' program. In the browser window will be a 'page' showing a title 'MGI PhotoVista for Windows' You can read as much of this page as you wish to but there is a lot of information that may not make a great deal of sense. I suggest that you close the browser window by clicking on the '**X' button** in the top right-hand corner. This then takes you back to the Digital Dream main menu screen. The installation of MGI PhotoVista is now complete.

Okay, we now have the MGI programs installed, and you are back looking at the Digital Dream main menu screen as shown in the next picture.

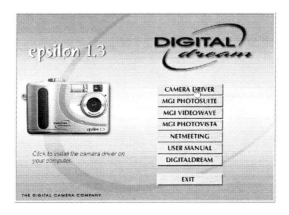

The next button in the list after MGI PhotoVista is one called **NetMeeting**. NetMeeting is a program that allows you to have a 'video phone' linkup to another person over the Internet using your digital camera and to share things with them such as a 'whiteboard' where you can sketch out a drawing or picture that you can both see simultaneously.

> **!** **I recommend that you don't attempt to install 'NetMeeting' just yet, because there are complications dependent on the different versions of Windows that you may be using. We do discuss the installation of this particular program in some detail later on in Chapter 10.**

The button labelled **User Manual** is a facility to read a copy of the User

Manual contained on the CD-ROM in digital form. If there are items of interest about the camera that we don't cover in this book, then you can look them up using this facility at any time in the future. To do this sometime later you need simply insert the CD-ROM again in the CD drive and the 'Autoplay' feature will bring up the Digital Dream Main Menu screens once more. If you have read the companion guide 'Using Email for the First Time' then you may recall that in section 4.1 we discussed file types and in particular the .pdf file type. The User Manual is one of these .pdf type files and when you press the User Manual button, the 'Adobe Acrobat Reader' program (version 4.0) will be loaded from the CD-ROM for you, in order to be able to view this file.

The final button labelled '**DigitalDream**' is a shortcut button to take you to the camera manufacturer's web site.

At this point we have finished installing the programs that we need in order to work with the camera. Click on the **Exit button** to close the 'Digital Dream' main menu screen and return to the desktop. Remove the CD-ROM from the CD drive and replace it into its paper cover. *Now put all of the booklets and the CD-ROM together in one large envelope and store it in a safe place.* One day you will need these items again, and if you do it straight away then you will know where in the future to find them! You might even consider making yourself a little note on the computer using the 'Notepad' program (as described in 'Using a Computer for the First Time', Chapter 4) to remind you where the 'safe place' was in a year's time!

Back at the desktop, you should notice that you have two extra icons showing, one for the MGI PhotoSuite 4 program and the other for MGI PhotoVista (the MGI VideoWave program does not put an icon on the desktop).

To complete the last part of the exercise, go ahead and shut down your computer and then restart it back up again. The purpose of doing this is to allow all of the changes that have been made as a consequence of the program installation processes to be incorporated into the workings of the Windows program itself.

When your computer has restarted then exercise 8 is concluded.

3.2   Connecting the camera to the computer

Before we go ahead and connect the camera to the computer, I want to first chat about USB connectors in general on the processor unit. Forgive me for getting deeper into the technicalities here but there are some important points for 'first-timers'. You can skip over the next five paragraphs if you know that your computer system definitely has two or more spare USB sockets for you to use.

The camera's connecting cable (item 12 in the list at the beginning of Exercise 1) has a USB 'A' type plug for connecting to a computer, so it is hardly surprising that your system must have at least one USB 'A' socket available at the rear of the processor unit. Most modern desktop computers have at least two such sockets, looking a bit like these...

Two USB 'A' Type Sockets

For the purpose of this book, if you also want to use a USB colour printer (as we do in chapter 5), then you are going to need two spare sockets – one for the camera and one for the printer. The theory of USB connections is that you can unplug devices not in use at any one time, but I advise that it is better to have a socket for each device if you can arrange it. Printers and scanners in particular are notorious for giving you problems if you unplug them and then use their USB sockets for something else!

If your processor unit does not have any USB sockets at all (possibly because it is an older model) then it may be possible to have a new 'card' installed at the rear to provide two or more. For example, I have an OPTi 82C861 card installed that gives me an extra 4 USB 'A' sockets. However, you must also check that you are running a version of Windows 98 (or later Windows versions such as Windows ME, Windows 2000, or Windows XP) in order to be able to use them. If you are using Windows 95, it is theoretically possible to have USB devices added but I do not recommend it – far better to upgrade to Windows 98 or an even later version. If you have Windows NT then you have no choice but to upgrade.

USB sockets on the processor unit can also be expanded by using a device called a USB 'extension hub'. Extension hubs are external boxes and often have four or more 'A' type sockets with a single connecting lead to an 'A' type plug. By plugging the 'A' type plug into one of the sockets on the rear of the processor unit you then effectively gain an extra three that you can use. You can even plug one extension hub into a second extension hub in a sort of 'daisy chain' (up to a maximum of five hubs theoretically), in order to increase the total number of USB 'A' type sockets available. However, I would like to sound a cautionary note here about such use of extension hubs. There is nothing to beat those USB sockets that are directly part of the processor unit itself. These are known as 'root' sockets as opposed to 'extension' sockets. They can supply higher levels of electrical power to peripheral devices and my own experience is that they give you far less bother than extension hubs.

Note

Some devices depend on this electrical power to function and have no other source of power.

If you are in any doubt about USB connections or the fitting of extra cards to your processor unit, then consult your local dealer.

Exercise 9 – Connecting the camera to the computer

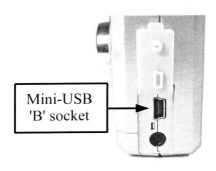

Mini-USB 'B' socket

At last we get to connect the camera to the computer. With all the preliminaries out of the way now, this really is simple and straight-forward. First connect the small plug end of the USB cable into the Mini-USB 'B' socket on the camera, as identified in this picture. Then connect the large plug end of the cable into a spare USB 'A' type socket on the processor unit (or extension hub, if you are using one, and the hub into the processor unit).

Now observe the rear of the camera. You should notice – without doing anything at all to the camera's controls – that first the indicator light on the back panel glows red, then it changes to green and the Monitor screen of the camera lights up blue with the message 'Mass Storage' displayed. If you have audio speakers working on your computer, and you are using Windows XP, then you will hear an interesting sound consisting of two notes (one following the other) with the low note first and a higher note second. This sound is a very useful diagnostic aid to tell you that the processor unit has detected a new USB device and furthermore has successfully set up a working connection with it. When you come to disconnect the camera, you will hear the same notes again but this time in the reverse order. Again, this is a useful diagnostic to tell you that the processor unit has detected its removal and has successfully removed the working connection with it.

If you are using Windows XP then you will also see a new window pop up, as shown in the following picture. Users of Windows 98 don't get to see it, but they do see a 'Found New Hardware' message.

If you do see this window, it is tempting at this point to click the OK button, but instead I want you to click the **Cancel button** so that you are back looking at the desktop display. If you accidentally click the OK button then the built-in Microsoft Scanner and Camera Wizard will start. Choose Cancel on the first wizard screen to close it. This 'Scanner and Camera Wizard' is certainly a useful and interesting facility to use and you may want to explore this some time later on your own, but not all readers will be using Windows XP so we won't describe how to use it here.

At this point, all users (with whichever version of Windows you have) should be looking simply at the desktop display on the computer's monitor screen. If any other program has begun, then close it so that you do see only the desktop.

As part of this exercise 9, we are now going to explore what the message 'Mass Storage' really means, for this is one of the very useful features of the 'epsilon 1.3' camera and others like it that behave as though they were an attached temporary disk drive to the computer.

On the desktop display, there is normally an icon called '**My Computer**' in the top left hand corner. Using the mouse pointer **double-click** on this icon to open it up as a window (or make a right-click on it and then select Open, if you find that easier to do). When the My Computer window opens, you should see an icon referring to a new disk drive with the label something like '**Removable Disk G:**' The precise drive 'letter' that your own computer will show you is likely to be different to 'G:' (more likely E: or F:). It will normally be the first free letter available. This next picture shows the window from my own system...

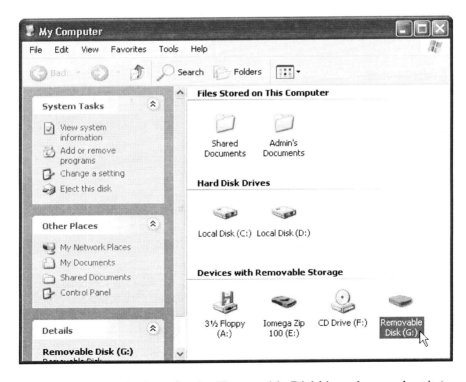

Now click once on the icon for the 'Removable Disk' in order to select it (as we see in the picture), then double-click (or again right-click and select

Open) on the icon to open that in turn. You should then see a folder called 'DCIM' as in the next picture.

Note
There are several ways to work with icons in the 'My Computer' window (and with the subfolders that we are about to witness). If you are not too adept at double-clicking with the mouse, there are simpler ways to achieve the same ends. For example, whenever something is selected (that is, highlighted blue as above) you need only press the **Enter key** on the keyboard. Such tips and tricks can all be found in the companion book *'Using a Computer for the First Time'*.

❗ **Now understand a very important point. The 'Removable Disk' is NOT a disk at all! It represents your camera. The computer thinks that your camera is another 'Hard Disk' drive – with folders and sub-folders and files, just like your C: drive. Whenever you see a reference to this 'Removable Disk' then you should mentally think 'camera'. This is what the message 'Mass Storage' actually means on the small display at the rear of the camera itself. It is telling you that the camera is now behaving as though it was a storage type of device for the computer.**

Let me add just a subtle point to the above. If you have any other electronic devices connected to your computer then they too may also be called 'Removable Disks' (if they have memory capability). You then have to be careful to identify the correct one for the camera. This will always be the one that has this 'DCIM' folder when opened. 'DCIM', by the way, stands for 'Digital Colour Image Map'. This sounds like gobbledygook to me. It's not a map – it's a folder!

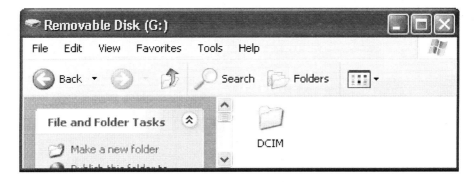

Double-click again now on the 'DCIM' folder and you should see yet another folder (a sub-folder) called '100V1310' (or it may alternatively be called 'epsilon'). Double-click on this sub-folder, and then you will see a number of 'objects' representing your individual camera pictures with names such as 'DSCI0001' or 'DSCI0002' etc. (Remember, if you are not too happy with the double-click, you can always do a right-click and then select open).

Precisely how these picture objects are displayed to you in the window depends on the version of Windows that you are using, and the '**View**' settings for the folder. If you are using Windows XP or Windows ME, then you will probably see them as '**Thumbnail**' pictures. If you are using Windows 98, then you will see them purely as 'Large Icons'. If you click on the 'View' menu option at the top of the window, you will see the different ways that you can display the photographs in the second section of the menu list. Windows 98 is fairly limited in this respect only having the options to show them as 'Large Icons, Small Icons, List or Details'. Windows XP is much more interesting and has 'Filmstrip, Thumbnails, Icons, List or Details'. The Filmstrip option is a particularly useful method of showing your pictures.

There are three key points to be aware of now:

1. **No matter how these pictures appear to you – whether you see them presented as Thumbnails, Icons, or a simple List – they are ALL files and you can manipulate them just the same as you would do for any other file, using for example such operations as 'Cut, Copy or Paste'.**

2. **To use 'Cut, Copy or Paste' on these files, you need to make sure that they are first 'selected' – that is, highlighted in blue. If you have more than one picture highlighted, then when you do a 'Cut, Copy or a Paste' operation, you will be doing it to all of those highlighted as one action.**

3. **The pictures that you are viewing now are STILL only in the camera. They have NOT yet been transferred to the computer. We get to do the actual transfer in Exercise 10.**

If you bear the above key points in mind then you will find it much easier to understand what is going on. If the operations of 'Cut, Copy and Paste' are still fairly new to you, then you should definitely read the companion book *'Using a Computer for the First Time'*.

Well, that brings us to the end of exercise 9. Close the window by clicking on the '**X**' **button** in the top right-hand corner and return to the desktop.

3.3   Transferring and saving the pictures

In this section, we will transfer the digital picture files out of camera and save them on the computer's hard drive. In deciding precisely where we shall put them on the computer, we need to be wise and give it some thought. What we really need is a new folder to drop them into, and because we will be taking even more pictures in the future, we may need several such folders. Our first little job then is to consider the computer's hard drive and whereabouts upon it we should think of creating these folders.

In the forthcoming exercise I will demonstrate creating new folders on your C: hard drive, because I know for sure that everybody has one. Some of you may have a D: hard drive and prefer to save them there instead. How do you know if you have a D: hard drive? Well if you open the 'My Computer' icon as a window (just as we did in the last exercise) then you can see your hard drives listed there. If you look back at the last picture but one, you can see an example taken from my own system. For those who do have a D: hard drive, follow the instructions in the next exercise to begin with and at the very end of it I will show you how you can move everything over from the C: to the D: drive.

Applying a bit more thought to our pictures and how we are going to store them, probably the best idea is this. Let us imagine that we take, say, thirty pictures with the camera on one day. What would be reasonable is to create a new folder specifically for that day, and then transfer all the pictures out of the camera and put them into this folder. The next day we may take thirty more pictures, so we will create yet another new folder and put the second batch into that one. For the third day, a third folder, and so on for each future day. We then end up with a series of folders.

Now each new folder has to have a name, so why don't we make the name something to do with the date when we took the pictures? That way, it becomes easier to go looking for a particular picture from potentially several hundred pictures. If we remember the date when it was taken, then all we need do is find the corresponding folder having the same name. We can then browse through that folder and pick out the picture that we want.

With this idea, you may not remember the date exactly, but if you have a rough idea then it cuts the searching down quite a bit.

Okay, we can do that. But there is just one slight modification to this idea that I want to recommend. It arises from the way that the computer normally displays folders on your monitor screen. Whenever the computer shows you a list of folder names, more often than not it will try and sort them according to their names. It does this by attempting to put the names into numerical and then alphabetical order. If we are to keep the folders appearing in true date sequence, that is with the oldest folder first and the newest folder last, then my recommendation is to write the date in a peculiar way. I am going to recommend that you write it as a pure number – no spaces, no full stops and no slashes (they can all cause complications) – just a simple number. This number will have six digits in it. The first two digits will be the year ('03' for the year '2003'). The second two digits will be the month ('01' for January, '02' for February etc.). The third two digits will be the day ('01' for the first day in the month, '02' for the second day in the month, and so on). To illustrate what I mean, here are three examples for the dates 4th, 5th and 6th of January 2003:

030104

030105

030106

Now it is easy to see how we can make the computer display any folders having these names appear in the right order for us. It's a bit like a digital clock without any hours, minutes and seconds, and having years, months and days instead!

To convert these names back to days requires a little effort, but it is not too difficult when you get the hang of it. Let us just do it for the one on the top of the list. The first two digits '03' signify that the year is '2003', the second two digits '01' represent the first month, that is January, and the third two digits '04' represent the fourth day.

This idea seems to work well now for the folder names. All we need to do is to group these folders together and we have a design that we can go and implement on your C: hard drive. Now the way that we group a set of folders together is put them all inside another folder. This latter folder is known as a parent folder, and the individual folders inside the parent are known as sub-folders. What seems very sensible is to name the parent folder

'Epsilon Pictures' (from the name of the camera), and to create the parent folder in the general data folder that all 'Windows' type computers have these days, which is the 'My Documents' folder.

This gives us now a complete folder structure, and just so that you get a feel for what this looks like from an overall perspective, the next illustration is a diagram of it.

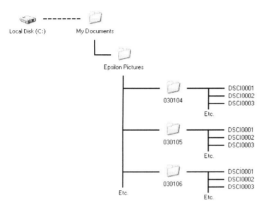

Let us just review this diagram, so that you fully understand what we have created...

- Starting at the top level on the left, you can see an icon for the C: hard drive, which in the diagram is called the **Local Disk (C:)**.
- Somewhere on the hard drive is the general data folder **'My Documents'**, which for our purposes is the top level.

- Underneath 'My Documents' is a **sub-folder** that we shall create ourselves called **'Epsilon Pictures'**. This is our **parent folder** for all the other sub-folders.

- Underneath the **'Epsilon Pictures'** then are several **sub-folders**, one for each day that we transfer pictures. In the diagram I have illustrated three such sub-folders called '030104', '030105' and '030106' respectively.

- Finally, within each of the day **sub-folders**, we have the digital picture files themselves, called 'DSCI0001', 'DSCI0002' and 'DSCI0003' etc.

This diagram also shows a solution for a problem that you may experience yourself sometime. If you take some pictures with the camera, the first picture that you take is held inside the camera as a file and automatically named as 'DSCI0001'. The second picture is named 'DSCI0002', and so on. Once you have transferred these to the computer and emptied the camera's memory, it will start the naming process all over again for the next set. The first picture of the second set will be named 'DSCI0001' etc. Now the problem that can arise is that you cannot have two files in a folder of the same type with the same name. If you attempted to transfer all your pictures into just one single large folder, the second set would try and overwrite the first set. *You would then lose the first set!* I think you can see from the diagram that we have solved this problem rather neatly. By putting the sets of pictures into different sub-folders, the problem never arises of having two files with the same name in the same folder.

Okay, so much for the design of the file structure. Let us now go ahead and create it.

Exercise 10 – Transferring and saving the pictures

Begin from the desktop. If there are any other windows open or other programs running then close them now.

Double-click on the 'My Documents' icon to open it as a window (do remember that if you have trouble with your 'double-clicking', you can always make a single right-click and then select 'Open' as an alternative).

Tip – If for some reason this icon has disappeared, you can still open it by clicking on the Start button and selecting the Run option. In the Open box, type 'My Documents' (including the quotation marks) and then click on OK.

You should then see a window with 'My Documents' in the title bar at the very top, as in this next picture.

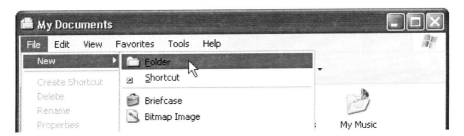

From the main menu bar at the top of the window, click on '**File**' and select '**New**', then slide the pointer sideways and click on '**Folder**', as demonstrated above.

This then creates the folder as shown on the left in the next picture, within the 'My Documents' window. This is going to be our parent folder called 'Epsilon Pictures'. Take care now not to click anywhere else or you will lose the so-called 'focus' of attention.

The 'focus' is currently in the name part underneath the folder picture, as shown in the left-hand picture. Notice that the initial name given is 'New Folder' and it is highlighted blue with a black flashing 'cursor' positioned over at the far right-hand edge of the lettering (look carefully, it's a bit hard sometimes to see it). Leave the mouse pointer alone for a moment and carefully just using the keyboard, type the words 'Epsilon Pictures' (remember to use a capital 'E' to begin with). You will notice that as soon as you type the first letter, all of the other letters in the highlighted name disappear. If you make a mistake in your typing, you can use either the Backspace key or the Delete key to correct the error. When you have finished your typing and you have it correct, then press the **Enter key**. The folder will now be renamed as shown in the previous picture on the right.

Note

For readers still a bit unsure about the keyboard keys then chapter 4 of the companion guide 'Using a Computer for the First Time' covers this subject in much greater depth.

Tip – If you end up with the folder named incorrectly, then use the mouse to right-click on its icon, and select the 'Rename' option. This puts the focus back into the name part and highlights it again. If you ever need to remove a folder completely, you can click on the folder's icon to highlight it blue, then press the Delete key on the keyboard. Click the 'Yes' button on the message that follows and the folder is removed entirely.

Now that we have the sub-folder 'Epsilon Pictures' created, double-click on this folder to open it up as a window. You should see that the title bar at the top of the window changes to say 'Epsilon Pictures'.

To make our first day sub-folder named according to our peculiar date idea, you use a similar procedure to the one we have just done. Click on 'File' from the main menu bar in the 'Epsilon Pictures' window, select 'New' and then click on 'Folder'. This pops up a new sub-folder with the name 'New Folder' highlighted in blue. In the same way as we did before, we now have to rename this sub-folder, taking care not to click the mouse inadvertently and lose the focus from the name box.

Go ahead now and name this folder using the true current year, month and day for the date that you are actually doing this exercise. For example, by typing '030107' you are representing the year 2003, the first month of

69

January (...01...) and the 7th (...07). Press the **Enter key** finally to complete the name. Don't be tempted to put anything else in this name other than numbers. It can create problems for you in the future.

When you have the day folder completed, double-click on it to open this folder as a window. You will then see a blank window, with your peculiar 'date' name as its title.

Okay, at this point we are ready to transfer the digital pictures out of the camera and put them into this sub-folder on to the computer's hard drive. We will do this using the **Copy** and **Paste** method of the invisible device known as the **Clipboard**. Keep your last window open, but minimise it now with a click on its **Minimise button** (which is the left one in the group of three found in the top right-hand corner). You will then see the window reduce to an icon on the task bar at the bottom of the screen.

From the desktop, double-click on the '**My Computer**' icon to re-open this as a window. Now double-click on the '**Removable Drive G**:' icon representing your digital camera (yours probably has a different drive letter). Double-Click on the folder named '**DCIM**' inside the window. Double-Click again on the folder inside that too. It may be named '100V1310' or it may be named 'epsilon'. When this latter folder opens as a window, then you see all the 'objects' representing your digital pictures again, be they icons, thumbnails or whatever. Remember – these objects are all **files** no matter how they are presented.

With these files visible in the window, go to the main menu bar near the top of the window and click on '**Edit**', then select the option labelled '**Select All**'. Instantly, all of the files are highlighted blue. This means that when we make a **Copy** action, they will all be copied at the same time to the **Clipboard**, not just one single file. Be careful now not to lose this highlighting by clicking the mouse inadvertently. Go to the main menu bar again and click again on '**Edit**', then select the option labelled '**Copy**'. This last action now places all the highlighted files on the invisible Clipboard and you don't have to worry any further about maintaining the highlighting (although it will still be there). Finally, close this window using the '**X**' **button** in the window's top right-hand corner.

Our files are still placed on the Clipboard even though the window that we took them from has itself now closed.

Click now on the minimised sub-folder titled '030107' or whatever you called your own particular one. It should be a rectangular icon on the Task bar at the very bottom of the screen. This action will restore it again as an open window on the desktop from its minimised state. Go to the main menu bar of this window and click on 'Edit', then select the option labelled 'Paste'. You will then see a new temporary message window pop up looking like this next picture...

What is happening here is that all those highlighted files that we placed on the Clipboard are being 'pasted' into the sub-folder. When the 'pasting' has finished, then we have achieved our major objective of getting a copy of all our digital pictures into the computer.

Close the '030107' sub-folder window (or whatever yours is called) using the 'X' button in the top right-hand corner. All windows should now be closed and we are back looking at the desktop.

This concludes exercise 10.

At this point, it is important to realise that all our digital pictures have now been copied across to the computer from the camera, but that the 'Copy' and 'Paste' commands did not actually affect the content of the camera. The original digital pictures are still held inside the camera filling up its memory. To finally get rid of them now, they need to be 'deleted' and this is the main purpose of the next exercise.

3.4   Deleting the pictures from the camera

Exercise 11 – Deleting the pictures in the camera

Begin this exercise from the desktop. If there are any other windows open or other programs running then close them.

Double-click on the 'My Computer' icon again to open it as a window.

Double-click on '**Removable Disk (G:)**' to open that too (remember your drive letter may be different). Double-click on the folder you see inside named '**DCIM**'. Then double-click again on the folder named '**100V1310**' (or it maybe called 'epsilon' instead). Again you can see the objects representing the original picture files.

Now first let us examine how we can delete individual picture files from the camera. Click once on the first picture file labelled 'DSCI0001' to highlight it blue. Then press the Delete key on the keyboard (normally found just to the right of the big Enter key). You should then see the following message...

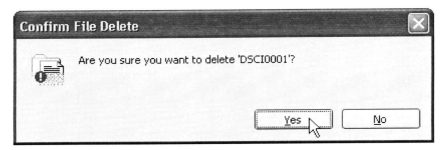

Click on the Yes button and the picture file will accordingly be deleted from the camera. It's as simple as that.

You may use the above procedure over and over again if you want to, each time deleting a different picture. However, let us now see how you can delete all of the pictures files in one action. Go to the main menu bar at the top of the window. Click on '**Edit**' and then select the option labelled '**Select All**'. You should now see the pictures files highlighted blue. You could press the Delete key again at this point, but I will show you an alternative using your mouse pointer. Go back to the main menu and click on '**File**' again, then select the option labelled '**Delete**'. You may or may not then see the screen shown in this next picture...

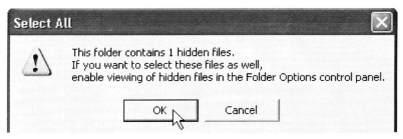

Click on the **OK button** if you do see it (don't worry if you don't, it means that your computer settings are set slightly different). You then see this following picture...

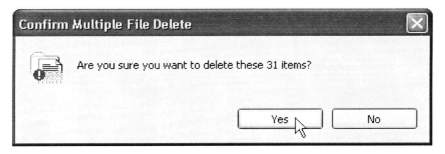

The number of items referred to in this message will vary according to the number of pictures currently in the camera. Click on the Yes button. Next you will see the following message...

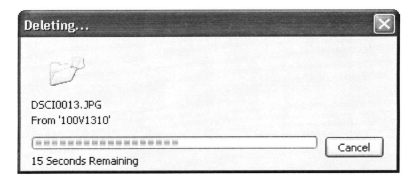

When it has finished, then all the picture files previously seen in the window will be gone. Not only are their 'object' representations gone, but also they are truly gone from the camera. To prove this, disconnect now the camera cable that is linking the camera to the computer at both ends. If you are using Windows XP and your audio speakers are operational, you will hear the 'two notes' sound again telling you that the computer has recognised the camera's removal. Turn the camera's Function switch to the Viewing position, as shown in this next picture.

Switch the camera on. First it will show 'Playback Mode' on its rear screen and then it will show the message 'No Image'. This is the final proof that the camera no longer has the pictures in its memory. Switch the camera off. This concludes exercise 11.

Just before we finally close this chapter, I would like to make a few concluding remarks about manipulating the camera contents from your computer.

First of all, some of you may be wondering why I did not suggest to you that you use the '**Cut**' option instead of '**Copy**' in Exercise 10, when we were transferring pictures. This would automatically delete the pictures inside the camera and there would be no need to delete them in a separate exercise as we did in Exercise 11. The short answer is that you can do this if you want to and it will save you time. However, the real reason why I did this in two stages is that the 'Cut' option can sometimes catch people out when they don't expect it. If you lose track of what you are doing with the 'Cut' operation, before you have successfully done a 'Paste', there is a small danger that you may lose the pictures completely. This is particularly true if you should be distracted midway through the transfer, and sometimes such distractions are not of your own making. For example, if you suffer a power failure on the mains supply just at the wrong moment, then your computer will just 'go off' and there is nothing much you can do about it. When you get power restored, are you really confident that the pictures were safely copied to the hard drive before they were removed from the camera? The answer is that you cannot be 100 per cent sure. Such dangers admittedly are quite slim, but if your pictures are very important, say, from a business point of view, then you may regret not taking that extra bit of time to copy them first, before deleting them. I know this from experience because it once happened to me!

Note

If the pictures you have taken are important, then it is always better to err on the safe side and transfer them in two stages – copy them first, then delete them later!

This leads us to another important point, which I shall emphasise again later in the next chapter...

Note

Never do ANY work on the original computer copies of your digital pictures! Always make additional backup copies first to safeguard the integrity of the original images.

I am referring here to those copies on your hard drive (not to those copies inside the camera). It is the copies on the hard drive that will become the 'originals' longer term, after such pictures have been deleted in the camera.

Another interesting point is that when you have emptied the camera of its pictures, it is possible to put some or all of them back again, providing that you have good 'original' copies saved within the computer. This is achieved in a manner that is the reverse of the situation of Exercise 10. By copying from the date sub-folders, you can 'paste' picture files back into the '100V1310' sub-folder (this may alternatively be called 'epsilon') of the 'Removable Disk' in the 'My Computer' window. If you do this, then you are actually copying the pictures back into the SmartMedia memory card. Why would you want to do this? Well there are two reasons that I can think of. First, you might want to take your camera to a friend's house and show her or him some pictures on their TV (in the manner demonstrated in Exercise 7). Second, you can remove the memory card from inside the camera if you want to, and take it to a high street store for printing. This illustrates once more why the camera is referred to as 'Mass Storage' and a 'Removable Disk'.

My final comment is for those people who have a D: hard drive, as mentioned at the start of this section. You can transfer the whole of the folder structure that we created across to the D: drive (including all of the picture files) simply using a 'copy' and 'paste' action. Here is how to do it...

> First, open up the '**My Documents**' window.
> Then click once on the '**Epsilon Pictures**' folder in order to highlight it blue.
> From the main menu bar, now choose '**Edit**' and select '**Copy**'.

This puts not just this one folder, but also all of the structure that exists at a lower level underneath, on to the Clipboard.

> ➢ Then go click on '**My Computer**' to open it as a window.
> ➢ Select the '**D:**' **drive** by double-clicking on it.
> ➢ When the 'D:' drive window is open, from the main menu bar, choose '**Edit**' and then select '**Paste**'.

What will then happen is that a complete copy of the 'Epsilon Pictures' folder, and all its lower structure, will be made to the 'D:' drive.

> ➢ Once it has finished with the copying, go back to the original '**Epsilon Pictures**' folder in the '**My Documents**' window and click again to highlight it blue.
> ➢ Then press the **Delete key** on the keyboard.
> ➢ When you see the **Confirm Delete** message, click the **Yes button** to send it and all its contents to the Recycle bin.

4

Adjusting Pictures with Software

4.1 Selecting the picture from a folder

The stage we have now reached is where our pictures are stored in a folder on the computer, and they have been deleted from the camera. If you compare this stage with conventional photography, it is similar to the situation where the exposed film has been removed from the camera and sent off to the chemist for processing. Normally you would now wait a few days for the film to be processed and then pop along to the store and pick up your finished photographs.

With our digital pictures, we could do the same as conventional photography and simply print these out on a colour printer just as they are. But one of the great advantages of digital pictures is that you now have the opportunity to examine what you have taken before you decide to go ahead and print them. Immediately, you can discover all of those mistakes made inadvertently, such as taking a picture of your own feet or maybe a featureless shot of an overcast sky – we have all done that before today! These can be identified and not printed in the final batch.

For those pictures that you do want to print, when you examine them in detail you often wish that the picture had been taken with just a small modification to it. Maybe it isn't framed quite right, and you would prefer the central figure to be appear a bit more to the left or right. Or perhaps there is something else in the picture that you don't really want to see in the final scene.

With digital pictures, you can now make some adjustments to them to improve the overall appearance of the final image. This can range from very simple amendments made in a few minutes to other more complex changes taking hours of careful manipulation. It all depends on the importance you attach to the pictures and how much effort you are prepared to put in.

In this next exercise, we are going to use the first of those user programs installed in the last chapter called MGI PhotoSuite. We will use it to view the pictures that you have already taken and select one ready to do some alterations to it. Then later in Exercises 13 and 14, we will use the same program to go ahead and make the changes, and save them back to the hard drive.

Exercise 12 – Selecting the picture to work with

There are two ways that you can choose to start **MGI PhotoSuite** running. You can either double-click on the icon for it (shown here) on the desktop ... or in a more long-winded fashion, you can click on the **Start button** in the bottom left-hand corner of the screen, select 'All Programs' or 'Programs' (depending on the version of Windows you are using), then select **MGI PhotoSuite 4,** and finally slide the mouse pointer sideways to make a single click on the smaller sub-menu option also labelled **MGI PhotoSuite 4** ...

This starts the program running and briefly you will see the pair of 'intriguing eyes' staring at you again, quickly followed by the opening screen that looks like this next picture ...

Note

If the program window is not displayed full size (covering the whole of the monitor screen) then maximise it now by clicking on the **Maximise button**, which is the middle one of the three in the window's top right-hand corner.

78

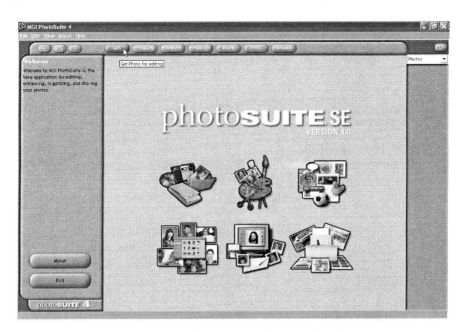

One of the really nice features of MGI PhotoSuite is that it is very easy to use. Near the top, just underneath the main menu bar for the program, there is first a set of three grey buttons towards the left, and then a further set of seven grey buttons in the centre. Our main controls are those of the second set of seven in the centre, but before we get into the detail of using them, it is worth just mentioning the functions associated with the set of three on the left.

At any time whilst using the program, if you click on a button and something happens to take you a step forward, but then you decide that you want to go back one step, click on this next button and it will be done...

 The icon is trying to indicate going a step backwards and then up a level. As we click on buttons, and get into the function of the button, we always think of ourselves as going 'down a level'.

If at any time you want to jump back to the starting screen (as shown in the last but one picture) then click on this next button. The icon here is representing 'home', because the starting screen is often referred to as the 'home' page.

 And finally, if you need a bit of help to understand any aspect of the program, then click on this button ...

Okay, the first button (left-most) of the set of seven in the top centre is labelled 'Get' and we use this one to select our digital picture folder and pick individual pictures for viewing within the program. Click on the Get button now. This will then change the far left panel of the program window to look like this next picture...

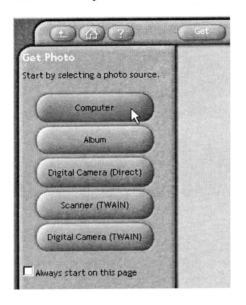

There are now five new buttons visible in this panel. There is not the space in this exercise to describe them all in detail, so I will limit my comments mainly to the first one labelled 'Computer'. However it is worth mentioning something about the others to avoid confusion. Let's do this first and get them out of the way:

- The **Album button** allows you to select pictures to work with providing that they have previously been organised into groups known as 'Albums'. We have not yet done so. All that we have done so far is copy the pictures into a folder.

- The **Digital Camera (Direct) button** is of not of any use with the epsilon 1.3 digital camera. It is used for other digital cameras. If you are using a digital camera other than the epsilon, then it may be worth having a click on this button to see if your particular camera is mentioned in the subsequent list.

- The **Scanner (TWAIN) button** may be of use if you have a scanner attached to your computer, for it provides a method to operate the scanner mechanism from within this program. Because it is not related to the use of digital cameras, it is beyond the scope of this book.

- The **Digital Camera (TWAIN) button** is again not of any use with the epsilon 1.3 digital camera. It is used for other digital cameras that do not have the 'Mass Storage' capability that we discussed in Exercise 9. TWAIN ('Technology Without An Interesting Name') was a software standard devised a number of years back to enable different software programs to link up with graphical hardware gadgets such as cameras and scanners. If you have a camera that uses the TWAIN method of communicating with your computer, then the camera's TWAIN software must be installed correctly first, before you can access the camera via this button. The process of installation adds the camera model number into the computer's own internal 'list of TWAIN devices' and then you can select which TWAIN device you want to work with.

Now back to the main plot. Click on the **Computer button** (shown in the previous picture), and you will see the '**Open' dialog box** appear.

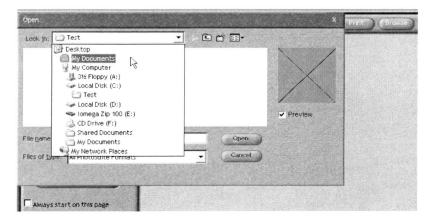

In the 'Look in:' box just under the 'Open' title bar, we need to have 'My Documents' displayed. If it isn't then click on the small 'down-arrow' on the right-hand end of the box and you will see a drop-down list as shown in the previous picture. Move the mouse pointer over 'My Documents' and click to select it.

Note If at the end of chapter 3 you moved the 'Epsilon Pictures' folder over to your D: hard drive, then you will need to select this D: drive into the 'Look in:' box instead.

With 'My Documents' now showing in the 'Look in:' box, click on 'Epsilon Pictures' to first highlight it blue, then click the 'Open' button as shown in this next picture.

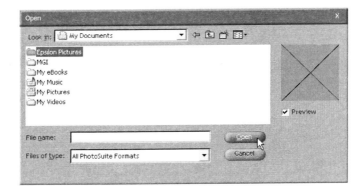

Everything now moves around as we descend inside the 'Epsilon Pictures' folder. The title 'Epsilon Pictures' moves up to the 'Look in:' box, and in the large white area below it, we see the sub-folders named according to the date convention that we established in Exercise 10. For your own situation, you may choose any of the sub-folders you wish. In my example I will choose a folder named '030109'. Click on your chosen sub-folder and click again on the 'Open' button.

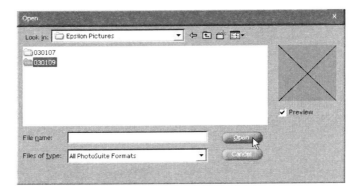

Now we descend inside the sub-folder. Its name moves up to the 'Look in:' box and in the large white area we see our individual picture files. When you first see these displayed, you will probably see them as a list, one after the other.

Click on the first file in the large white area labelled 'DSCI0001'. As soon as you have done so, then you can see a small copy of the picture showing over in the 'Preview' pane over on the right-hand side. This 'Preview' image is very useful, for it reminds us what the file actually contains. Click now on the second file labelled 'DSCI0002' and you will see what I mean.

Okay. I now want you to browse through all of the picture files in your folder slowly. Carefully inspect them in the 'Preview' pane and choose one that you wish to work with for the exercises in this chapter. You can do this simply by clicking with the mouse pointer, selecting them each in turn. Or a better method is to use the set of arrow keys on your keyboard...

With the arrow keys, you can move about in all four directions inside the folder. To help you make a suitable choice you should note that in Exercise 13, I am going to illustrate how to 'crop' a picture – that is, to select a rectangular portion of the complete image, and then chop off the bits outside of this portion. This is an easy method of removing an unwanted part of the picture that currently exists at one side or the other, or even at the top or bottom. So, in making your choice of picture to work with, if you have any good portraits that include a 'head and shoulders' view then this will be a good picture to use in the coming exercise.

Select your chosen picture file by highlighting its name in blue, then click on the Open button, as shown in this next picture.

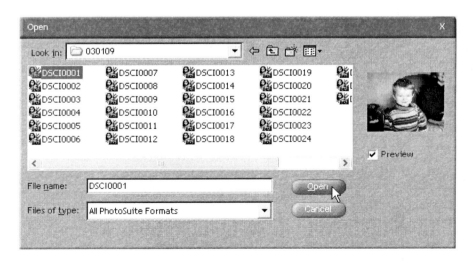

This will then open up the picture into the main working area and you can now view the picture in its full glorious detail.

! ■ One very important point you should now understand is that this picture is an ORIGINAL. You should always avoid MAKING CHANGES to an original, because once you have done so you will have lost information that you may want again in the future. If you make a mistake with your changes, and you don't have the original picture to go back to, you will be – as we often say – 'up the creek without a paddle'!

To avoid working on an original picture, we are now going to save the picture under a <u>different</u> name. By saving it under a different name, we are effectively making a completely separate copy of the picture, and this will leave the original file alone untouched. Once you have saved it as a different named file, the program effectively 'swaps' over to using the new copy in the working area. You can see this by keeping an eye on the title bar at the very top of the program window. If you look now in the top left-hand corner before we have saved it (see next picture), you will see it titled as 'Dsci0001 – MGI PhotoSuite 4' (your own screen will show whatever number your own chosen file was called). When we save it as a different name, the new name will appear here. This is one way that you can always be sure of the actual file that you are working with.

Click now on File from the main menu bar, and select the option '**Save As...**', as seen in the following picture.

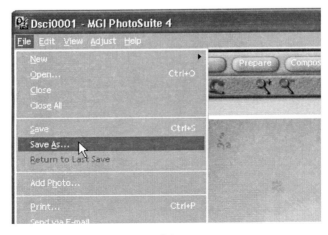

Notice that we use the 'Save As' option and *not* the 'Save' one. 'Save' will not allow us to rename the file. It only saves any changes you may have made back to the original file – and that is the last thing you want to do!

The 'Save As' option will then display the 'Save Photo' dialog box, as seen in this next picture...

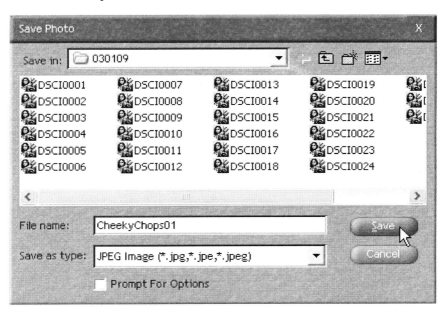

When this first appears, the old filename will be shown in the **'File name' textbox,** just left of the **Save button,** and it will be highlighted. If you are careful not to disturb the 'focus of attention' (by inadvertently clicking with the mouse), the first key that you press on the keyboard will then remove the old filename from this box and show you the first letter that you typed. Go ahead and type a complete new name for your picture. In the above, I have used 'CheekyChops01'. This illustrates a habit that I have developed whereby I give names to files and add '01' to the first version of it on the end. In the future I can then save further versions by changing the number to '02' instead, or '03' etc. This allows me to track all of the changes that I make to my work independently. You may also notice that another habit I have is not to use spaces in the filename, but to use capital lettering instead to identify the separate words (notice the capital 'C' in 'Chops'). The reason I don't use spaces is that sometimes you accidentally press the Spacebar key twice instead of once when making a new filename. Now when you see a filename written on a computer display, it is very difficult to judge whether there are two spaces in the wording or only one. Computers can forgive humans a few things, but they won't forgive you missing out a space if there should be one there, and this can lead to all manner of problems. That is why it is easier not to use spaces in filenames at all. However, if you want to use spaces then by all means do so – but don't say I didn't warn you about it when funny things happen to you. When you have finished typing your new name, then click the **Save button**.

You now see the new file in the working area. It looks identical to the old one – because we haven't made any changes yet – but you should notice that the name on the window title bar in the very top left-hand corner shows your new name and not the old. This is confirmation that you are no longer working on the original picture file.

This concludes Exercise 12.

Note
If you get a strange pop-up menu titled 'JPG Advanced Settings' appearing when you saved your file, the reason is that the little checkbox marked 'Prompt For Options' was somehow ticked on the Save Photo dialog box, when it should normally be cleared. You only need click the OK button if you do see this menu.

4.2   Cropping the picture content

Having selected your picture as shown in Exercise 12 and renamed it, we now make alterations to improve the overall picture's appearance. The 'cropping' action is one that 'cuts' out and retains a selected portion of the picture.

Exercise 13 – Cropping the picture

Begin with the newly named version of the picture open in the working area, as at the end of Exercise 12.

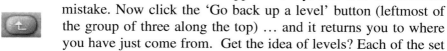

In the panel down the left-hand side of the screen you will see three buttons and a heading that says 'Prepare Photo' (as in the above picture). This section of the program is the view obtained whenever you click on the **Prepare button** (the second button of the group of seven). You automatically enter this section after you use the **Get button** to open a picture.

Click the first button from the left-hand panel labelled '**Rotate & Crop**'. This will reveal a sub-section in the left panel with four new buttons. Click the **Rotate button** and watch what happens. Okay, that was a deliberate mistake. Now click the 'Go back up a level' button (leftmost of the group of three along the top) … and it returns you to where you have just come from. Get the idea of levels? Each of the set of seven buttons at the top is like a 'major' level, and the subsequent buttons that appear down the left-hand panel are options for 'dropping down to lower levels'. The jargon for this method of moving around the program is called navigation.

Okay, this time click the **Crop button** (last of the four down the left). A new left-hand panel appears. Also, and more important for our exercise, the picture shown in the working area has a new dotted line running all the way around the outside edge There are also small 'dots' at each corner of the dotted line and in the centre of each side. This dotted line defines the Selection Area of the picture for the 'cropping' operation. It always begins with the whole picture area enclosed, and we narrow down the selection by using the mouse pointer to make a Drag action upon the dots. By dragging upon one of the dots, we move the dotted line in a given direction. Let me illustrate how this happens. Placed your mouse pointer into the working area of the picture, and just to the right of the dot located in the middle of the left vertical side, as in the picture on the left below.

 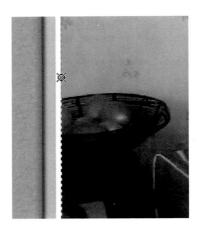

The mouse pointer changes its appearance when over the picture and on the 'inside' of the 'selected area' to a hand with a 'curled index finger'. It is the very tip of the curled index finger (the fingernail if you like!) that is the important part of the mouse pointer. The rest of it is not that important! Now very carefully move the 'fingernail' of the mouse pointer on top of the dot and again you see things change, as in the previous picture on the right. The hand is now a cross symbol, but only while you are precisely over the dot. Taking great care not to lose the cross symbol, click and hold the left mouse button to start a Drag action. Do not let go of the mouse button or you will end the drag. Still pressing the button, slide the mouse over towards the right – about maybe two inches (5 cm.) – and then let go of the mouse button. You can now move the mouse pointer off the dot and away further to the right. You should then see that the dotted line defining the left side of the Selection

Area has accordingly moved over to the right, and it is now positioned at the point where you ended the Drag action, as in the following picture.

Okay, that has the left side sorted out. Now go ahead and do the same type of thing for the other three sides (top, right and bottom), again using the dots in the centre of them. Try and frame your portrait 'head and shoulders' picture so that you cut out any objects at the picture's edges and leave your subject nicely centred within the dotted line's Selection Area. You may repeat the drag actions as many times as you want to. If when moving a 'side' you decide that you have gone too far then move it back a bit. By the way, if you make a drag action over the dots in the corners, you will move two adjacent sides simultaneously. When you have finished positioning the whole rectangular dotted line frame, you should then click the circular button in the left-hand panel (in the 2nd section) labelled '**Crop**'.

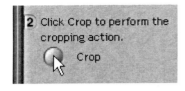

Wait for the mouse icon to change to the hourglass symbol and then revert back again to an arrow pointer. During this time, your computer is performing a lot of fairly intensive mathematical calculations to eliminate the information on the outside of the Selection Area and leave you with the chosen image. When finished, your revised image in the working area is automatically adjusted to fill it out the available space.

Now if you are not satisfied with what you have done, you can undo the 'changes' in the working area by clicking on this 'Undo' symbol at the top of the working area...

If you ever use this **Undo button**, then your picture is restored to its appearance just before the 'crop'. The button to the right of it is the **Redo button** and becomes available after you have undone something. The Redo button gives you the choice of applying your changes for a second time, without having to readjust the dotted line rectangle again. Try them out if you feel like it, but end with the changes applied.

When you are finally content with your handiwork, click the **Return button** in the left-hand panel. This takes you back to where you were at the beginning of the exercise.

Before we finish, we should now save the changes that have been made back to the newly named file on the hard drive. This is a very important point to note. All the work that you do with a picture, in the working area of MGI PhotoSuite, is held in the **RAM memory** of your computer system and **NOT** in the file on the hard drive. It is only when you deliberately perform a **save** that the new image in RAM memory is actually transferred to the file on the hard drive. If you accidentally try to close the Photosuite program before you save the last changes, then it will prompt you to do so before closing, but it is not good practice to rely upon this prompt. To save the alterations, click on **File** from the main menu bar, and select the '**Save**' option. Note that we use 'Save' this time and not 'Save As', as we did at the end of Exercise 12. 'Save' will always save to the file whose name is in the very top left-hand corner of the program's title bar.

This concludes Exercise 13.

4.3 Resizing the picture and saving it

Having made some changes to a picture by cropping out the parts that you don't wish to see, we are now going to consider how we can change the overall size of it. There are many occasions where you will want to change the size of digital pictures and for a variety of reasons.

The topic of size with digital pictures can be a little mystifying. This is because we don't measure them directly in units of length (centimetres or inches). Instead we measure them as a number of pixels for their width and height, and then use another factor called resolution (measured in pixels per centimetre or per inch) to change that number into a physical length. Let us spend a few moments just discussing this business in more detail, so that you fully understand what is going on.

The pictures that you take with a digital camera are at the outset stored in the camera's memory. In Exercise 10, we saw how to transfer these from the camera to a computer. These pictures are contained within an object that we call a file and in Exercise 12 we opened one of these files to see the picture contained inside it. The original file that we transferred from the camera has a 'natural size' to it. The natural size for the epsilon 1.3 camera is based upon the total number of pixels contained on the special 'light sensitive electronic chip' (which we talked about in section 1.2). If you have not altered the camera's Image Size settings, the picture in the original file will be composed of 1280 pixels wide and 1024 pixels high.

What happened to the picture after we 'cropped' it and saved it back to the file? The answer is that we simply chopped bits off and practically this means that the resultant picture ended up with fewer pixels wide and fewer pixels high. In my own example of the new 'CheekyChops01' file, the picture inside it has now only 579 pixels wide and 683 pixels high. Once a picture has been cropped and then saved back to the file on the hard drive, the pixels that were taken away by the cropping action are lost from that file permanently. This fact emphasises once again why you should never work on the original file but always on a copy. You never know when you may want to use the original picture in the future.

The action of cropping is one way that the number of pixels in a picture can change, but it is not the only way. There is also another method by which they can change called resizing. It has nothing to do with cropping, and is able to both reduce the number of pixels in picture and maybe increase them too if you wish. Resizing maintains the overall picture content. It simply uses a mathematical technique to modify the number of pixels that go to make up the picture. If you change the number of pixels in the width (either by increasing or decreasing them), then you must also do so for the height in a fixed proportion, if you are going to keep the overall shape of the picture.

Does resizing change the picture quality? Yes it does. If I make the picture size bigger then there will be more pixels in the file after I have done so than beforehand. Now you don't usually get something for nothing, and this is certainly true of digital pictures. In order to create more pixels, the MGI PhotoSuite program will do some mathematics. It will guess (using a very clever guessing procedure) at what the colours and intensity should be for the new pixels in the resized picture based upon the original information in corresponding areas of the former picture. The guess will never be as accurate as for a camera with a larger chip that has an equal number of them in the first place. This is a subtle factor that leads to a theoretical deterioration when the picture is made bigger. In the end, you are seeing something that wasn't actually there and has only been guessed at. If I go the other way and make the make the size smaller instead, then there will be fewer pixels in the file after I have done so than beforehand. To remove some pixels, the MGI PhotoSuite program will do some alternative mathematics. It will guess (using another clever guessing procedure) at what the colours and intensity should be for the reduced number of pixels based upon the original pixels that are being replaced. Fewer pixels always lead to a deterioration of picture quality and is more obvious to appreciate.

The deterioration of picture quality with resizing is something that you must bear in mind to keep your pictures at their best. For example, if you resized something larger and the resize it again smaller back to the size you started from, the two operations will successively affect the picture quality adversely.

Well, if you have managed to stay with the discussion so far, I am nearly done. There is just one additional point to mention and that is 'scaling'. Computer programs that work with digital pictures often have a scaling feature to apparently change the size of picture before printing them out on a printer. This is a very useful feature and to all intents and purposes is similar to resizing. It appears to change the picture by increasing or decreasing the width and the height just the same. The substantial difference from the user's point of view is that scaling only changes the picture temporarily for the duration of the print. It does not normally affect the contents of the file on hard drive. Resizing, on the other hand, is a way of permanently affecting the file.

Okay, we now have two operations that appear similar – **resizing** and **scaling**. When should you use one technique and when should you use the other? This really depends on the job that you are trying to do. More often than not, you can get perfectly good results by scaling before printing, so for one off print jobs where you are not likely to keep repeating the task in the future, then scaling is quicker and will sort things out for you. It also guarantees you the best quality prints that can be created for that particular picture. If however your task is to send the picture as an attachment to an email, and 'post' this to a relative or friend over the Internet, then resizing may be what you need to do.

Note

The issue of an inappropriate picture size attached to an email is discussed in section 4.3 of the companion guide *'Using Email for the First Time'*, and in section 9.2 of this book.

In this last exercise of the chapter, I will demonstrate how to resize a picture. In section 5.3 of the following chapter, I will show an example of scaling.

Exercise 14 – Resizing the picture and saving it

Begin with your selected picture open in the working area of the MGI PhotoSuite program, as at the end of Exercise 13. If you have closed the program down after the last exercise, then retrace the early steps of exercise 12 to open it up again but this time select the cropped file (mine is called 'CheekyChops01') from the **Open dialog box**.

Okay, from the main menu bar, choose '**Adjust**' and then select the **Resize...** option, as shown in the next picture.

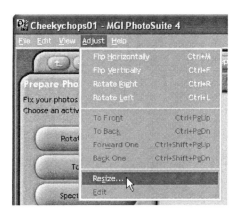

The three little dots by the way, after the word 'Resize', indicate that there is a further menu to come once you have made your selection (this is a common little indicator that you may see with quite a few of the selections on different menus). Here it is...

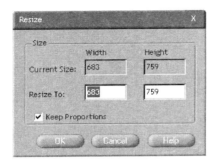

Notice that this **Resize pop-up menu** shows you the 'Current Size' (in pixels) of the picture that you have open in the working area. This is a useful point to remember if you have any picture file (from any source – it doesn't have to be from the digital camera) that you would like to know the pixel size of. If you only want to inspect the number of pixels, you can then close the pop-up menu using the **Cancel button** to avoid making any changes.

Now we will specify a new size for the picture. Generally, you can alter either the height or the width as it suits you. In this exercise, I want you to change the height. Using the mouse pointer, double-click on the number shown in the lower white **Height box** (or right-click and choose 'Select All', if you find that easier to do). This will highlight the number for you in blue ('759' in my example). Then using the keyboard keys, type in a new height number of 400. I have chosen this number for a practical reason and I would like you to use the same number for this exercise. This choice will change the picture in my case to almost half of what it was after we cropped it. Notice that the width has automatically changed itself to a new number (your own width number is now likely to be different to mine). This happened because the 'Keep Proportions' textbox is ticked. If you ever want to change the width and height to something where the proportions are not maintained then you need to 'uncheck' this box with a click first.

Finally, click the OK button to activate the resize calculations.

What you should now see happens quite quickly. Down at the bottom of the screen, just above the Task bar, the MGI PhotoSuite program has a grey bar known as the **Status Bar**. In black lettering it normally displays the size of the picture in Kilobytes (KB) and also the full pathname of the file that you have open. What you may have seen if you were watching is a 'progress bar' (a block of squares progressively

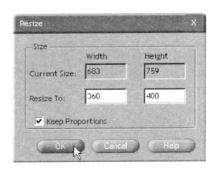

increasing in their number) whiz along the Status Bar in the place of the full file pathname. If you have been very observant, you might have notice that the quoted size of the picture, as now shown on the Status Bar, has decreased. The picture shown in the working area itself will also change.

Just to show you how things have changed, and in case you didn't catch the quoted size of the picture beforehand, click now on the Undo button towards the top of the working area (as shown in the following picture on the left). This 'undoes' the changes, and you can examine the situation before the 'resize'. Now click the Redo button (as shown in the next picture on the right). The changes are applied again.

  If you flip back and forth several times between clicking the 'Undo' and 'Redo' buttons (have a go and try it), you soon appreciate the way in which the picture size has altered from before to after. When you have done with flipping back and forth, leave things in the 'redone' situation (the after case) and you have the smaller quoted picture size.

There is another small point that you can also observe now if you care to. The filename on the right hand side of the Status bar now has a little asterisk (*) symbol against it. This means that there are changes that have been made to the picture, but not yet saved back to the original file. I don't want you to save them to the original file. I do want you to save them to a completely new file – and in my example, I will save them to a file named 'CheekyChops02'. This is the point I made in the discussion before the start of this exercise, when I was explaining that resizing actually loses some of the quality of the file. By not overwriting the initial file, we can avoid losing information. And you never know when you may need this information for a different, future purpose!

Let us now complete the exercise by saving the changes back to the hard drive. In passing, I want to emphasise the same comment that I made at the end of Exercise 13 – when you work with a picture in the working area of MGI PhotoSuite, you are not affecting the hard drive file directly. Your work is held in RAM memory within the computers processor unit, which is temporary memory. It is not until you use either the 'Save' or the 'Save As...' options that the files on the hard drive get altered.

Note This fact may have very important implications for you. If you do a lot of work and do not save it back to the hard drive, then you run the risk of a mishap occurring and you may lose a complete days work! You can never tell when a power failure is going to shut your computer down instantly!

Click now on File from the main menu bar, and choose the 'Save As...' option. When the 'Save Photo' dialog box appears, enter your revised file name in the 'File name:' textbox. Make a check that the 'Prompt For Options' checkbox is not checked (click on it if it is to clear it) and finally click on the Save button, as shown in the following picture.

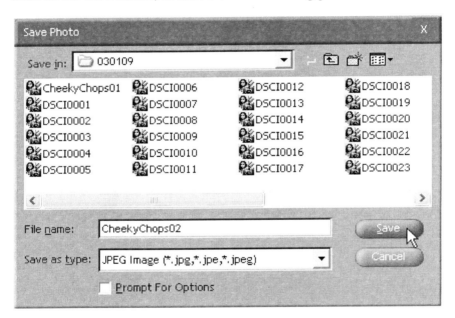

The dialog box will close and the new picture file is then created on the hard drive.

Note Although we have made the picture smaller in this exercise, you can use the same technique to make any picture bigger. If you enter new numbers for either width or height that are greater than those quoted as current values, then the picture size will increase.

This concludes Exercise 14.

We have now reached the end of this chapter about 'Adjusting the pictures with software'. As you will have noticed, there are literally dozens of features and facilities in the MGI PhotoSuite program that we have not even mentioned. My essential purpose in this chapter was not to teach you all about this program, for that could take a whole book in itself! What I wanted to do was to introduce you to it and to show you how to do three jobs that are very common for everyone dealing with pictures from a digital camera, namely:

✓ 1. To be able to select a particular picture and view it in detail on the monitor screen. You can then decide if the picture is worth printing (either as a whole or maybe even one object within it). You can also decide if there are any facets of the picture that you would like to modify.

✓ 2. To be able to re-adjust the 'framing' of a picture so that the placement of your central subject appears in just the way you would like it to appear. This allows you to remove objects from the outer edges altogether if you choose to.

✓ 3. To be able to resize the resultant image, so that you can then use the picture for other particular purposes. There are many occasions where your original picture is either too large or too small. Sending pictures via email is a classic example of a situation where they are often too big and you would like to resize them smaller. By shrinking them to half size first before you attach them to an email, when they are received at the destination they will appear clearly visible and in full view to the reader without them having to detach the picture and print it themselves.

In the next chapter we complete the last stage in producing a digital photograph by printing pictures out on to photographic quality paper.

5

Printing on an Inkjet Printer

5.1   A quick guide to printers

To produce our own colour photographs from the digital pictures that we have taken with the camera, we are going to need the help of a particular type of printer known as an Inkjet printer. The printer model that I am using is the **Hewlett Packard (HP) Photosmart 7150** – a particularly fine piece of equipment and one that I can readily recommend. It is not the most expensive on the market, and not the most sophisticated in terms of features. But it is a good quality printer specifically designed for photographic work, and it will give you some stunning results. It will also serve as a good general-purpose printer for all the other non-photographic work that you may wish to do with your computer. We will cover the use of this printer in some detail within the forthcoming sections of this book.

Note
If you decide to buy a new printer, make sure that you also purchase a printer lead to connect it to your computer. Printer manufacturers invariably don't include such a lead. Most new printers use a USB type of lead and they come in varying lengths. Buy one of sufficient length, bearing in mind where you intend to site your printer as a part of your home installation, but be aware that printer manufacturers often specify a maximum length. With the HP Photosmart 7150 this maximum is 3 metres.

Now, you may have a printer already attached to your personal computer that could be suitable for the job we have in hand, but if you are new to this technology how can you be sure that it is of the correct **Inkjet** type?

Well, the first idea that comes to mind if you are in doubt is to read the name on the label or case. However, I have noticed that many printers will

98

tell you the maker's name and the model number, but they don't always spell out explicitly whether it is of the inkjet type or not (if you see the word 'jet' anywhere, then it will be). If you have the original manual to hand then reading this should answer the question. But I suspect that quite a number of readers may have second-hand equipment – possibly donated from other sources – and chances are that the manual has long since disappeared. Another idea is to look up the model number in the adverts of a computer magazine. This may give you a clue. But if you can't find it listed anywhere then you will still be no wiser.

Note If you can't find your model of printer listed in a current computer magazine, then you may be in trouble in any case! The market in printers is very fast moving these days and spares for them, such as replacement ink cartridges and the like, can quickly become difficult to obtain for older models.

For those readers who haven't a clue about printers and may be wondering what kind they have bought or have been given, I will quickly run through the different types that you may come across and how they function, so that you can make your mind up what type it is and whether you need to replace it or not.

In the early days of personal computing, the most common type of printer that you would meet was the **Dot Matrix** printer. This worked by using a group of very small 'needles' internal to a printing 'head' that individually stamped against an ink ribbon and made small dots (arranged in a matrix on the paper) to form the letter, numbers and symbols. This type of printer is of no use for digital photographs.

The **Daisy Wheel** printer was another type of printer similar to the Dot Matrix in that it too used an ink ribbon. Instead of a group of 'needles', it used a spinning plastic disc with the letters, numbers and symbols embossed on the end of the 'petals' radiating outward from the centre of the disk. As the appropriate 'petal' passed underneath an impact hammer, the hammer would stamp it against the ink ribbon. This printer is also of no use for photographs.

Later, in the mid-eighties, **Laser** printers were developed. Though you cannot easily see the inside workings, these use a beam of light to optically scan over the surface of a rotating drum leaving a small electrical charge in all the right places. As the drum rotates, it then picks up black printing powder (called 'toner') attracted by the electrical charge on the surface. When paper is passed through rollers and makes contact with the drum, the powder is transferred to the paper. The drum itself is then 'cleaned' of charge and made ready for the next page to be printed. The paper continues on through another set of heated rollers that 'fuse' the black powder into the paper's surface. Laser printers can produce good quality black and white images, but colour laser printers are quite expensive. If your printed paper feels particularly warm when it first comes out of the printer than it's almost certainly a laser.

Note
A device called an LED printer is, for our simple purpose, to be considered as the same thing as a laser printer. They just use different ways of creating the beam of light.

If you have a standard black and white laser printer, you should consider purchasing a colour Inkjet printer to compliment the output of your work. You can have more than one printer connected to your personal computer, and you can easily select which one to use for a particular job.

Some of the very latest printer models offer combined functionality of scanning, printing, photocopying and faxing. The printer included in these gadgets may be either an inkjet or a laser type. If it does colour printing then it's almost certainly an inkjet.

That brings us finally to the Inkjet printer itself. Now it is worth spending a few moments describing how these work, because they need maintaining with new ink cartridges on a periodic basis. Just how periodic depends obviously on the workload demand that you place upon them. There are also a few tips and tricks that you should be aware of to get the best out of your printer, and you will understand these tips and tricks better if you have some rudimentary understanding of how they work.

An **Inkjet printer** squirts very fine drops of ink directly from the print head onto the paper. It does this while moving the print head backwards and forwards across the width of the paper very quickly, and the paper itself is traversed slower through the machine. In this manner, the print head can eventually reach every part of the paper's surface area and ink drops can be deposited in all the right places. Because there is no physical contact between the print head and the paper (the ink remember is squirted at the paper) then this type of printer is very quiet in operation. All you hear is a 'whoosh' kind of sound as the print head glides back and forth across the paper's width.

Inkjets can print just in black and white, and when they do so, the black ink cartridge will be used to supply the ink drops necessary for squirting at the paper. When colour pictures or coloured document text is required, a colour cartridge is employed. The colour cartridge consists of three (and for some printers maybe even more) separate colour compartments within the cartridge each filled with different coloured inks. These inks are squirted either independently, or simultaneously, to form the required colour rendering on the paper. The quality of this colouring process has been highly developed in recent years, such that the final printed works produced today can reach photographic standard. What distinguishes a true 'photo' type of inkjet from an ordinary one is the smaller size of the ink drops and the special qualities of the inks used. The whole business of inks, paper and their qualities is discussed further in Chapter 8. Photo printers may have other special photographic features, such as direct printing from a digital camera's memory card, or maybe a direct cable link to a camera (so that you don't necessarily need to use a personal computer). There may also be special arrangements made with the paper tray, such as a separate compartment for small photographic sized paper.

If you've never seen a modern inkjet printer print out a digital colour picture, then boy, are you in for a treat!

Well that's a quick overview of printers at this moment in our history, and a quick description of how they work. From this you should be able to observe your own printer should you have one, and decide what type you have. And now with an idea of how an inkjet printer works, you can better understand the use and fitting of ink cartridges.

To be complete, I will mention that there is another type of printer used by professionals for photographic work called a dye-sublimation printer, but these are more expensive than inkjets.

5.2 Getting the printer ready, inks and paper

In this section, we will cover setting up the Hewlett Packard Photosmart 7150 printer from scratch and make it ready for use. Like most other modern printers, it uses the USB standard to connect it to the computer. This supersedes the 'parallel port' connector that many earlier designs used.

 If you wish to know more about these types of printer connections, see section 1.5 of the companion book *'Using a Computer for the First Time'*.
Note

In setting up the 7150, the manufacturer specifies that your computer system should meet certain minimum requirements (as do other manufacturers for their own printers). These requirements are specified on the front page of the booklet listed as item 8 in the forthcoming Exercise 15. Two points specifically worth mentioning are that your computer system must be using Windows 98 (or Windows 2000, ME or XP) with at least 64 megabytes (preferably more) of RAM memory.

Exercise 15 – Preparing the printer

Open up the box containing the new printer, and carefully remove the contents. It should contain the following items:

1. the printer itself
2. an AC power adapter, and a power supply lead/cord
3. two ink cartridges (types hp57 and hp58) each wrapped in its own sealed white packet
4. a small odd-shaped black plastic device. This is a protector for an ink cartridge
5. a CD-ROM that contains the software needed for your computer in order to work with the printer
6. a set-up guide sheet for quick reference
7. a booklet titled 'basics guide' for the printer
8. a booklet titled 'software set-up and product support'
9. some free samples of hp printer paper.

As I mentioned in the last section, what you will not find in the box is a USB type connecting lead to connect the printer to your computer. If you don't possess a spare lead then I'm afraid you will have to go out and buy one. A

typical USB lead for a printer is shown here. Notice that the left hand end (USB 'A' connector) is much broader than the right hand end (USB 'B' connector). If you do buy one, get one of sufficient length to easily reach from the printer to the computer's processor unit, but no more than 3 metres maximum length.

Note

It is important that you do not connect the printer to the computer until we are ready to do so. The reason is that USB connected equipment requires special computer software to operate, and this is to be found on the CD-ROM. There is a special sequence of events to install the software correctly and it is triggered by plugging the USB cable into the computer. If you do this prematurely, then the sequence will get out of step.

Before we go any further, it may be wise to check that your computer's processor unit does have a spare USB 'A' socket for use with the printer.

Two USB 'A' Type Sockets

Most recent desktop computers have two such sockets at the rear of the processor unit such as these. If your computer does not have a suitable USB socket (either because they are both occupied, or your computer is an older model), it may be possible to have a new 'card' fitted into one of the card slots at the rear to provide two or more new ones. In my own computer, I have a card with an extra four sockets, giving me six in total. Such extra sockets will certainly come in handy for the future – believe me! Consult your local dealer for more details about such cards.

Another important note – The USB system allows for external devices called USB 'hubs' to provide extra USB sockets. My personal advice is never connect your printer to the computer via a USB hub. Always connect it direct using a socket on the PC itself. This can be an additional 'card' added into one of the processor units rear slots, as we have just mentioned. There are several technical reasons behind this advice, but this is not the place to go into them. If you are interested in knowing more, have a look at my web site (www.billhall.me.uk).

Okay, we are ready to start our preparations. First of all, position the printer in the place where it is going to permanently reside. Ideally, this should not be too close to a radiator and it has to be somewhere where there is a mains power socket within reach. Do bear in mind that you are going to use this printer extensively throughout its lifetime so don't just dump it anywhere. If you haven't space on the same surface top that you are using for your monitor and keyboard, then you might want to invest in a small side table. Keep enough space clear on your working surface for placing books (such as this one!) and for managing finished printed pages or photographs that you will produce in due course.

Carefully remove all the pieces of sticky tape that are attached to the printer. These have held everything in place during transit.

Plug one end of the mains power supply lead/cord into the AC power adapter, and the other end into a mains supply outlet. Don't switch it on just yet. Then plug the thin lead from adapter into the white Power Socket on the rear of the printer as shown here.

Face the front of the printer. Observe that the dark grey paper tray has a sliding lever with a light grey knob on the right-hand side (visible under my hand in the next picture). Its purpose is to engage or disengage a special compartment for 6in x 4in photographic prints. Make sure that this lever is in the position nearest to you and furthest away from the printer mechanism (this is the disengaged position).

Now lift up the paper tray lid until it 'clicks' into the open position, as shown in the next picture. This lid is actually the bottom of the OUT tray, where your finished prints will be placed after they have been printed. The tray underneath this lid is the IN tray, where your normal sized printing paper (for example, A4) is placed before being printed.

In this next picture, look carefully at the points I have marked by the two white arrows...

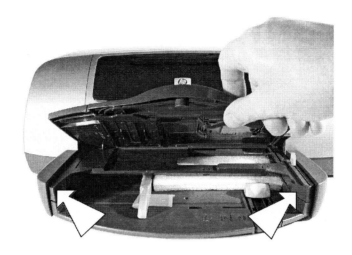

Using your thumbs at these points, very gently apply pressure outwards in order to lift up the whole plastic assembly (including the lid) and then take hold with your hands to slide it forwards towards you. Carefully remove it altogether from the printer and make sure to place it somewhere where it won't get broken!

There is normally another piece of sticky tape at the bottom of the paper tray holding the light grey side-guide lever in position. Remove that too and then slide the side lever as far to the left as it will go.

At this moment, you should notice a rectangular piece of white foam. Its position is demonstrating where the unused printer paper normally sits. Holding it in place is another light grey end-guide lever. Slide this lever towards you now as far as it will go. This end-guide lever is sliding inside yet another dark grey slide, which will also extend when the guide lever is fully out.

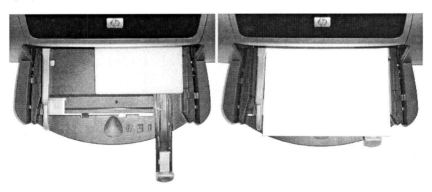

Remove the white foam and replace it with a small stack of plain A4 size inkjet paper in the tray (say 10 sheets), as shown in the right-hand picture above. You can now discard the foam. Position the paper so that it is up against the right-hand edge of the tray, and push the stack gently forwards (away from you and towards the printer mechanism) until it reaches a natural 'stop'. Slide the left-hand guide lever now a little towards the right to 'snuggle up' to the paper and hold it square in position, and slide the end-guide forwards to 'snuggle up' to the end of the paper. These guides are now set for A4 paper. If you should choose to use some other sized paper in the future – for example A5 – then the procedure for setting the guides is precisely the same.

 Tip – When printing, if the paper fails to be drawn into the printer, then the reason will most likely be that the paper is not far enough forward in the tray.

Now gently replace the plastic assembly that you put to one side back into position. **Don't use force**. If it doesn't immediately drop back into its original position, take it out again and try once more. This assembly is a delicate piece of plastic that may break if you are ham-fisted! Just check when you think you have replaced it that it is sat down correctly again, as shown in the picture last but one (the one with the white arrows).

Close the paper tray lid down once more.

Note

In future, you will not have to remove the plastic assembly in order to replace the paper, but knowing how to do it will serve you in good stead should any paper become subsequently jammed.

To restock the paper tray with the same sized paper, you need only lift up the lid, slide in your new paper and close the lid again.

Okay. Now we will install the ink cartridges.

Power On/Off button

Switch on the mains power at the outlet, and press the Power On/Off button on the front panel...

There are three indicator lights on the front panel that now begin to flash in rotation, and 'whirring' noises can be heard from inside. Lift up the 'Smokey glass' top cover of the printer (where you see the 'hp' logo) and wait for the two internal ink cartridge holders to reposition themselves in the middle of the mechanism. The 'whirring' noises will then stop.

Flip up the latch of the blue (left) cartridge cradle, as shown in this next picture.

Remove first the ink cartridges labelled 'hp57' from its sealed white packet. It should have a blue top to it. Using the pink tag as shown in the following picture, pull off the clear protective plastic completely, but take great care not to touch the shiny print head shown here underneath the cartridge, nor the electrical contacts on the end. You can discard the tag.

Now carefully insert the cartridge into the blue holder numbered '57' from the front side by aligning the top lip of the cartridge with the groove in the grey plastic, as seen in the next picture.

The electrical contacts on the end of the cartridge go in first, so that you can read the writing on the cartridge top (that is, the writing does not appear upside down).

Now here comes the tricky bit. When you try to push the cartridge fully into the holder it gets stuck halfway! The first time I tried to do this it just would not go in. The secret for success is shown in the above picture. Gently push it in as far as it will gently go, then gently press down on the back edge with you finger and push it in a bit more. As you push down, the cartridge 'cockles up' at the front and you should feel it

then go past the obstruction. Close the blue latch. As you pull the latch down, it presses down on the cartridge to secure it in the holder.

Now have a look again at the last picture. Notice that the grey latch on the right has two numbers on it – '56' and '58'. You can put either a cartridge labelled 'hp56' or labelled 'hp58' into this one. The printer is only supplied with an 'hp58' cartridge, which is the photo colour cartridge and is the one we will now insert, but you can go purchase an 'hp56', which is a pure black ink cartridge. The idea here is that you only use the 'hp58' for photographic type work, and you use an 'hp56' for simple black text work with documents.

Note

The ability to use either 'hp56' or 'hp58' cartridges in this grey holder is the reason why you have been provided with that odd-shaped black plastic device (item 4 in the unpacking list). If you decide to switch them over at any point, this protector is somewhere for you to 'park' the unused cartridge and keep it in good shape for later use.

Now install the 'hp58' cartridge in the same manner as we have just done for the blue 'hp57'. Close the grey latch when you have done so.

Now comes the moment of truth! Close the top cover and wait. What you should hear is more 'whirring noises' and after a minute or so, a strange blue glow can occasionally be seen through the 'Smokey glass' cover window. After about three minutes, a printed 'Calibration Test Page' magically comes out of the printer into the top tray, as shown in this next picture.

At this stage, we have now prepared the printer mechanism physically (often referred to as the hardware). Our next task is to install the printer software on the computer. This we do in a particular sequence, which you should follow carefully step by step.

Remember **not** to plug the printer cable into the computer until we are ready to do so.
Note

If your computer uses **virus-checking software**, you should disable it before you continue. Instructions for how to do this vary from product to product so you need to check with your own product's information.

Tip – If you can see a virus-checker icon visible on the Task bar (in the bottom right-hand corner near the clock), then right-clicking on it may display an option to disable it temporarily.

Now open the CD packet and carefully remove the HP Photosmart CD-ROM (item 5 on the un-packing list at the start of this exercise). Remember, no fingerprints allowed on the shiny side! Place the CD-ROM in the CD drive of your computer (printed side uppermost) and close the drive door. Wait for a short while and the 'Autoplay' feature of the CD-ROM drive should automatically start the installation program running (if it doesn't then read the advice given in Exercise 8).

When the installation program runs, the first screen that you see is shown in the following picture on the left. Click on the top button marked 'Install HP Photosmart printers software' (notice that the mouse pointer changes from an arrow to a 'hand' when over the button). After a short while, you will then see the picture on the right.

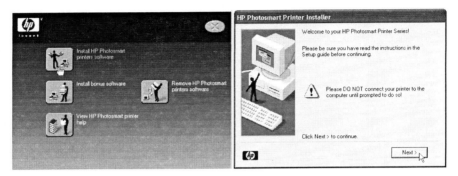

Click on the Next button. The program will then do a little check to make sure that your computer system meets the standard of minimum requirements for the installation to continue.

Note

If for any reason it fails to meet the minimum standard requirements, then you will see a message telling you so. Read it carefully to see where it falls short, and take appropriate remedial action. Item 8 in the list at the start of this exercise specifies what the minimum requirements are. Consult your local computer dealer if you need help to correct the problem.

Assuming that your system **does** meet the requirements, the screen you should now see is shown in the following picture on the left. The progress bar seen in the middle of this screen will gradually move from left to right, and similar progress bars will appear one after the other in quick succession.

At one point the program screen may vanish completely, and you may wonder what is going on. If you observe the hard disk indicator light on the processor unit, you should see that this is merrily flashing away, meaning that the processor is still working on the installation task. Eventually, the screen shown in the next picture on the right will appear ...

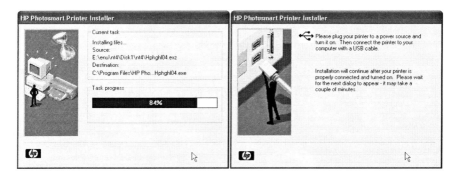

This is the point where we are going to physically connect the printer cable to the computer. First, make sure that the power to the printer is switched on and wait for the green indicator light at the right-hand side of the **Power On/Off button** to settle and glow steady. Then insert the narrower plug end of the USB printer cable into the USB 'B' socket at the rear of the printer (this socket is visible on the picture illustrating the power socket that we met before). Finally, insert the wider USB 'A' plug into a USB 'A' socket at the rear of the computer's processor unit. It does not really matter which USB socket you choose because the processor unit will automatically sense and detect the one that you have chosen (but bear in mind the point I made about not using a 'hub' that I made earlier in the section). Wait for the installation program to sense that the printer has now been connected.

Several things happen quite quickly and it varies a little depending on whether you are using Windows XP, Windows 98, or another Windows versions as to precisely what you will see. If you have had a printer previously installed on your computer, then Windows XP users may see a message asking 'Do you want to set the HP Photosmart 7150 series as your default printer?' Click on the **Yes button** if you do see it. Making this the 'default' printer means that it will automatically be the chosen printer when we want to do any printing work in the future. Windows 98 users will see a 'New Hardware Found' message. Wait for the 'driver information database' to be built and for some other files to be copied. This copying may take a few minutes.

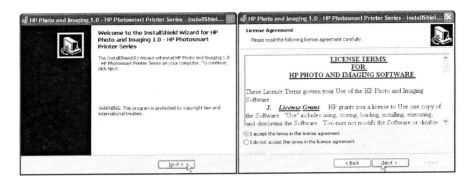

Eventually, all users will see the 'Install Shield Wizard for HP Photo and Imaging' screen as in the previous picture on the left. Click on the **Next button** and soon after you then see the adjacent picture on the right.

In theory, you now read through all the small print in the 'license terms' (I have yet to meet anyone who has actually done so!). When you are ready, click inside the small circle to the left of 'I accept the terms in the license agreement' to put the dot inside it. Then click on the **Next button,** as shown in the previous right-hand picture.

The installation procedure will now show you the screen on the following left. Click on the Next button. You then see the adjacent screen on the right. Click on the Install button.

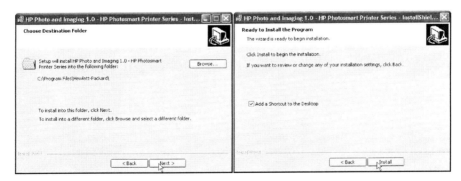

More screen messages now follow in quick succession, displaying a progress bar as files are copied from the CD-ROM to your hard drive. It will take a few minutes to copy all of the files required. Finally you see the screen shown in the next picture on the left. Click on the **Finish button**.

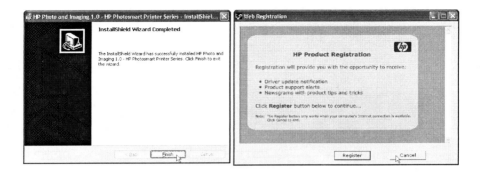

What happens then depends again on the version of Windows you are using:

● For Windows XP users, some time after clicking the button you will see the product registration screen on the above right.

● For Windows 98 and ME systems, you will see a screen that invites you restart your computer. First make sure that you remove the CD-ROM from the drive and then click the Restart button. Your computer will respond by automatically closing down and restarting itself. When it does restart, it will display the desktop with two windows already opened. One of these is the product registration screen, shown in the previous picture on the right.

Note

If users of Windows 98 or Windows ME restart the computer without removing the CD-ROM first, they will likely see yet a third window displaying the very first installation procedure screen again. This is because the CD drive will start up the 'Autoplay' action for the CD-ROM once more, after the restart. The remedy here is simply to close this unwanted window by clicking on the grey oval 'X' button visible in the window's top right-hand corner. You can then continue as normal.

From the window displaying the previous picture on the right, the installation program now invites you to register your printer product over the Internet using Hewlett Packard's web site. For the moment, I want you to choose the **Cancel button**. A simple message then appears with three options to remind you to register either 'Tomorrow', 'In a month's time' or 'Don't remind me again'. Choose whichever option is convenient for you and then click the **OK button**.

Okay, at this moment the printer is fully installed on your computer. You will also see a browser window open. If this is not showing full screen, then click on the Maximise button to make it so (the middle one of the three located in the top right-hand corner).

You can now see a screen that invites you to print a test page on the printer. Move the mouse pointer anywhere over the area shown in this following picture and make a 'click' to start the sequence for the test page

First a pretty picture of some houses can briefly be seen, and this is quickly followed by a Print window that pops up over the top of it.

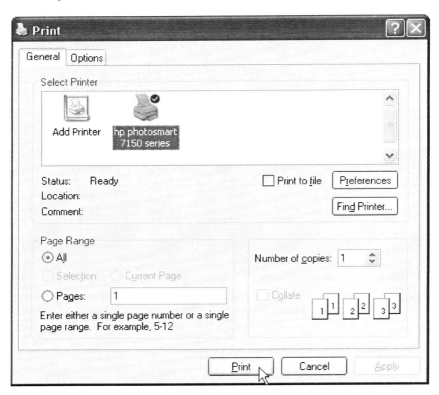

The print window for Windows XP has a **Print button**. Windows 98 is slightly different and has an **OK button**. Whichever version you are using, click on the appropriate button and printing of the test page will be set in motion.

You will then see a further window on your monitor with images representing the status of the printer's ink cartridges (both the hp57 cartridge and the hp58). If you now care to observe the printer itself, you will shortly see the green indicator light begin to flash and 'whirring' noises start to come from within the mechanism. The green indicator light is flashing to show you that it is accepting information now down the USB cable and storing it in the printer's own internal memory.

Eventually, you will hear a rhythmic sound coming from the printer, as the print head glides back and forth over the width of the page being printed. Tiny drops of ink are being squirted onto the paper with each pass. Finally, your test page is ejected into the Out Tray and the green indicator stops flashing and returns to a steady glow. The test page is revealed to be a colourful picture of some wooden clapboard houses in Buenos Aires, Argentina.

At the end of printing, the window showing images of the ink cartridges disappears and you are left with the screen image of the houses as seen in the test page. Close the window by clicking on the '**X' button** in the top right-hand corner and you are then back at the normal Windows desktop.

The installation procedure is now complete. Win XP users will now have to remove the CD-ROM from the CD drive and put it back in the paper envelope

Note   Remember to keep all the booklets, CD-ROM and other small items somewhere safe for future reference. I usually put mine together in one envelope and I have a standard file where all such computer information is kept. One day in the future you will need these items again – so do take good care of them!

This concludes Exercise 15.

5.3   Printing your first photo

At this point, you should now have a colour inkjet printer attached to your computer and ready to use for printing your digital pictures.

Exercise 16 – Printing your first digital picture

Begin this exercise from the desktop. Start the MGI PhotoSuite program running again, as we did for Exercise 12 in Chapter 4. If the program is not displayed full screen then click on the **Maximise button** (the middle one of the three in the top right-hand corner of the window), so that it completely fills the monitor screen.

Click on the **Get button**. The left-hand panel will now show you the five buttons for selecting a Photo Source. Click on the **Computer button**. Up pops the **Open dialog box**.

Back in section 4.3, we discussed digital picture sizing and I promised later to show you an example of Scaling. We shall do that here in this exercise, so I now want you to leave alone the files that we created by Cropping and Resizing and choose another of your digital pictures from the original set that we transferred to the computer. If you have not altered anything since Exercise 14, then your list of files will now probably be displayed in the large white box of the **Open dialog box**. Should that not be the case then you should click on the down arrow symbol at the right side of the 'Look in:' box (we call this a 'drop down list box for obvious reasons) and select 'My Documents'. Then click on 'Epsilon Pictures' to highlight it blue and click the Open button. Then select one of the 'date' sub-folders with a click, and click again on the Open button. Now you see your list of picture files.

Choose one of the files that you would like to see printed as your very first digital photograph. Remember that you can browse through them each in turn by using the group of four 'Arrow keys' on the keyboard (as we did in Exercise 12). To browse, you must start with a click of the mouse on the first file in the list to highlight it (we say that this puts the 'focus' of attention inside the large white box). Then if you keep pressing the 'Down Arrow' key repetitively, it will go through all the pictures in sequence and show you a sample of the picture in the Preview pane. If you pause on one picture for about one second, you see a small box pop-up to tell you more details about the picture.

In this exercise, I am shall choose 'DSCI0007'. To open the chosen picture file into the working area of MGI PhotoSuite, first make sure the file is highlighted and then click the **Open button** once more, as shown in this next picture.

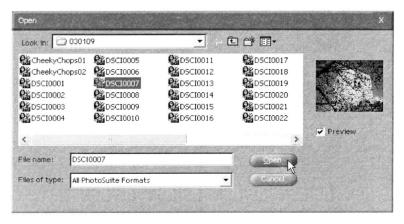

Your picture then appears in its full glorious colour in the working area.

From the horizontal group of seven buttons at the top of the screen, click the **Print button**. A little bit of screen shuffling then takes place, and the left-panel changes to offer two buttons. Click on the top one simply labelled '**Print**'. This opens the '**Print Preview**' sub-section, as seen in the following picture.

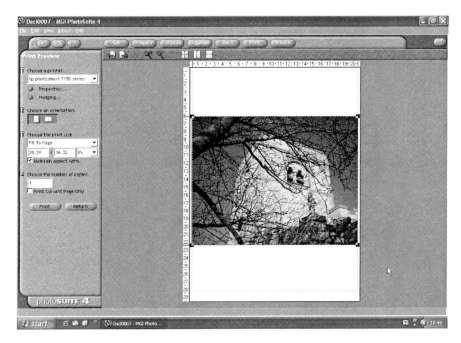

Before we go any further, you may recall from the last chapter that I placed great emphasis on the fact that you should never do any work or alterations on an original picture. We have just selected one of the 'original' images and loaded it into MGI PhotoSuite – should the first task not be to save it under a new filename for safety? The key issue here concerns the danger of making changes to an original picture. Click now on **File** from the main menu in order to see the list of options to choose from. What you will notice is that all the options in the list for saving back to the hard disk are 'greyed-out' and not available for you to choose. Therefore there is no danger for us in using this **Print Preview** section of the program of affecting the hard drive copy of this file we have chosen. Click anywhere in the grey part of the working area just to make the list disappear.

From this **Print Preview sub-section** of the program, we can do all the necessary work to scale the picture and prepare it ready for printing.

Many of the functions of the controls in the left-hand panel are self-evident, so I will not dwell upon each of them in fine detail. I will only briefly describe their functions and give you the pleasure of playing around with them at a later time. Taking the controls in turn as they are numbered, let us begin an overview of them:

- **1. Printer Selection Box.** If you have more than one printer attached to your computer (for example a Laser and an Inkjet), then you select the one to use from a list that appears when you click the 'down arrow' at, the right side of this box. The name that finally shows in the box is the one that will be used. Underneath it are two smaller controls labelled 'Properties…' and 'Nudging…' Clicking the small 'Properties…' button brings up a pop-up window known as the 'Printer Driver' menu, and this window is not part of the MGI PhotoSuite program, but a separate 'driver' program whose functions are specific to the manufacturer and type of printer you are using. The small 'Nudging…' button is a fine-tuning control to very accurately line up the image that will be printed onto the paper in the printer. You won't normally alter this control unless you are printing things like peel off 'labels' where a small misalignment can appear very visible on the finished work.

- **2. Orientation.** Printer manufacturers have now settled upon two delightful jargon words to describe how the image that you are about to print will be orientated on the paper – **Portrait** and **Landscape**. These words describe the way your image is printed in relation to the paper

118

direction. You choose between them by clicking the little icons in the grey box. The left one is 'Portrait' and the right one is 'Landscape'.

Paper is normally fed into the printer mechanism with its 'narrowest edge' first. The **Portrait** option will print your image arranged just as you can see it in the working area. The top goes into the printer first and comes out first.

Click on the little **Landscape** icon and see the effect. Observe that your view of the working area now appears as though the paper has been rotated by 90 degrees. This is slightly misleading and only done for your viewing convenience. Practically what happens is that the left side now goes into the printer first and comes out first. Now click on the Portrait icon to change it back again.

● **3. +.** Here you can see alternative methods for Scaling the image of your digital picture. You can either use a preset option from the 'drop down list' box, or you can type in your own dimensions in the two boxes below it.

Note **There seems to be a software 'bug' in this control and it does not always behave itself**. What I have found is that sometimes you need to click on the white 'units of measurement' box to 'elbow' it into responding properly.

● **4. Number of Copies box**. Here you ask for more than one copy in the same print run.

The small tick box titled 'Print Current Page Only' underneath is only for situations where you have several items that could be possibly printed, for example, if you create an 'Album' with several pages of digital pictures, then this tick box is limiting the print to only what is shown on the screen.

With that brief overview of the list of controls, lets now describe what you can see in the working area.

The large white space in the working area represents the paper in the printer (it's a preview of it). Along the top and down the left side you can see two rulers to help you judge whereabouts your image is located on the paper, and the actual size of the paper itself. The units shown in my illustrations are all in centimetres.

Note The units used for the rulers are determined by the way in which your Windows system is set for the basic computer itself. It is governed by the 'Regional Settings' within 'Control Panel'. If you want to change the units then you must adjust them by first opening the 'Regional Settings' icon within 'Control Panel', and then making your change.

The paper size is actually determined by how the printer has been set up. If your printer is not set up for the paper you are using (A4 is the normal size in Europe, Letter 8 ½ by 11 is the normal size for North America) you can change it using the 'Properties...' button under the 'Printer Selection box' in control No.1 (there is often a tabbed page labelled 'Layout' or 'Paper' within 'Properties', which allows you to change sizes).

One final point to mention about the working area concerns a thin light-grey line that you can see running right around the inside edge of the paper. The line is shown in this next picture and indicated by the mouse pointer.

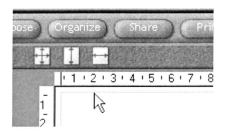

The line represents the 'printable area' for the paper and forms a border that is 3mm (1/8th of an inch) from the paper's edge at the top, left and right edges. You may notice that it is slightly wider, 12mm (1/2 an inch), at the bottom edge. The theory is that you should arrange for the image of your digital picture not to cross this border, or you run the risk of printing ink not on the paper but on the printer's rollers, and this can lead to smudges. The border is slightly wider at the bottom because this is the last piece of paper available for the printer's rollers to grip the paper before it finally ejects it into the Out tray.

Okay, we are now ready to prepare our picture for printing. We will do this by considering how each of the controls numbered 1 to 4 in the left-hand panel should be adjusted. When we have done that we can then press the Print button to activate the printing.

Control No. 1

Most readers will have only one printer connected to their computer, and you should see the make and model number shown in the Printer Selection box. If you have more than one and the desired inkjet is not showing, then select it in the manner that we described previously in the overview.

Click on the '**Properties ...**' **button** just below the box. A new 'Printer Driver' window opens showing you features about your specific printer. For the HP Photosmart 7150, the window has five 'tabbed' pages. You can change tabbed pages by clicking the tab label at the top. The important points to check are:

    a. that the quality is set to the 'best' or 'highest' setting

    b. the paper type is set to either 'automatic' or to 'photo glossy'

    c. the paper size is correct (A4 in my example).

Now the method for checking these points will be different for different makes of printer. With the Photosmart 7150, you can check points a. and b. from the first tab labelled 'Quality'. The standard settings are usually 'Normal' for quality and 'Automatic' for paper type, so go ahead and change the quality to '**Best**' by clicking on it. Click then on the tab labelled 'Layout' and check that the paper size is correct (A4 for my example).

There are a myriad other settings that you can adjust. I will leave these for you to explore at a later time. The important points are the three mentioned above, and with these now set to their appropriate values we 'apply' them to the printer by clicking the **Apply button** at bottom of the window. This may be 'greyed out' if you haven't changed any settings (indicating that there is nothing to apply!) so don't worry if that is the case. Finally click the **OK button** at the bottom of the window to close it and return to the MGI PhotoSuite control panel.

Control No.2

This control should already be set to **Portrait** and we leave it at that setting. We demonstrated the two different orientations in the overview discussed previously.

Control No.3

The boxes shown as part of this control allow you to modify the size of the picture image by preset or numerical means. Again, I will leave you to experiment with these by yourself at a later time. In this exercise, we investigate an alternative method of changing the size and position of the image on the paper by directly using the mouse pointer in the working area.

The image when you first begin will be centred both vertically and horizontally on the paper, and the size of the image will be expanded to fill the full width between the two extremes of the thin light-grey line defining

121

the printable area. The paper we will finally use for our 'photographs' will be 'Photo Glossy' paper and is more expensive than the ordinary kind used for general text type of work. As such, it is wise to take care not to waste it, so I am going to alter the size and placement of the image to leave enough room to get two images on one sheet. We will finally print our first photograph in this exercise, and a second one in Exercise 17. Then in Exercise 18, I will demonstrate how you can cut these photographs out very cleanly from an A4 sheet, and trim the edges to give you two stunning individual photographs.

Place the tip of your mouse pointer over the little black square at the bottom right-hand corner of your picture. Notice that when you do so, the pointer icon changes to a sloping 'double-headed arrow', as shown in this next picture.

Click on the mouse and keep the button held so that you are performing a **drag action**. Now move the mouse up and to the left, following the diagonal path of the sloping icon. You should see the dotted line surrounding you picture also move. Keep the drag action going until the dotted line is indicating a new size of about one quarter of the original picture size (the length of each side becomes about half of what they were). As long as you maintain the drag, you can slide the mouse back and forth to judge the new size with a degree of care. It doesn't have to be exact, try and guess it approximately. When you think you are about right then let go of the mouse button and the drag action terminates. The picture will now resize itself smaller. (If you let go of the drag too soon, don't worry about it. You can always pick up the corner again in the same way and start another drag action going.)

Now that you have the picture smaller, we can try to move its position. Place the mouse pointer into the centre of the newly sized picture and notice that the pointer icon now changes to a 'four headed arrow' symbol, as shown in the next picture. Click the mouse button and keep it held to perform another drag action. Move the mouse so that the rectangular dotted line slides up to the top left corner of the white paper area to leave a border of about 1cm along the top and down the left side. There are two lines also moving on the rulers to guide you more precisely, as shown here...

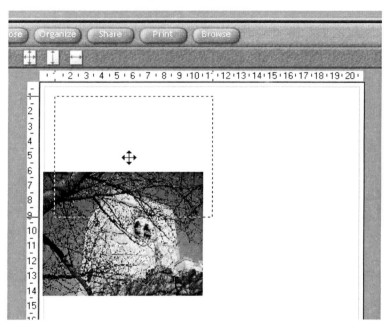

Then let go of the button to end the drag. Observe that the picture location now changes to occupy the position defined by the dotted line rectangle. (Again, if you don't get it quite right on the first attempt, start another drag in the same way to make a correction).

Okay, with the picture now repositioned, we can make the last adjustment, which is to resize the picture bigger to better occupy the available space on the paper. Now this is where you need to watch the left-hand ruler more closely and do a small calculation. We want to be able to get a second picture onto the same A4 sheet of paper and also need to leave a boundary for cutting it out. You will find that it is the height that we need to take care with. There will be plenty of space in respect of the width. The height of A4 paper is almost 30cm, which puts the centreline at approximately 15cm. If we place one picture in each half then we should be OK. With a boundary of 1cm at both the top and bottom of each picture, plus another 0.5cm for clearance, that means that the picture height should be 15cm − 2.5cm equals 12.5cm. The bottom edge of the picture will then be the picture height of 12.5cm plus the top boundary of 1cm, equals 13.5cm on the ruler. We must therefore now expand the bottom edge of the picture by dragging it down to the 13.5cm mark on the left ruler. Move the tip of the mouse pointer to point over anywhere at the bottom edge of the picture, preferably in the middle of it. Notice that the symbol changes again to a vertical 'double-headed arrow' symbol, as shown in the following picture. Click on the mouse button and keep pressed to perform the last drag action. Move the mouse down the paper, watching the marker in the ruler on the left. When the marker is in the centre between the numerals '13' and '14' (as shown in this next picture) then let go of the mouse button to end the drag.

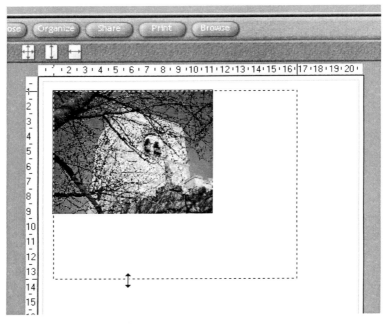

Again you will see the picture change its size to fill out the dotted line.
Our picture image adjustments are now finished.

Control No.4

We are nearly ready to make a print, but there is one last thing that we must do. We need to change the paper in the paper tray to 'Photo Glossy' paper.

If you are using the HP Photosmart 7150 printer, this paper is known as 'hp premium plus' 240 gm/m2.

Remove the existing stack of ordinary print paper from the printer's 'In' tray and carefully replace it with a few sheets of A4 Photo Glossy paper. Because it is photographic paper, you should avoid putting any fingerprints on the glossy side.

! **■** **Take great care to make sure that you have this the correct way up. For the 'HP Photosmart 7150' printer, the 'correct way' is for the most <u>glossy side to appear face down</u> in the tray (dull side facing upwards so that you can see the 'hp' logo).**

The HP Photosmart printer pulls the paper into the mechanism and flips it over before printing, so this is the reason why you place it face down in the In tray. When it flips it over then it will then have the glossy side facing upwards and directly under the ink cartridges. If you are using another manufacturer's printer, the 'correct way' may be different. Those printers that have an 'In' tray at the back of the printer (rather than the front as with the 'HP Photosmart 7150') are likely to need the paper placing glossy side face up. If you are not sure then you must consult the printer's instructions.

Check, and readjust the guides if necessary, to make sure the glossy paper is squarely positioned in the tray so that it feeds evenly into the printer mechanism. The guides must not trap the paper, or you may experience a problem when it attempts to pull it inwards.

Looking back at the left-hand panel on the monitor screen, check that the number of copies box is showing '1'. **Okay, This is the big moment!** Now click the **Print button** as shown in this picture.

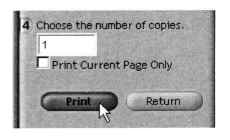

You then see a message saying 'Printing in progress', and the printer will soon start making whirring noises. There is nothing more that you need do now other than wait for the printing process to go through its motions. Depending on the type of printer you are using, you may see another screen showing you the status of the ink levels in the ink cartridges (this happens with the HP Photosmart 7150). These 'supervisory information' screens are normally automatic and they will disappear when the printing process is complete.

Finally, your magnificent digital photograph will appear in the Out tray in its full glory!

Close the MGI PhotoSuite program by simply clicking the '**X' button** in the far top right-hand corner of the window. You will then arrive back at the desktop.

This concludes exercise 16.

5.4   Printing another and trimming your photos

In this section, we investigate printing another digital picture on the same sheet of A4 glossy paper as the one we have just used. This shows you how you can optimise the use of this fairly expensive paper. The problem then arises of cutting out your pictures so that they become true photographs. You can, of course, do this simply with a pair of scissors, but there is a much easier and neater method using a device called a 'personal trimmer'.

In the final exercise of this chapter, I will introduce you to a brilliant personal trimmer from a company called DAHLE. Their **Personal Trimmer Model 507** is a fairly inexpensive device, currently retailing at under £40, and is well worth purchasing one for the amount of effort that it will save you. It also gives you a very neat and professional finish to your photographs and is completely safe to use.

Exercise 17 – Printing your second digital picture

The computer aspect of this exercise is identical to that for last one (Exercise 16). For this reason, I will not illustrate all of the steps again in detail but simply help you by describing what needs to be done. If you need to refresh yourself about the way to do things, then refer back to the previous exercise.

Begin this exercise from the desktop. Start the MGI PhotoSuite program running again, as we did before. Click on the **Get button** and click again on the **Computer button** that then appears in the left-hand panel.

Using the **Open dialog box**, select for this exercise another of your original digital pictures. This will become your second photograph so pick one that has some good colours to show you what the printer can really do.

With the picture now open in the working area, you get a better chance to inspect it. If you want to change your mind, then you can 'close' the picture by clicking on File from the main menu and then selecting the **Close**

option (you use the **Close All option** for occasions where you have opened several pictures). You can then choose another. If you don't close a picture first and go ahead to 'get' another, the first picture will still be held in the program's memory. This doesn't cause a problem particularly, but may reduce the total amount of 'free memory' available for the program to work with, and you may then notice that the program slows down a bit in its overall response time. (If you have several pictures open at once then you would notice this even more).

Okay, click again on the **Print button** in the group of seven buttons at the top of the screen. Then click the **Print button** that appears in the left-hand panel. You now have to follow the same steps considering each of the numbered controls in the panel:

1. Check that the printer's name is correct in the selection box, then click the 'Properties' button below it. Make sure that the 'Quality' is set to 'Best', the paper type is 'Automatic' (or 'Photo Glossy', whichever), and the paper size is correct (A4 if appropriate).

2. The normal setting is **Portrait** and you can see that this has already been set for you by looking at the vertical paper direction in the working area.

3. Again, you should manipulate the size and position of the picture image using the mouse pointer and the three 'drag' actions that we described in Exercise 16. Make them exactly the same for this second picture and then we will see in a moment how this will fit with the paper used for the first picture.

4. **This step is the one slightly different from before**. Remove the existing stack of glossy paper from the 'In' tray. Now place the single paper sheet containing the first picture into the 'In' tray – but this time feeding the end with the blank 'half' into the tray first. Remember, you must put it in the 'correct' way up, which is face down for the HP Photosmart 7150. Readjust the guides if necessary to make sure the paper is square in the tray and fully inserted. (If the printer fails to pick it up, then it is likely that you haven't put it far enough in).

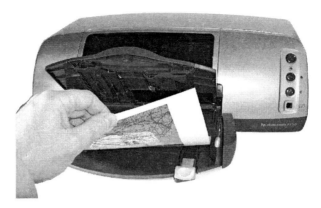

With the paper now inserted in the printer and the second image correctly positioned on the computer screen, we are now ready to print the second photograph. Click the **Print button** underneath the controls in the left-hand panel.

The 'printing in progress' message will appear on the screen, and the printer mechanism will soon start printing again. After a few minutes, the paper will be ejected into the out tray, and you will have two images printed on the same sheet of paper upside down to each other and separated by a white border in between of about 1.5cm each.

This concludes Exercise 17.

Exercise 18 – Cutting and trimming your pictures

The **DAHLE 507 Personal Trimmer**, shown in this picture, is a simple but effective device for cutting and trimming paper. It is ideally suited for working with digital printing and allows you to easily print several pictures on a single sheet of paper. You can use the trimmer to both separate them out and to trim their borders individually. This produces professional looking photographs that you may then mount in a conventional photo album.

The trimmer has a flat blue bed for the paper to rest upon, and a cutting head with a black handle that slides up and down an aluminium guide. To operate the trimmer, place the trimmer in front of you in the way shown in the above picture, so that the aluminium slide is on the right side (if you are right-handed). Pull the black handle towards you as far as it will go, until it is resting in the 'home' position in the bottom 'end stock' (the one nearest to you). Then slide the paper onto the bed from the left and tuck one corner underneath the clear plastic strip so that the clear plastic strip is over the top of the paper, as shown in this next picture.

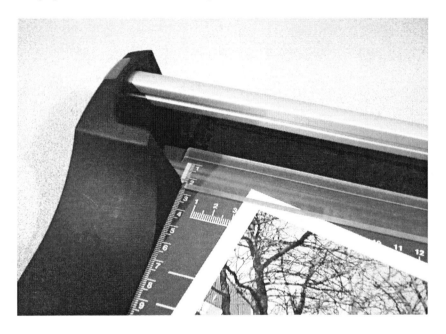

Now feed the paper all the way underneath the plastic strip and square it up to the top 'end stock' so that approximately one half of the paper is resting on the blue bed, and the other half is hanging over the right hand side, as shown in the following picture.

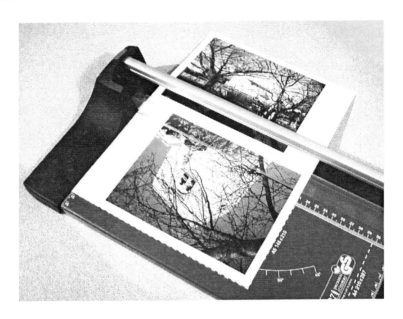

The trimmer will shortly slice the paper precisely along a line down the right edge of the plastic strip, so reposition the paper now squarely against the top 'end stock' and as far under the plastic as it needs to go, in order to make the cut down the central border between the two pictures.

When you are ready to make the cut, place the palm of your left hand on the flat part of top 'end stock' and let the weight of your upper body hold the trimmer firmly down on the table. Then with your right hand, slowly but firmly slide the cutting head up from the bottom stock all the way to the top stock. Leave it there while you remove the paper from the bed. You should now have neatly separated the two pictures with a nice clean edge. When you have completely removed the paper, you should then slide the cutting head back to the bottom stock, ready for the next time you want to use it.

You may now repeat the trimming action to trim all four edges of each picture. How much white border you decide to leave around the picture is entirely up to you, but try make and each border edge of equal width.

When you have finished, you should have two very professional looking photographs.

This concludes Exercise 18.

Before we leave this chapter on the printer, I want to mention that Hewlett Packard also provides some excellent software on their CD-ROM, besides that required for the printer itself. Space does not permit me to go into details, but one program of particular interest is the 'Memories Disc Creator'. If you have a CD-Writer on your computer, and a DVD player that supports the Video CD format (most new ones do), you can make your own CDs to play back on the DVD player. This will let you watch your pictures on TV as a 'slide-show' presentation, and accompanied with music of your choice taken from your own audio CDs!

If you get chance to try it out, you will find it is truly amazing!

6

More About the Camera

6.1 The other camera controls

In chapter 2, we introduced the basic controls for the camera and this allowed us to switch the camera on and off, take pictures and view them on the camera's own Monitor Screen. In this chapter, we will discuss the remaining controls and their functions.

Further controls on the front

The Flash Bulb and Viewfinder Window are fairly obvious items so I have not bothered to label them here, nor have I labelled the main controls that we have described before. Three items that are not so obvious are shown in this next picture.

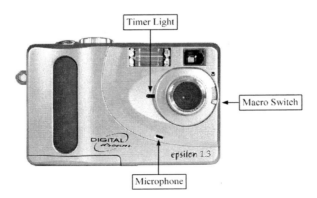

Flash Bulb

The flash facility is described in Exercise 19, section 6.2.

Viewfinder

As with most cameras, the Viewfinder is simple enough to use. Though the Monitor Screen will show you the picture you are about to take, you may often find that using the Viewfinder instead helps you keep the camera steadier when it comes to pressing the Shutter Button.

Timer Light

The camera has a built-in 'Self Timer' mechanism that can automatically take pictures after a preset delay (normally 7 seconds). The red Timer Light is an indicator that flashes to warn you when it is operating. We will discover precisely how to use the timer in Exercise 20. The classic use for the timer is to take a picture including yourself (where you trigger the camera and then dash to join the group type of photo), but another good idea – if you often suffer camera shake when you press the button – is to use the timer feature for taking an ordinary shot. You can then hold the camera perfectly still and let this automatic feature effectively press the button for you.

Macro Switch

The camera will normally take pictures in good focus from as far away as the horizon right up to about 1 metre (3 ft) away. Any closer than that and things start getting a bit blurred. The Macro Switch can alter the focus so that you may take close-up pictures with a focus between 16cm (6½ in) and 24cm (9½ in), with the optimum at 20cm (8 in). A typical example is where you want to photograph a small object. We will see how to use this feature in Exercise 21. In the previous picture, the Macro Switch is shown in the 'not active' position, and to activate it you flick the switch up towards the 'tulip symbol'. However, you must not forget to flick it down again to take ordinary pictures or you will have some very blurred ones!

Microphone

If you study the symbols marked on the rotary Function Switch (on the top of the camera), you can see that the fourth position shows a 'movie camera symbol' and the fifth position shows a 'microphone symbol'. The built-in microphone is active when either of them is being used. The first of these functions is used to record a short 'Video Clip' and we talk about this in section 6.3. The second function is used to record a short 'Sound (only) Clip' and we talk about that in section 6.4.

Further controls on the rear

Here is the rear view of the camera ...

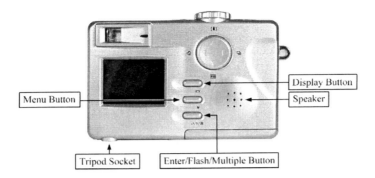

Display Button

Speaker

Menu Button

Tripod Socket

Enter/Flash/Multiple Button

Speaker

The built-in loudspeaker is used to play back sound recordings made either during a 'Video Clip' or a 'Sound (only) Clip'. It also provides the 'beeps' and 'pips' heard when you press various controls.

Tripod Socket

This socket is a standard fitment that will fit either the small tripod that comes with the 'Gift Pack' version (see item No. 6 listed in Exercise 1, section 2.1) or it can be used with any standard camera tripod purchased from a high street store. You can purchase a very reasonable full sized tripod for about £16, and if you intend to take a lot of pictures I recommend that you obtain one.

We shall now describe the functions of the three buttons on the rear panel. They are a bit more complicated because they do different things depending on which position the Function Switch has been set to. For reference, here are the functions that may be chosen by rotating the knob to place any symbol next to the red dot on the camera top.

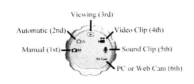

Viewing (3rd)

Automatic (2nd)

Video Clip (4th)

Manual (1st)

Sound Clip (5th)

PC or Web Cam (6th)

Display Button

If you have the Function Switch set to either 'Manual' (1st position), 'Automatic' (2nd position), 'Video' (4th position) or 'Sound' (5th position) – in other words, the picture or sound recording functions – then the Display Button acts in the following way:

- **Press it once** – the symbols displayed on the Monitor Screen will

disappear, so that you can see the picture on the screen more clearly.
- **Press it again** – the whole screen goes dark and is now in the 'power saving' condition.
- **Press it once more** – the screen comes back on again and the symbols re-appear.

The Display Button has this 'three step' action continuously. If you press it over and over again you will cycle around the three states of 'Symbols, No Symbols, and Blank Screen'. If you are out and about and want to force the camera into the power saving condition (without waiting for it to automatically time out after a minute) then press it repeatedly until you see the screen go dark.

If the Function Switch is set to 'Viewing' (3rd position) then the Display Button simply toggles between the 'Symbols' and 'No Symbols' states. When set to 'PC Cam' (6th position) it has no effect.

Menu button

The Menu button operates in conjunction both with the Circular Button (the one with the four direction arrows of up, down, left and right) and the Enter Button (also used for Flash and Multiple Picture viewing). Remember that to use the Circular button, you need to press down on the appropriate edge of its rim to choose the required direction. There are two different ways that the Menu Button works:

Delete All

Delete One

Guard One

Mark for Printing

a. Viewing pictures

If you have the Function Switch set to 'Viewing' (3rd position) and the menu is switched off, then pressing the Menu button will switch it on and show you a vertical list of symbols on the Monitor Screen, as in this picture.

The symbol that is highlighted yellow is the menu option currently selected. You can change the selection by pressing either the 'up' or 'down' directions on the Circular button. If you press the 'left' and 'right' directions instead of 'up' or 'down', then it will not affect the menu selection, but it will change the currently selected picture on the Monitor Screen. Your four choices from the menu are:

- **Delete All** – this deletes ALL of your pictures (as discussed in section 2.5). The icon represents a waste bin and there are many items shown in the bin to remind you that it works on many pictures. Be very careful when this option is shown yellow or you might inadvertently delete all the pictures in the camera when you didn't want to!

- **Delete One** – this deletes the picture currently shown on the Monitor Screen. The waste bin icon shows only one item to remind you that it works on just the one picture. After a picture has been deleted, the numbering is automatically adjusted for those remaining.

- **Guard One** – this marks the current picture as 'guarded' so that you cannot accidentally delete it. If there is a picture in your camera that is very special, then it may be wise to mark it as guarded. To 'un-guard' a picture you choose this selection a second time and it toggles the state back to 'un-guarded'.

- **Mark for printing** – this marks the picture as 'requested' and then using the 'up/down' directions of the Circular Button you specify how many prints of this particular picture you want. The option is only used when you intend to remove the SmartMedia memory card from your camera and send it off to a high street store for printing, or if you choose to requests prints over the Internet by sending them 'on-line' to an Internet company's web site.

When you have selected one of the four choices, you then need to press the Enter Button to put the choice into effect. The menu action will not happen if you don't press it. The Enter button is effectively the 'entry' of your choice to the camera.

Finally, you switch the menu off by pressing the Menu Button again.

b. Recording pictures (and sound)

Exposure   Setting

When the Function Switch is set to any of the recording positions (1st, 2nd, 4th and 5th positions), press the Menu Button and it now shows a different type of menu, as shown in this picture.

White Balance   Format

Again, the selected menu choice is highlighted yellow. To change selection, use the 'left' and 'right' direction arrows on the Circular Button, and for any given selection, use the 'up and 'down' directions to alter the values for it.

The four menu choices are:

● **Exposure** – this governs the amount of light allowed through the camera's lens when taking a picture. When the Function Switch is set to 'Manual' (1st position) then you can adjust the value shown up or down from +2.0 to -2.0. When the Function Switch is set to 'Automatic' (2nd position) you cannot vary it here (the value will be fixed at '0.0'), but the camera will automatically vary it for you just before taking a picture by sensing the average amount of light in the scene.

● **White Balance** – this is a colour compensation facility to automatically adjust the camera's response to colour, based upon the lighting that may be in use at the time of taking a picture. Different light sources (such as daylight, tungsten lamps or fluorescent lamps) each have a natural tendency to make objects and pictures appear slightly 'tinted' either towards the 'red' end or towards the 'blue' end of the colour spectrum. By choosing a value for this menu option, you can compensate for the tinting and achieve a more uniform colour appearance overall. When you have correctly compensated for the type of light source, then white objects that are present within your pictures will have a more natural appearance. The effect of 'tinting' is particularly noticeable on close-up objects. The light of daylight has a lot of blue in it and the light from tungsten lamps has a lot of red/orange colour.

● **Setting** – there are several different settings that you may alter (Date/Time, Date Style, Beep, Video System, Image Size, Quality, Self Timer, Language, Power Saving). To make an alteration, first highlight the setting name (using the 'up/down' directions and take note that there are some more names off the screen), and then press the Enter Button. This will then allow you to modify the chosen setting using the direction arrows of the Circular Button. When you have modified a setting, press the Enter Button again to save it and return to the previous menu screen. You may then use the 'left' and 'right' directions of the Circular Button to choose a different menu selection.

● **Format** – this facility allows you to re-initialise the whole internal memory structure of the camera, as it would exist when first purchased.

It is primarily of use if you should obtain a SmartMedia card that has already been used by some other electronic device (and may subsequently have a format not compatible with the camera). Be careful with this because if you do choose 'Yes' here, you will lose ALL existing pictures just as surely as if you had deleted them. The word 'Format' in this context has the same meaning as with floppy disks and hard drives of a computer. Indeed, you may remember that when we were discussing the transfer of pictures, we talked about the epsilon camera acting as a 'Mass Storage' device. When plugged via the cable into a USB socket of a computer, the camera effectively becomes a new removable disk drive.

Note – For more information about the process of 'Formatting' read section 8.2 of *'Using a Computer for the First Time'*.

Note

When you have changed a value for any of the menu items, you then need to press the Enter Button to put the change into effect. The menu item will not change if you don't press it. For most menu items, pressing the Enter Button will also switch the menu off (the exception being 'Setting'). You may also switch the menu off by pressing the Menu Button again.

In the normal situation, when the menu is not showing, you will notice a number of 'icon' symbols displayed on the Monitor Screen in the top left-hand corner. These symbols indicate the camera's current settings and you can find a list of their meanings on page 6 of the User Guide, held on the Digital Dream CD-ROM.

The Enter/Flash/Multiple Button

In the descriptions of facilities provided by the Menu Button, we have seen how the Enter Button acts as a 'now go and do it' button, once a menu item has been selected and a new value set for it. This principle of preparing for a change and then committing the change by pressing the Enter Button is very similar in action to a computer and its keyboard's 'Enter' key. It allows you to change your mind at the last minute. If you switch the menu off before you press the Enter Button, then the changes are discarded.

This same button has two other uses that we should describe for completeness. These are for controlling use of the 'Flash' facility and for viewing 'Multiple Pictures' on the Monitor Screen. *These uses are only available when the menu is **not** being displayed on the screen.*

With the menu off and the Function Switch set to either 'Manual' or

'Automatic' recording positions (1st or 2nd positions), the button controls the Flash facility. It has three settings that are selected each in turn by further presses of the button. This action cycles around in a loop after the last one to return back to the first one. The three flash settings are:

Forced   Auto   Off

When set to 'Forced', the flash will always take place when the picture is taken. If set to 'Auto', the camera will decide for itself based upon the amount of light it is receiving. When set to 'Off', the flash will never occur. When changing from one setting to another, there may be a small delay while the electric charge required for the flash builds up, and you may see the power on/off indicator light flash red and green during the charging period. You will not be able to take pictures during this delay period.

With the menu switched off and the Function Switch set to 'Viewing' (3rd position), the button controls the Multiple Picture display facility. It has two settings:

- Monitor Screen shows one large picture
- Monitor Screen shows nine smaller pictures.

Press once for one of the settings and press again to choose the other one.

The Circular Button

We have mentioned the Circular Button a number of times now and described the use of the 'direction' arrows marked on the button. These direction arrows of 'up', 'down', 'left' and 'right' are used for control of the highlighted options when the menus are visible, and for moving from one picture to another when 'Viewing' pictures on the Monitor Screen.

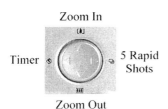

Zoom In

Timer

5 Rapid Shots

Zoom Out

The same button has other uses when the menus are not visible. 'Icon' symbols displayed around the edge of the button give you an indication of what they are.
When menus are not visible and the Function Switch is set to 'Manual' or 'Automatic' recording (1st and 2nd positions), the Circular Button has the functions labelled in the above picture and we will now describe them.

The **Zoom** facility in the epsilon 1.3 camera is known as a 'digital zoom'. This means that the picture is enlarged using the electronics of the camera to magnify it, rather than using a special optical zoom lens. Press on the 'Zoom In' button edge to magnify the picture, press on the 'Zoom Out' edge to reduce it back again. The image quality with digital zoom is never as good as an optical zoom, for with digital zoom you are effectively reducing the total number of pixels in the final picture, but it is a much cheaper option to manufacture. With an optical zoom, the image is magnified before the picture falls upon the camera's light sensitive chip (see the first picture in section 1.2) so the final picture still has the same number of pixels in it, irrespective of whether the zoom is 'in' or 'out'. The normal condition for the epsilon camera's digital zoom setting is 'x1' (zoom fully out) and you can zoom in to a magnification of 'x4'. When you are not in the normal condition, you will see a thin yellow marker on a vertical scale displayed on the right of the Monitor Screen. This is an indicator of the amount of the current zoom setting. The magnification is also displayed numerically. Unless you wish to specifically use the zoom facility, you should take your normal pictures with the zoom set fully out.

The **Self-Timer** facility is also controlled by the Circular button. You switch this on by pressing the left button edge, and then the Shutter Button will actually start the timer running when you are ready to use it. The detail of how to use this is illustrated in Exercise 20. If the timer facility is switched on, then you will see the same 'icon' symbol as shown in the previous picture repeated on the Monitor Screen. Keep an eye out for this symbol because it is so easy to accidentally catch the button and switch the timer facility 'on' unintentionally. Sometimes, you may wonder why your camera won't take a picture properly when you press the Shutter Button. The answer may well be that the timer is 'on' and it will take a beautiful picture of the ceiling about seven seconds after you start scratching your head wondering what on earth is the matter!

The last use of the Circular Button is to prepare the camera for taking '5 Rapid Shot' style pictures – that is five pictures in rapid succession, spaced about one second apart. Press the right button edge to switch this feature on, or press it a second time to turn it off. The Shutter Button controls the start of the picture taking action when you are ready to use it. This facility is very useful where you have 'Sports' style action and you want to try catching the action in full flight. Another good use is for taking pictures of very small children who refuse to stay still. By taking successive rapid shots, you might just be able to catch an instant when they are not wriggling about! As with the 'Self-Timer', the 5 Rapid Shot facility 'icon' symbol (shown in the previous picture) is visible within the Monitor Screen display when it is active. It is also easy to switch this on accidentally, so if you take 5 pictures looking very similar when you are not expecting to, then chances are that you have unintentionally pressed the right side of the Circular Button and switched this feature on.

6.2   Taking good pictures

In this section, we will discuss the practical side of using the camera and see if we can improve your technique for taking good pictures, as well as learning how to use some of the features described in the last section. Don't be concerned if the text gets a little too technical in parts for your liking. Just skim over such details and proceed with the exercises.

Flash

Flash is obviously of great value to you when the circumstances surrounding the picture scene are such that there is not much light available. If you are indoors and it is dimly lit, or outdoors on an evening in the winter, then Flash will provide extra light to illuminate your subject. Its useful range is limited to about 3 metres (10 feet) maximum. However, you will need to be careful using it indoors because digital cameras are a lot more sensitive than many conventional film cameras and it is very easy to get too much light into your picture. In an average room with a tungsten room light on, then the camera may not need additional lighting. You have to experiment here to get the balance right.

There are also occasions when using Flash is not essential but does prove to be advantageous. If you are indoors during daylight hours and taking a portrait against a brightly lit background (a window for example, showing daylight outside) then the 'Automatic' electronics of the camera will try and cut down the light such that the average overall meets its target value. This often results in a very dark appearance of the principal portrait subject. In these circumstances, forcing the camera to fire off the Flash can compensate for the brightly lit background and give you a resultant picture with a much better final effect.

Shutter Speed

When you use the camera inside and are not using the Flash facility, you will be surprised how sensitive your digital camera can be. This sensitivity can lead to problems with fuzzy pictures. The reason is connected with shutter speed and long times of the shutter mechanism being kept open during the true picture taking period. If you wish to avoid these problems, you need to have a better understanding of shutter speed, and it is not something that you control directly on the epsilon 1.3 camera, but you can control it indirectly. We will discuss how you can control it shortly.

The shutter speed is displayed on the Monitor Display when you 'half-press' the Shutter Button (read Exercise 2, section 2.2, again if you need a refresh of what 'half-pressed' means). It is shown as something like 'S=6' meaning that the shutter speed is 1/6th of a second. 'S=120' means that the speed has changed to 1/120th of a second. The actual time is always the reciprocal of (one divided by) the displayed number. The true meaning of shutter speed is the length of time from the instant that the shutter opens to the instant that it closes. We say that the speed is fast when the time is very short, and slow when the time is very long.

Now if you think about it, if you don't keep the camera perfectly still (and lets face it, who can do so when holding it at arms length as you often will with a digital camera) then such movement of the camera while the shutter is open will always give you a blurred picture to some degree. The shorter that the time is (that is, the faster the shutter speed) then the less is the chance of camera movement causing such blurring. My rule of thumb for you is this – if the shutter speed is longer than 1/10th of a second, then you must take extra care to hold the camera very still throughout the picture taking period. This is where two tricks can come in handy – either use of a tripod, or use of the self-timer mechanism to press the button for you (avoiding any chance of movement by the act of pressing the button itself). We will talk more about these two tricks in a moment.

A shutter speed of 1/10th of a second will be shown to you when you have 'half-pressed' the Shutter Button but not yet fully pressed it. It will be seen visible in the Monitor Screen as 'S=10'. If the 'S=' number is higher than '10' then things are a little less critical, but if it is lower than '10' then you have to be extra careful to get a good quality picture.

Note

Note – If for any reason the 'S=' number is not visible in the display when you half-press the Shutter Button, then you will not be able to take a picture at all. There are several reasons why this can occur; one may be that the camera is in the middle of recalculating the speed to use, another is that it is readjusting itself in some other way. Wait for a moment then try it again.

Why am I stressing this point about Shutter Speed? Well it goes back to what I said earlier about digital cameras being a lot more sensitive than conventional ones. This sensitivity 'lures you into a false sense of security' because you can see what appears to be a very good image on the display screen. **But it only appears like this in low light conditions because it lengthens the Shutter Speed timing to VERY long times such as 'S=6' or 'S=4'.** Now these very long times mean that there is much more chance of camera movement occurring between the start and end of taking a picture. For example, 1/4th of a second is slow enough for you to clap your hands twice, let alone shake the camera about!

The improved sensitivity is something to admire and take advantage of. But when taking pictures in low light situations, you must be very careful not to move a digital camera, or you will be disappointed with the final result. This brings us back to using a tripod. Even if the subject matter is awkwardly placed and you cannot get the legs of a tripod spread apart for your picture, a tripod's bulk will often help you keep the camera still. Many have been the times when I have taken pictures with the camera attached to a tripod, and had the tripod legs folded up half-resting under my arm. This has proven itself to be far better than trying to hold the camera still on its own.

Now the trick of using the 'Self-Timing' mechanism to help keep the camera still is a good one, but it has a few points that need mentioning. The normal use of this facility is to set the timing going, then for you to rush around to the 'lens side' of the camera and join in the picture! That is the reason why the 'default' setting for the timing is set to '7 seconds', for you obviously need such a time to get yourself organised in position in front of the lens. However, this '7 seconds' is just a bit too long for our trick. I find that if I don't alter this, then my hands start shaking about after '5 seconds' waiting for the accursed thing to 'go off' (I mean take the picture!). For this reason, I always adjust the 'Settings' (we covered this in section 6.1) to reduce the time for the 'SELF TIMER' down to '2 seconds'. If you are using the Self-Timer in this way, then when you press the Shutter Button, your picture will be taken very soon afterwards. You notice also, when using the Self-Timer, that the indicator light on the rear panel begins to flash alternately red and green. The indicator will flash red once for each second of the timing period, and then flash red one final time to show that the shutter mechanism has opened. It is when the Monitor Screen display goes blank that your picture has finished being taken (the shutter actually closes) so you must keep the camera perfectly still until at least you see this effect happen. The screen remains blank while the picture is being processed by the internal electronics, then it goes blue for a short while, then it will finally show the live scene again.

If you want to control the shutter speed, you cannot do this directly, but you can do it indirectly. In either 'Manual' or 'Automatic' recording, when you 'half-press' the button, you then freeze the shutter speed to the value that is shown. If you maintain the shutter half-pressed, then this shutter speed is 'held' frozen and will not change – even if you move the camera to point at something completely different. It stays 'held' until either you go ahead and actually take the picture, or release the button. One technique to control it therefore is to point the camera slowly in different directions whilst 'half-pressing' the button now and again and watching the speed value alter as you do so. When you see the speed value you are looking for, then maintain the button 'half-pressed', but point the camera now in the correct direction for your scene and frame your subject matter as you truly want to see it, in either the Viewfinder or on the Monitor Screen. Finally, fully press the button to take the picture.

In using this technique, you will discover that the speed will shorten (that is, become a higher number such as 'S=100') as you point the camera nearer to a bright scene, and lengthen (become a lower number such as 'S=6') when you point the camera towards a dark scene. Normally the camera will decide the correct shutter speed automatically for you for any given scene, but the technique highlighted here is your method of biasing this one way or the other if you wish to. Much depends on the subject matter you are concentrating upon. I find this technique particularly useful for pictures of a nice sunset landscape. First I point the camera towards the horizon where the sun has just gone down, then I tilt the camera slowly up a bit (brighter) and then down a bit (darker), and repeatedly half-press the button to freeze a variety of specific speed settings. When I have a setting frozen, if I then like the brightness and contrast on the Monitor Screen, I finally frame the clouds in all their glorious colours – and then press fully to take the picture. Again, the beauty of a digital camera is that you can take several experimental shots one after the other, and not worry about wasting film. You can also get a quick assessment of your results by viewing them either on the camera, or soon afterwards on the computer.

Picture Brightness

One effect that you may see with the camera, particularly when light levels are low, is that the picture brightness as seen on the Monitor Screen becomes much brighter at the instant that you half-press the Shutter Button. What is happening here is that the button action is forcing the camera to recalculate its settings for shutter speed, and the resultant calculation is bringing up the brightness level to compensate for a dimly lit picture. This is very noticeable at such low light levels where the 'steps' in brightness are accentuated by the fact that the human eye sensitivity to light is not linear (human eyesight itself is much more sensitive to differences in lower light levels than higher ones). To get a good picture, you should be careful to let the camera 'settle down' to a light level before committing yourself to taking the picture. If you experience this 'sudden brightness effect' occurring, half-press the Shutter Button a few times. Soon after you will see the level begin to stabilise. Wait for it to become more consistent on the display then take your picture. Remember again, at low light levels, the shutter speed will be quite long so you must keep the camera very still at the precise moment of taking the picture to get it in sharp focus.

Okay, we have talked quite a bit about the camera and its controls. Let us now put some of the theory into practice.

Exercise 19 – Taking pictures with and without Flash

Begin the exercise with the camera switched on. If it is connected to the computer via the USB cable then disconnect it.

Turn the Function Switch to the 'Automatic' (2nd) position, and make sure that the '5 rapid shots' facility is not switched on (see section 6.1 to learn how to switch it off).

Forced

Auto

Off

Now press the 'Enter/Flash/Multiple Button' (the bottom one of the three on the rear panel) once. Have a look at the Monitor Screen. If you can see the 'Forced' Symbol as shown in this illustration in the display amongst the other symbols, then the Flash facility is set to 'forced', meaning that it will always fire when you take pictures. If you see either the 'Auto' Symbol or the 'Off' Symbol, then press the button again either once or maybe twice, until you can see the Forced Symbol.

Now select yourself a 'portrait' to point the camera at. If you haven't got a willing person available to volunteer as your subject, then choose an inanimate one such as a vase of flowers. Your subject ideally should be about 2.0 metres away (6½ feet). Half-press the Shutter Button, and keep it held for two or three seconds. You should see the display change to show you the 'S=' number when the button is half pressed. You should also see the 'Forced' symbol appear at the side of it. This is reminding you that the Flash bulb will definitely be used in the coming picture. Now slowly squeeze the Shutter Button fully down to take the picture and hear the beep sound.

After you have taken the picture, you will see that the rear panel indicator light flashes red and green alternately during the 'flash recharge' period. The Monitor Screen goes blank and stays blank until the end of the recharge period. Eventually the screen will appear blue for a while, and then the display goes back to normal showing you the subject scene again. You will not be able to take a second picture with flash until the display goes back to normal.

Now turn the Function Switch to the viewing position, and have a look at your handiwork. The quality of the picture you have just taken will depend on the ambient level of light and the distance your subject is away. If you find it is over-exposed with light (far too much white) then the distance between camera and subject needs to be increased. Once you get beyond 3 metres (10 feet) then you can still take a picture, but it starts becoming dark if the ambient lighting is very low.

Note – If you try to use the '5 rapid shots' feature, then this automatically turns the Flash facility to 'Off' when you do so. If you try switching the flash on when you have the '5 rapid shots' feature active, then pressing the Enter/Flash/Multiple button has no effect. In short, you can't use flash with '5 rapid shots'!

Okay, so much for using flash in a 'forced' condition. Press the Enter/Flash/Multiple Button once again. Notice that the symbol shown in the display now changes to the 'Auto' Symbol accordingly. Here in this condition, if you try to take a picture, the decision whether to use flash in no longer 'forced' but dependant on the amount of ambient light in your scene. If the camera should decide to use the Flash facility in 'Auto' mode, then again you will see a symbol appear to the right of the 'S=' number when you half-press the Shutter Button.

Press the Enter/Flash/Multiple button once again. Now you should see the 'Off' Symbol in the Monitor Screen. Set yourself up again to take the same 'portrait' picture as the last one. Half-press the Shutter Button again, and witness the 'S=' number shown on the screen; however notice that the flash symbol does not appear this time to the right of it. If the number is below '10' then you must try maintain the camera as still as you can do, in order to keep the picture in good focus. Finally, press the Shutter Button fully to take the picture. Again, the screen goes dark after the picture is taken, but it is now much quicker returning to normal because it doesn't have to recharge the Flash facility.

When the screen is back to normal, turn the Function Switch again to the 'Viewing' (3rd) position. Have a look at your latest picture, and compare it with the one previously taken with the flash. Sometimes it is difficult to see the true effect on a picture using the camera's monitor, so you might like to transfer these pictures to the computer for a more detailed look at them. Read Exercise 10 again if you need a reminder how to do this, and you can then view the pictures using the MGI Photosuite program, as we demonstrated in Exercise 12.

This concludes Exercise 19.

Exercise 20 – Taking a picture using the Timer

Begin the exercise with the camera switched on and not connected to a computer.

Turn the Function Switch to the 'Automatic' (2nd) position. Check that the Flash facility is 'Off' by looking at the Monitor Screen. You should see the Flash 'Off' symbol (shown in the previous exercise) visible somewhere in the list of symbols along the top left-hand corner.

Now press the left edge of the Circular Button (it has the 'Timer' Symbol next to it) to switch the Self-Timer facility on. You should see the Timer Symbol (shown here) appear in the Monitor Screen's list of symbols. If you don't see it then it may have been on previously in which case you have just switched it off, so press the left edge again to put it back on.

Okay, we now have the Self-Timer facility switched on ready to use. The next time that we press the Shutter Button, it will not take a picture immediately, but will start the timer running. However, before we go ahead and do that, we ought to demonstrate how to set the timer period to a suitable value. We will do that first.

Press the Menu Button (the middle one of the three buttons). The

Monitor Screen will now show the menu with 'Exposure' selected. Press the right edge of the Circular Button twice to move the yellow 'highlight' to the third menu selection of 'Setting'. You should see that 'Date & Time' is highlighted. Press the bottom edge of the Circular Button (the down direction) six times. You should then see 'Self Timer' highlighted. Press the Enter Button (the bottom one of the three) once. You should now see a number highlighted (probably '7' if it has not been altered before). Now press the top edge of the Circular Button (the up direction) five times to change the number to '2'. Each time you press it, you will notice the number decrease in value by one. Press the Enter Button again (the bottom one of the three). This is the action that actually commits the change of setting to the camera. Finally, press the Menu Button once (the middle one of the three) to remove the menu display from the Monitor Screen.

The camera's Self-Timer period has now been altered to '2' seconds, so that when we press the Shutter Button, there will only be a delay of 2 seconds before the shutter mechanism operates to take the picture.

Okay, now I want you to select a suitable subject for a 'test' picture, either inside or outside. The ideal would be outside during the daytime so that there is plenty of light about. Make sure that the main subject for your picture is at least two metres (6½ feet) away – a landscape scene would be a good one for the test.

Hold the camera ready to take the picture and frame your subject, then 'half-press' the Shutter Button so that you can see the 'S=' number in the display. Now, holding the camera still, gently fully press the Shutter Button and listen for the beep. When you hear it watch the green indicator light. All of a sudden, you will see it alternate between red and green; the Monitor Screen will go blank for a while, then turn blue, and finally show you the live scene again. Your picture was actually taken just before the instant that the Monitor Screen went blank.

Now turn the Function Switch to the 'Viewing' (3rd) position to have a look at your handiwork. You should see a picture now where the focus is quite crisp. The fact that you didn't press the Shutter Button at the precise instant that the shutter mechanism opened should have resulted in your being able to hold the camera quite still at the critical moment.

To complete the exercise, we ought to now switch the 'Self-Timer' facility off again. Turn the Function Switch back to the 'Automatic' (2nd) position. Wait for the Monitor Screen display to settle then press the left edge of the Circular Button. You should now see the 'Timer' Symbol disappear from the display.

If at this point you want to alter the timing period back to '7' seconds, then you can follow the same procedure that we described earlier. Else if you prefer to leave it at '2' seconds then don't bother.

This concludes Exercise 20.

Exercise 21 – Taking a close-up picture

Begin the exercise with the camera switched on and not connected to a computer.

Turn the Function Switch to the 'Automatic' (2nd) position. Find the little Macro Switch on the front of the camera just to the right of the lens. Flick it up into the top position nearest the 'Tulip' Symbol. We have now adjusted the focus of the camera so that it is very short range. Objects that are precisely 20cm (8in) away from the lens will be in sharp focus, Objects that are anywhere between 16cm (6½in) to 24cm (9½in) away will be in reasonable focus (but not as sharp). Objects outside of this range will be in blurred focus. In the Monitor Screen, you will now see a 'Tulip' Symbol like this amongst the other symbols.

Check that the Flash facility is 'Off' by looking at the Monitor Screen. You should see the Flash 'Off' symbol (shown in Exercise 19) visible somewhere in the list of symbols along the top left-hand corner.

Now select an object to use as the subject for your next picture. I am going to recommend that you try first of all a newspaper article from an ordinary newspaper, maybe with a photograph in it as well as text. Now to do this precisely, you will need to use a ruler. If you haven't got a ruler handy, then use the camera itself to do the measurement for you. The camera body's broadest measurement (across the width of the rear panel) is 9½cm (3¾in), so twice this length is very close to 20cm(8in). Place your newspaper article flat on a table and in good light. Using your ruler measure a distance of 20cm (8in) above it (or the distance of two camera broadest widths) and place the camera lens, as exact as you can judge it to be, at this distance with the lens pointing at the newspaper article. Be careful now not to get into the light shining on the newspaper. If you are, then turn things around so that you get the best light (use a table lamp if that helps, but don't allow the lamp to shine directly into the camera's lens).

Now go ahead and take a picture by pressing the Shutter Button. If your Self-Timer facility was left switched on from the last exercise, then you will probably end up with an even better picture than without it.

149

Okay, turn the Function Switch now to the 'Viewing' (3rd position) and examine the picture. If it looks good, then you are ready to move on to try close-up pictures of some other objects. If it doesn't look so good, then you might want to have another go. To read the actual print from the article, you will probably have to wait until you transfer it to your computer.

This idea of taking digital pictures of newspaper articles is great for quickly capturing information you might want to read later. It is much faster than scanning them with a computer scanner device. You must remember however that such information content is subject to copyright laws and should be respected as such.

That is all there is to taking close-up pictures. Try other objects around the house. Also try experimenting with a lamp to illuminate these objects. Finally, you might want to go outside in daylight on a nice sunny day and try and take some pictures of flowers in your garden. This next picture is one that I took of Norma's crocuses.

When you have finished your close-up pictures, don't forget to flick the Macro Switch on the front of the camera back to its original position away from the 'Tulip' Symbol or your ordinary pictures will not be in focus.

Check that the Flash facility is 'Off' by looking at the Monitor Screen. You should see the Flash 'Off' symbol visible somewhere in the list of symbols along the top left-hand corner.

This concludes Exercise 21.

Exercise 22 – Taking 5 Rapid Shot pictures

This exercise really needs to be conducted in daylight and outside. Begin the exercise with the camera switched on and obviously not connected to a computer.

Turn the Function Switch to the 'Automatic' (2nd) position. Press the right edge of the Circular Button and you will see the '5 Rapid Shot' Symbol (shown here) appear in amongst the other symbols in the left-hand corner of the Monitor Screen.

The camera is now prepared. The next time that the Shutter Button is fully pressed, 5 pictures will be rapidly be taken, one after the other and one second apart. When the camera is set up for this facility, it automatically turns off both the 'Self-Timer' facility and the 'Flash' facility.

You should now choose a subject for the next series of pictures and one where you want to capture something in motion. However, there are a few points that you need to be aware of if you are to get good pictures. First, because the Flash facility is not available, your subject needs to be in good lighting. Ideally this will be sunshine daylight outside. Second, having good lighting will also set the shutter speed to a short interval so there will be less likelihood of blurring. Third, if you are trying to capture motion – for example, a cyclist in a race – you will need to try track the subject in their motion to further reduce the chance of blurring. Keep the camera lens pointing at the subject for as long as you can. This will blur the background, but you might just catch a really good shot of the cyclist as they pass you by.

For the sake of experimentation, I suggest you now go outside and observe road traffic as it passes by you in the street. Remember that the whole '5 rapid shot sequence' will take at least 5 seconds to complete. When you see a car coming down the street, fully press the Shutter Button and then keep the camera pointing at it as it approaches you and passes by. When you press the button, the first thing you will notice is that the Monitor Screen goes blank immediately and stays that way. Over the next 5 seconds, a picture will be taken every second. When the camera finishes, the Monitor Screen will first go blue, then go back to displaying a live scene again.

When you have taken your rapid shot pictures, turn the Function Switch to the 'Viewing' (3rd) position to examine your handiwork. The first picture displayed will be the last one that the camera took. As you repeatedly press the left edge of the Circular Button to view the earlier ones of the same sequence, you will see all 5 pictures in turn.

After you have viewed them, turn the Function Switch back to the 'Automatic' (2nd) position. Then press the right hand edge of the Circular Button once more in order to switch the '5 Rapid Shots' facility off. Notice that the '5 rapid Shots' Symbol disappears from the list in the top left corner of the Monitor Screen.

This concludes Exercise 22.

6.3 Video Clips

As well as being able to take still pictures, the camera can record short video clips that include sound a sound track. The next exercise demonstrates how to make them. The picture detail recorded in the video clip is reduced from that we have experienced with our still digital pictures (from 1280 x 1024 pixels to 640 x 480 pixels), but nevertheless provides an interesting method of capturing short moments in time that you can then transfer to the computer for long-term storage.

Exercise 23 – Making and viewing a Video Clip

Begin the exercise with the camera switched on and not connected to a computer.

Turn the Function Switch to the 'Video Clip' (4th) position. As with the last exercise, the Flash facility will not be available so the exercise needs to be conducted in reasonable lighting. You can do this indoors providing that either natural daylight or a room light are giving sufficient illumination to see well. When the Monitor Screen settles down, you will see the 'Movie Camera' Symbol appear in the top left-hand corner.

Fully press the Shutter Button and listen for the beep to start the video clip recording. As soon as you do so, you will see a legend titled 'Rec' (meaning recording) appears at the bottom of the Monitor Screen and a counter appears in the top right-hand corner, counting upwards in 'seconds'. Remember that the sound microphone will also be recording at this time. Move the camera slowly around the room, or around the garden if you are outside, and speak aloud describing the scene as you do so. After about 10 seconds or so, fully press the Shutter Button a second time. This stops the video clip recording.

We will now replay the video clip. Turn the Function Switch to the 'Viewing' (3rd) position and watch the video clip replay itself. Any time during playback, you can press the right edge of the Circular Button to pause the playback sequence. Press it for a second time to continue the playback sequence. If you want to stop playback before the clip reaches its natural end, then press the left edge of the Circular Button.

Your video clip recording is now held as a file within the camera's memory, just like your still pictures are held as files. The only difference is the type of file. Should you choose to do so, you can transfer the video clip recording to a computer by using the same copy and paste technique outlined in Exercise 10 of section 3.2. The recording made in the camera's memory is stored as a file type known as '.avi' . You can replay these files back on a computer using the 'Windows Media Player', which is a special program for this purpose. To play back on the computer after you have transferred it, all you need to do is double-click (or right-click and select 'Open') on the copy of the file that you pasted into your computer's folder. Obviously, your computer must be equipped with loudspeakers to hear the sound part being replayed and they must be switched on and operational.

This concludes Exercise 23.

6.4 Sound Clips

Another very clever feature of the camera is the ability to digitally record a short 'Sound (only) Clip' via a built-in microphone. This is an alternative camera function to that of taking pictures, and the sound clip is stored in the memory of the camera so that you may play it back at a later time. It is just like using a handheld tape recorder. For example, imagine that you take a particular picture and you want to have a record of the circumstances in which it was taken so that you don't forget. You can make the sound recording directly after taking the picture, and when you play it back in the future, it will remind you again of the details by repeating what you said at the time. This next exercise demonstrates how to make these sound clips.

Exercise 24 – Making and listening to a Sound Clip

Begin the exercise with the camera switched on and not connected to a computer.

 Turn the Function Switch to the 'Sound (only) Clip' (5th) position. When the Monitor Screen settles down, you will see the Microphone' Symbol appear in the top left-hand corner.

Fully press the Shutter Button to hear the beep and start the sound clip recording. As soon as you do so, you will see that a legend titled 'Rec' (meaning recording) appears at the bottom of the Monitor Screen and a counter appears in the top right-hand corner, counting upwards in 'seconds'.

Now speaking in a natural voice, simply count out aloud from one to ten. The microphone is quite sensitive so you don't need to speak directly into it. When you have finished, fully press the Shutter Button again to stop the sound recording. Your sound clip recording has been made.

We will now replay the sound clip. Turn the Function Switch to the 'Viewing' (3rd) position. As soon as the camera settles down, your sound recording will automatically play itself back to you. Any time during the replay, you can press the right edge of the Circular Button to pause the playback sequence. Press it for a second time to continue the playback sequence. If you want to stop the playback before the clip reaches its natural end then press the left edge of the Circular Button.

Your sound clip recording is now held as a file in the camera's memory, just like your pictures are held as files. The only difference is the type of file. Should you choose to do so, you can transfer the sound clip recording to a computer by using the same copy and paste technique outlined in Exercise 10 of section 3.2. The recording made in the camera's memory is stored as a file type known as a '.wav'. You can replay these files back on a computer using the 'Windows Media Player', which is a special program for this purpose. To play back on the computer after you have transferred it, all you need to do is double-click (or right-click and select 'Open') on the copy of the file that you pasted into your computer's folder. Your computer must be equipped with loudspeakers to hear the sound clip being replayed and they must be switched on and operational.

When you have taken more pictures after making the sound clip recording, they too will be stored as more files in memory. If you should then switch the camera's Function Switch to the 'Viewing' position, the last job that you did with the camera is the first one that is displayed on the

Monitor Screen. By searching back and forth amongst your pictures, using the left and right directions of the Circular Button, you can again seek out the sound recording file. It will be shown on the Monitor Screen with a picture looking like this.

This picture is trying to symbolise a loudspeaker indicating that it is a different type of file than either still pictures or video clips.

When you are recording a sound clip, before you start recording, you can normally see a large number such as '4183' in the top right-hand corner of the Monitor Screen. This is telling you how many seconds worth of recording time are currently available for you to use before you will run out of free memory. It obviously depends upon how big is the size of any SmartMedia memory card fitted inside the camera, and how many pictures or video clips you have already taken. However, I think you will agree that '4183' is a lot of sound recording time – 69 minutes and 43 seconds if my mathematics are correct!

This concludes Exercise 24.

This also brings us to the end of the chapter. One function that we have not yet described is that of 'PC Cam' (personal computer camera), which is the 6th position of the Function Switch. This is covered in Chapter 10.

7

More About Adjusting Pictures with Software

7.1   Enhancing pictures

In chapter 4, we learnt how to select a picture from a folder, cut off parts of it that we didn't want using 'cropping', then resize the image and save it back to the folder. In this present chapter we will learn a few more techniques that you can perform with software to process the picture and produce a more desirable final image. We begin with how to enhance a picture to optimise the brightness, contrast and colour balance.

Exercise 25 – Enhancing a picture

Begin the exercise with the computer switched on and showing the desktop. Start the **MGI Photosuite** program running. If the program is not displayed full screen size then maximise it by clicking the **Maximise button**, which is the middle one of the three in the window's top right-hand corner.

For a change, we will select the picture to work on using a slightly different method of 'getting' it than we did in chapter 4. Move the mouse pointer over the first of the six pictures shown in the centre of the screen, as demonstrated here.

Notice that the mouse pointer changes to a 'hand' symbol. Click on it and you will then see the familiar **'Get Photo'** menu of buttons appear down the left-hand side. Click on the **'Computer' button** as shown in the next picture.

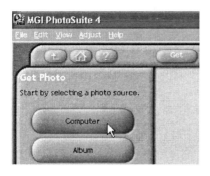

The **Open dialog box** then appears so that you can choose the picture you wish to work with. As we witnessed before, you need to have 'My Documents' showing in the **'Look in: box** (just under the title bar) to start with. If it isn't then click on the 'down arrow' at the right-hand side of the box, so that a drop down list appears. You can then click on 'My Documents' within the list and the list will disappear, leaving 'My Documents' in the Look in: box.

Now choose the 'Epsilon Pictures' folder with a click to highlight it in the large white box below. Click on the Open button to open the folder. The name 'Epsilon Pictures' shows in the Look in: box and we can see the various sub-folders in the large white box. Click on any one of these to highlight it blue (your own sub-folders will obviously be different to my illustration here). Then click the **Open button** again, as shown in this next picture.

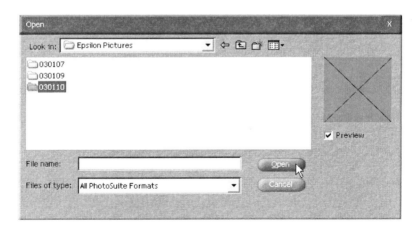

The folder now opens to reveal the list of individual picture filenames in the large white area.

At this point you need to choose one of these picture files as your example to work with. Ideally, to show the full benefit of the **'enhancement'** process, you should pick one that is maybe a bit on the dark or grey side –

possibly one taken outside on a dull day. For my demonstration I will choose a picture of 'Dover Castle' in the county of Kent, England, which happens to be named 'DSCI0007'. Click on your own picture file to highlight it blue. Then click the **Open button** one last time and the picture will appear in the working area of MGI Photosuite. You now see that the menu buttons change down the left-hand side to show those for the **'Prepare Photo' menu**.

In keeping with the philosophy announced earlier in the book, we are not going to do any work on this 'original' picture but only on a copy of it. We can make such a copy very easily by saving the picture with a new name. The picture then in the working area of MGI Photosuite will be this new 'named' copy and not the original picture, so any work we do upon it cannot affect the original. Let me illustrate precisely what I mean.

If you look now at MGI Photosuite's title bar (the blue bar at the very top of the screen), in the left-hand corner it now says something like 'Dsci0007 – MGI Photosuite 4' (yours will be different according to the file that you selected).

This is telling us that the file we currently have open in the working area is the 'original' file as it was when taken out of the camera and transferred to the computer. Click now on **File** from the main menu bar, and choose the **Save As... option**.

You then see the **Save As... dialog box**. The filename will be highlighted blue in the **'File name:' box**. Using the keyboard, type a suitable new name for the copy that you are going to work with. I will call my example 'DoverCastle01'. The instant that you type the first key then the old name disappears and you see your typing appear in this box, as shown in the next picture.

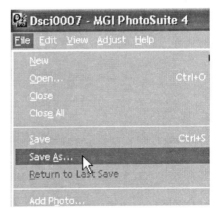

When you have finished typing the new name, make sure the little 'Prompt for Options' checkbox is not ticked (if it is, click on the inside of it to clear it) then click on the Save button.

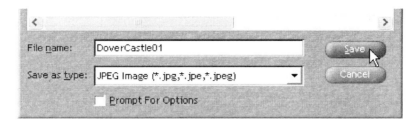

If you watch the bottom right-hand corner of your monitor screen, you may catch a black 'progress bar' suddenly making an appearance to show the progress of saving a new copy of the digital picture back into the sub-folder on the hard drive. Finally, the progress bar disappears, and you are back viewing the same picture (apparently) but now the MGI Photosuite's title bar has changed.

It shows your new name, indicating that the picture in the working area is a copy of the original, and not the original itself. The important point here is that from this moment onwards, any changes that we make to the picture will not affect the original picture but the named copy instead.

Okay, we are ready to enhance the picture and see what effect this has. Click on the **'Touchup' button** from the left-hand panel and then click on the **'Enhance' button**. You should be able to see a left-hand panel that looks like this following picture.

As the panel says 'Your photo has been enhanced automatically' and you should see a change take place in the overall appearance of the picture.

The amount of change is hard to predict, for it depends on the degree of contrast and brightness in the original picture. You can examine the 'before' and 'after' views by clicking on the little **Preview checkbox** in step 1 of the panel, to clear the tick symbol. This deselects the changes. When you click again on the same checkbox, the tick symbol will re-appear and the changes are re-applied.

Another important point to appreciate at this stage is that although the enhancements are shown to the picture that you can now see, they have not yet truly been made in the working area proper. If you decide not to keep the changes, all you need do is click on the **'Return' button** at the bottom of the left-hand panel and you will return to the **'Prepare Photo'** screen, with the working picture reverting to as it was before. If you do want to make the changes then you must click the **Apply button** in step 2 of the panel (as shown in the last picture) to apply them to the working area and then click on **Return**. Bear in mind also that such changes are not yet applied to the 'DoverCastle01' file on the hard drive. For that to happen, we must perform a **'Save'** from the **'File'** menu on the main menu bar – but more of that later.

To illustrate the degree of enhancement that can be achieved, the following picture is a composite I have artificially created of the 'before' and 'after' changes to my 'Dovercastle01' example...

The left half of the picture is the 'before' and the 'right' half is the after. Quite impressive I think you will agree.

Okay, our picture has been enhanced in the working area and if we chose to do so, we could now make some further alterations using other functions that the program offers. They are several possible functions available by clicking on the **'Touchup' button**, such as:

- Remove 'Red Eye' (the red effect sometimes seen when flash is used to take a portrait picture).
- Remove Scratches (more appropriate to working with old photographs).
- Remove Blemishes.
- Remove Wrinkles.
- Touchup Filters.

The last one in this list allows you to make changes to Brightness and Contrast independently if you wish to. The 'Enhance' function that we have just demonstrated has a good try at doing everything for you, but there are occasions where you may need to 'tweak' them individually. You might also want to apply some special effects available from the **'Special Effects' button**. Sadly, space does not permit us to investigate these functions any further so I shall leave you to experiment with them by yourself at a later time.

The last thing we need to do in our exercise is to commit the changes made in the working area back to the file on the hard drive. Click on **File** from the main menu bar and choose '**Save**', as shown in the next picture.

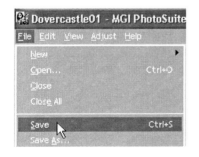

Now a black progress bar will indicate that the program is saving your work back to the hard drive for a permanent record, and it is the file with the name shown in the top left-hand corner that accepts this data.

This concludes exercise 25.

7.2   Adding text

Exercise 26 – Adding a text caption and drop shadow

This exercise is all about text and how to add it to a picture. Just adding plain text is easy enough to do, so to add a bit of panache, we will investigate how to add a 'shadow' behind the lettering as though the sun was shining on the text and casting a shadow underneath it. This is a useful way to make the letters stand out from the detail in the picture, particularly when you want to use a light colour for the letters themselves. It is known as 'drop shadow'.

Begin the exercise with the computer switched on and showing the desktop. Start the **MGI Photosuite** program running. If the program is not displayed full screen size then maximise it by clicking the **Maximise button** (the middle one in the top right-hand corner).

You should be fairly conversant with opening a picture into the working area so I will not show illustrations of every button that you use to do it. At the program's opening screen, click on the **Get button**. When you see the sub menu buttons in the left-hand panel, click on the **Computer button**. The **Open dialog box** then appears. You now need to select a picture to work with and one where you would like to see a title caption. More than likely, the sub-folder that you last selected from will be visible in the **Look in: box** at the top of the dialog box and you may choose any picture from the large white area under it. If it has lost its way, then click the down arrow at the right of the **Look in: box** and choose 'My Documents' again. Then highlight the folder 'Epsilon Pictures' and click the **Open button**. Repeat this procedure with a sub-folder until finally you can see the list of picture files.

Now highlight the picture file that you want to add a caption to. This next illustration shows the **Preview checkbox** as ticked (with a click if need be) and is a useful guide to picture content. Here I choose 'DSCI0009'.

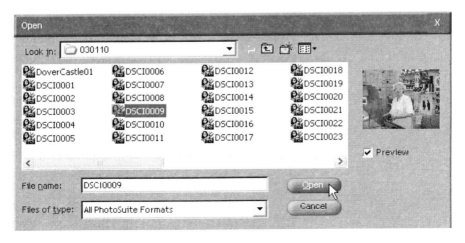

When the picture opens into the working area, the first job that we must do is save it with a different name to protect the original, just as we did in the last exercise. From the menu bar at the top, click on **'File'** and then select **Save As...** and choose a new name for the copy we will work with. I am going to save my example as 'OldRoadFisheries01'. The reason why I add the '01' bit on the end is that I can in the future make additions or alterations to the picture, and then use '02' or '03' etc. to give me several different versions of the same picture. When the name is correct in the **File name: box** then click the **Save button**.

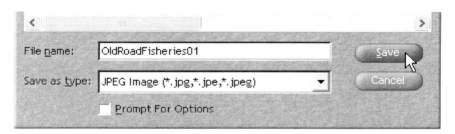

Notice that the **Prompt for Options checkbox** is not ticked. If yours is, then clear it by clicking on it, or else you will see another pop-up dialog box about 'JPG Advanced settings'.

Okay, with the picture selected in the working area, we are ready to begin a procedure to add a text caption. Click now on the **Compose button** in the group of buttons above the picture. You should see a new set of buttons in the panel down the left-hand side. Click on the **Collages button**. This will bring up a new left-hand panel, as shown in the next illustration.

The 'Current Photo' option should show the 'dot' in the small circle. If not, click on it to put one there. Click the Next button. There is a short delay while the screen then rearranges itself and further buttons appear in the left-hand panel. Click on the **'Add/Edit Text' button.**

At this point in the procedure, we are ready to finally add text. Using the mouse pointer, move the pointer arrow to the location on the picture where you would like to see the text caption appear, then make a click on the picture. You instantly see a **'text' box** appear on the picture like this one that I placed in the bottom left-hand corner.

Now it may be a little difficult to see the text clearly here, particularly if the picture is creating a dark background to it. The first thing I am now going to do for my example is change the colour used for the letters to yellow and I recommend you do the same. This is achieved by clicking on the small black square in the left-hand panel, as shown at the bottom of the next picture.

What happens next is that a **Select Color grid** appears, presenting a range of different colours for you to choose from. For this exercise, select bright yellow with a click of your mouse pointer on it. This removes the grid and changes the colour of what was the 'small black square' in the panel to yellow. You will also notice that your text in the picture has changed colour as well.

 Note – Remember that if you make a mistake at any stage, you can simply 'undo' the last step that you took by clicking on the 'undo' button (the left one of the two just below the Get button).

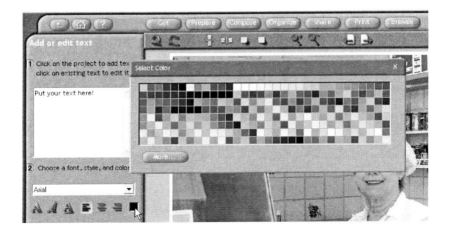

To change the actual text itself, we click with the mouse pointer in the white area of the 'Step 1' section of the left-hand panel, so that a vertical 'cursor' appears just behind the exclamation mark following the word 'here!'. Notice that the mouse pointer symbol changes to an 'I' type symbol when in this box...

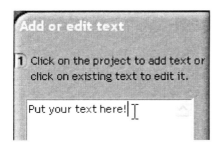

When you see the vertical cursor, you can then use the 'Backspace' key (sometimes called the 'Rub Out' key) that is situated on the keyboard directly above the Enter key (and usually directly below the F12 key) to rub out the phrase 'Put your text here!' and then replace it by typing the text for your caption. Go ahead and do this for your own caption, choosing something appropriate.

Did you notice when rubbing out that the letters also disappeared on the actual textbox over the picture in the working area? When you type you new letters for your replacement caption, they each appear in it too, one by one.

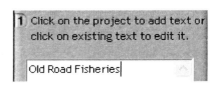

When you have completed your text there are some other controls in the 'Step 2' section of the left-hand panel that you may choose to alter its appearance if you wish to. You can choose a new letter style in the Font box (currently showing 'Arial') and there are six further control buttons underneath it, to the left of the small yellow square. The functions of these buttons are, in the order left to right:

> 1st button – Alternate 'Bold' on or off (click once for on, once for off)
> 2nd button – Alternate 'Italics' on or off
> 3rd button – Alternate 'Underlining' on or off
> 4th button – Push the text over to the 'Left' in the textbox
> 5th button – Centre the text in the textbox
> 6th button – Push the text over to the 'Right' in the textbox

Click on the 5th button and watch your text move slightly over, so that it becomes centred. Now looking at the textbox, there are four basic things you can do with it. Three are shown labelled here and involved the little blue 'handles' around the textbox. The fourth is the movement of the complete textbox using the 'hand symbol'.

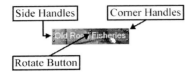

All these things involve a **drag action** with the mouse pointer, whereby you press and hold the left mouse button when performing the action and then let the button go when you have finished. With your own caption, make an attempt to increase the size of the text by dragging on a **Corner Handle**. Corner Handles maintain the height to width ratio of the lettering as it changes, whereas Side Handles change it in one dimension only – either height or width, depending on which side you choose. Notice that when over a handle, the mouse pointer symbol changes shape. When you are not over a handle but are over the textbox, then the pointer takes the 'hand' shape

Now position the mouse over the textbox to show a 'hand' symbol and then perform a drag action to pull the textbox a little upwards, then to the right, then down and then to the left. Notice that as you are performing the drag that the hand symbol changes slightly to a hand with its index finger only extended. It is as though the index finger is pulling the text about! Finally leave the textbox in a position in the left-hand corner of the picture so that it is pleasantly positioned as a final caption for your picture. Don't get too close to the picture edges because we are shortly going to apply some 'drop shadow' to it and you need a little space for that (leave a gap of about 1cm or ½in).

When you have finished all the work you want to do with the text caption, click the **Return button** under 'Section 2' in the left-hand panel.

Okay, this returns us to the Compose menu and its set of buttons in the left-hand panel. Click on the button labelled 'Adjust Objects'.

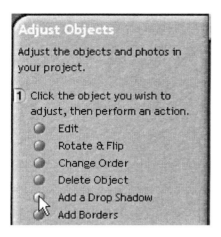

This then reveals a new control panel. Click on the 'Add a Drop Shadow' button.

And then click on the bottom right square. These squares are indicating the position of the shadow relative to the main object...

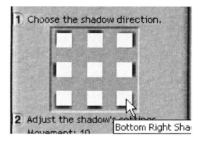

Now below the squares in 'Section 2' are three '**Spiral' slider controls** that you may alter by performing a **drag action** on them and sliding them left or right. The three slider controls are for:

- **Movement** (value set at '10') – how far away the shadow is from the main object.
- **Opacity** (value set at '100') – how strong the shadow appears.
- **Diffusion** (value '20') – how fuzzy the shadow is.

Have a play around with these controls in turn by slowly dragging them left or right and watching their effect on the shadow that appears underneath the lettering of your caption. When you have finished getting a feel for these controls, leave them so that they have the following values:

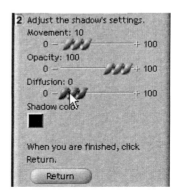

- ✓ Movement is set back to '10'
- ✓ Opacity is set back to '100'
- ✓ Diffusion is set to a new value of '0'

If we chose to, we can also alter the colour of the shadow by clicking on the small black square underneath the 'Diffusion' slider. This works in a very similar way to that we saw before by popping up the **Select Color grid**. However, for our example we will leave it set to black so that the yellow lettering of the caption stands in strong contrast with the black of the shadow. This makes the caption stand out from the underlying picture quite well.

Finally, click on the **Return button** to go back to the 'Adjust Objects' panel and click again on the **Return button** to get back to the **'Compose' menu.**

At this stage, I want to emphasise the point that I have made several times previously, which is that the changes you have made to the picture have been made to it as seen in the working area of the program, but not yet to the picture file on the hard drive. If for any reason you should end the program and not make a save back to the hard drive, then you could lose the work that you have done. If this has taken you a long time then you might appreciate how frustrating that can be! Our next task therefore to complete the exercise is to perform such a save to the hard drive. However there is a slight complication involved in this caused by the nature of the way that the MGI Photosuite program works. This complication can be confusing so you need to pay close attention to this next point I want to make.

❗■ Up until this moment, all of the picture files that we have been dealing with – be they picture files inside the SmartMedia memory card of the camera, or be they files transferred to the hard drive on the computer – have all been the same type known as a '.jpg' (pronounced 'dot jay peg' or simply 'jay peg') type. This file type has largely been hidden from your viewing (but has occasionally cropped up and you may have spotted it). What we are about to see is the MGI PhotoSuite program getting a bit clever and wanting to create a new type of file known as a '.pzp' file (pronounced dot pee zed pee). This is a type specially made just for this particular program and is referred to by the program as a 'project' file. For the purpose of this exercise, I am not going to work with '.pzp' files but stick with '.jpg' files. That is not to say that you should not use '.pzp' files, for there are some very good reasons why you may want to use them. My only reason for doing so is, first of all, to be consistent with the work we have done beforehand, and, second, to avoid complicating matters by

introducing a new file type midway through the exercise. In Chapters 9, we will be learning how to email pictures to your friends and family. Chances are that they will be able to view your pictures very easily if you send them as '.jpg' types. They probably won't be able to see pictures if you email them as '.pzp' file types – that is, unless they happen by chance also to be using MGI PhotoSuite or some other program that knows about this new file type.

When we perform the next task of saving the picture, the program is going to encourage us to save our work as a '.pzp' project file. We shall need to override this encouragement and that is the bit that can be confusing. Towards the end of Exercise 27, I will explain a bit more about '.pzp' files and why you should consider using them for your future work.

Okay, with that point, made let us move forward. To save your work, click on **File** from the main menu bar, and select the **Save As... option**. When the dialog box pops up, it will be different from the last time you saved your work. If you look closely to the title bar of the dialog box it says 'Save Project', as shown in this next picture.

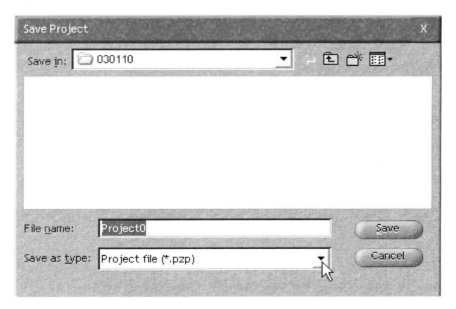

There are one or two points about this picture that can be confusing. The first is that the large white box is empty. Where have all the other files gone that were in this folder? The second is why does it say 'Project0' in the file name box? The answer to both these questions lies in the point I made a moment ago. You cannot see any of the other files in the folder because the 'Save as type:' box is showing 'Project file (*.pzp)'. We call this behaviour of the box a 'filter'. It filters out all of those files that match this **file type** (that is the '.pzp' type). There are other 'filters' that can be selected by using the drop down list that opens when you click your mouse on the 'down-pointing' arrow at the right-hand end of the box (see my mouse pointer in the last picture). Click now on this arrow on your own monitor screen. You will then see the list as shown in the following illustration:

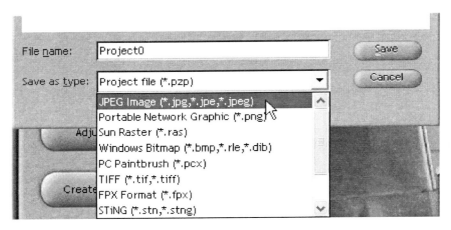

What we need to do is pick out the 'JPEG Image (*.jpg,*.jpe,*.jpeg)' filter and it is the first in the list, so you need to use the scroll bar on the right and drag it upwards to make the 'JPEG Image' filter visible. When you can see it, click on it and it will replace the former filter in the Save as type: box. As soon as you have the new filter selected, then you will see all of the picture files that we know are held in the same sub-folder.

Phew! That was a relief! Imagine how you would feel if all your picture files had disappeared without trace!

Okay, with the **Save as type** now changed to our familiar '.jpg' type, we need to alter the **File name: box** above it that is currently showing 'Project0'. Why is it saying 'Project0'? Who ordered that name? Well, it comes from the program's concept of working on a 'project' and we shall learn more about this in Exercise 28. For now, we will simply ignore this suggested name and replace it with the name we chose at the start of the exercise. In my own example this was 'OldRoadFisheries01'. You can make the replacement in one of two ways. Either you can click in the **File name: box** itself and rub out 'Project0' with the **Backspace** or **Delete keys**, and then type your own example's file name, or you can look in the large white box that now shows (thank heavens) all your picture files and click on the file name you saved early in the exercise. This latter method will then automatically pop the name into the **File name: box**. Finally, make sure that the **prompt for Options** checkbox is <u>not</u> ticked (click on it if it is to 'un-check' it) and when you have things correctly set, then click on the **Save button**, as shown in this next picture.

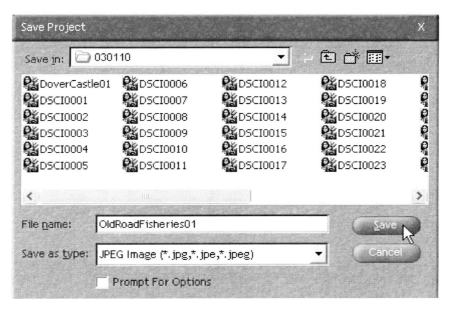

You are then likely to see a message box that says something like 'The file named 'OldRoadFisheries01.jpg' already exists do you want to overwrite it?' (The exact message varies slightly with the version of Windows that you are using). Click on the **Yes button** and your picture is saved.

If you want to print out your picture you can do so. Here is what my final picture looked like.

[Bill - should the file name in pic725 above be 'OldRoadFisheries01'?]

That concludes Exercise 26. When you close the MGI PhotoSuite program, you will probably get a message asking you if you want to save 'Project0'. You can safely click the **No button**, because we saved our work as a '.jpg' file instead.

Exercise 27 – Adding a speech bubble

Sometimes you may take a picture with your camera that would look quite funny if you could add a speech bubble to it and read someone saying something or making a quotation. I mean here the sort of thing that you see in comic strips or magazines. Or you may simply want to add a greeting to a picture that you intend to email to friends and family, such as 'Happy Birthday'. In this exercise we will take the business of adding text to a picture one stage further and show you how this can be done.

Begin the exercise with the computer switched on and showing the desktop. Start the **MGI Photosuite** program running and displayed full screen size.

From the opening screen, click on the **Get button** then on the **Computer**

button. Select the picture that you would like to work with from the **Open dialog box** by clicking to highlight it. Then click the **Open button**. Your picture opens up into the working area, just as we have seen before in the last two exercises.

Click now on the **Compose button** from the group of buttons along the top. Then click on the **Collages button** from the left-hand panel. The **Current Photo option** should be selected having the dot in its little circle. Click the **Next button**. A new set of buttons appears in the left-hand panel. Click the **Add Props button**.

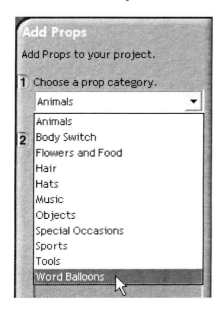

The left-hand panel now displays the **Add Props menu** and in Section 1 it asks you to choose a props category from the drop down list box. Click on the down-pointing arrow at the right side of the box and the list appears. From the list you can now see a number of different categories. Select the **Word Balloons** category by clicking on it, as shown in this next picture.

The list then disappears and the chosen category is displayed in the box. What you will also see are three styles of 'Word balloons' in Section 2, and you are invited to perform a drag action in order to add one of these objects onto your picture.

Move your mouse pointer over the top of the oval-shaped one and press and hold the left mouse button to begin a drag action. Keep the button pressed as you now move the mouse pointer over onto your picture in the working area and carefully position it into the spot where you want it to appear. Now release the left mouse button and you should see the 'Word balloon' pop-up.

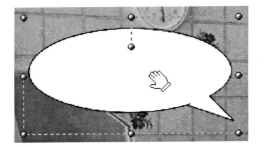

If the 'Word balloon' is not quite located exactly where you want it to be, you can perform another drag action to move it into final position, providing that your pointer is still over the balloon and shows the 'hand' symbol. Again, if you do use the hand to drag it, the instant you start the drag action, then the hand symbol changes slightly to show the extended index finger!

The size of the balloon may also be altered by dragging upon the side or corner 'handles'. If your speech text is going to be longer than will fit into the size that now appears, you might want to increase it a bit. However, don't be too bothered yet about the final size because we can come back later and adjust it if necessary.

When things are looking reasonable, click the **Return button** in the left-hand panel. This takes you back to the **Compose menu**.

Now we add want to add our text. Click the **Add/Edit Text button**. This works just the same as in the last exercise. Position your mouse pointer in the very centre of the word balloon in your picture and then click it. Suddenly a textbox appears, again saying 'Put your text here!'. Reposition your mouse pointer inside the white box of Section 1 in the left-hand panel. Note that the pointer symbol changes to the 'I' symbol once more when you have it inside the white box area. Place the pointer at the end of the text (after the word 'here!') and click to make a vertical cursor appear. Then use the keyboard's Backspace key (that is the one just above the Enter key and often directly below the F12 key) to rub out the existing text. Finally, carefully type in your new wording as you wish to see eventually in the speech bubble. As you type, so the words actually appear inside the balloon on the picture.

When you have completed your typing in Section 1, you can choose to alter the style and appearance from the controls in Section 2. If you need a reminder of what these controls do and how they work, flip back to the previous exercise and jog your memory.

Okay, with the text appearing over the top of the balloon, chances are that your text is too big to fit inside the balloon neatly. If this is the case, you can adjust the text size using the side and corner 'handles' of the textbox. The corner handles in particular are useful because they maintain the height/width ratio of the text. The other trick you may want to juggle with is the number of lines of text that you use and how many words appear on each line. Don't be afraid to click your mouse pointer back into the white box of Section1 in the left-hand panel. This puts a vertical cursor back there and you can edit the text formation by rubbing things out and typing new things in, as you feel appropriate. Creating additional lines of text (I mean for example, line 2 or line 3 etc.) is achieved using the **Enter key** just as you would do with a word processor program.

When your text is finished, press the **Return button** in the left-hand panel and this returns you back to the **Compose menu**. Now it is here that you can make the final adjustments to both text size and to balloon size. The combination of these two items is what I refer to as the complete 'speech bubble' and each one is a separate 'object' in its own right. I mean here that the 'text' is an object on its own, and the word balloon is an 'object' on its own. Both are individually adjustable. How? Well that can be slightly tricky, but is simple enough when you catch on to what is actually happening. Let me explain…

Looking at your picture now, you can probably see the 'handles' surrounding the textbox. This is because the textbox was the last thing that you did any work with. You don't see the 'handles' for the word balloon, but you can make them re-appear with a bit of carefully mouse pointing. There is a little trick here that is important to know about in order to be successful in switching between the 'word balloon object' and the 'textbox object'. The trick concerns the very tip of the mouse pointer symbol. When you see the mouse pointer displaying an 'arrow symbol' then it is fairly easy to know where the very tip of it actually is! But when the mouse pointer becomes a 'hand symbol' then it is not so easy to know where the very tip of it is. The answer is the **Fingernail of the Index (First) Finger** – or at least where the fingernail would be if you could see it in the symbol!

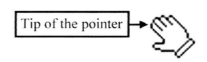

To make the 'handles' for the word balloon object become visible, you need to click with the mouse pointer <u>anywhere inside the balloon that is NOT on top of the text</u>. Try it now. Position your mouse in the balloon where the tip is over a white part of the balloon background and make a click. If you have done it correctly, you will then see the handles for the 'word balloon object' appear. Let us now switch back to the 'textbox object'. *This is where you have to be very precise! Position the mouse pointer so that the fingernail of the index (first) finger is* **exactly** *over a black letter (any black letter) and make a click.* You may have to try this several times to get it right! When you do, then you will see the 'handles' for the 'textbox object' re-appear.

As I said before, it's a bit tricky. But when you get the hang of it, you can then easily switch back and forth between these two objects that make up the complete speech bubble. And when you can do so, then you will be able to drag upon the 'handles' for each of these individual items and adjust them accordingly. Complete the job by making these adjustments to your own picture, such that your text fits inside the balloon, but is still big enough to be easily readable.

Okay, with the main task completed for this exercise, it simply remains for us to save the picture back to the hard disk again. Click on **File** from the main menu bar and select the **Save As... option**. You will then see the **Save Project box** pop up on the screen.

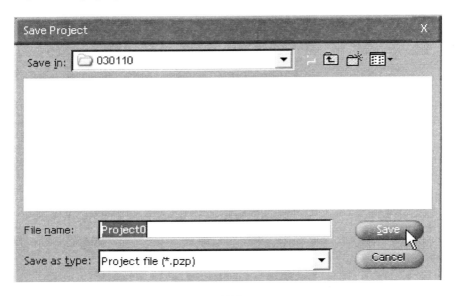

Now this time, instead of saving the picture as a '.jpg' file type, we are going to save it as a project file – that is, as a '.pzp' file type. Accept the suggested project name already in the **File name: box** and simply click on the **Save button**. For a brief moment, you see the black progress bar appear while your picture is saved to the hard drive.

Note – If you intend to email your picture to yours friends or family, then you should consider saving it as a '.jpg' file type instead. Copy the procedure outlined at the end of the last exercise to see how this is done.

You may be wondering what the real difference is between saving your picture as a '.pzp' file and saving as '.jpg' file. The answer is that saving as a '.pzp' file type will preserve the 'objects' in the picture as individual items. These objects are such things as the 'textbox object' and the 'word balloon object' that we talked about before. By preserving these, I mean that if you re-open a '.pzp' file at any time in the future (long after you previously saved it to the hard disk and closed the program down), then the objects will still be there for you to make further adjustments to. You can even remove these objects from the picture altogether. On the other hand, if you save a picture as a '.jpg' file, then this is a universal file type that lots of other programs know about and can work with, but the drawback is that all of the 'objects' get flattened out into the very pixels of the picture itself, and you cannot come along at a later time to re-open the file and play around with them as separate objects.

If you would like to print out the picture before we finish the exercise then go ahead and do so.

Finally, close the **MGI PhotoSuite** program and return to the desktop. This concludes Exercise 27.

Note – If you would like to see for your self the difference between '.pzp' files and '.jpg' files, you might like to re-open the file saved in the last exercise and see that when you do so, you can click again on either the textbox or the word balloon to see their object 'handles' again. Try the same thing on the file saved in Exercise 26 and you will not be able to bring back the handles.

7.3 Creating new pictures

Exercise 28 – Creating new composite pictures

In exercise 17, we saw how to print two or more pictures onto one sheet of paper. We did this by printing out the first picture, and then returning the same paper back into the printer to print the next one into unused paper space. The danger with this technique is that you can easily miscalculate their sizes and placements, and end up printing part of one of them over the top of another.

In this exercise, we are going to learn how to create a large single composite picture consisting of two or more digital pictures, so that you can print them all at the same time. Starting with a blank page, we will first add one and then another. We can then resize and arrange these pictures as we please to make them all fit neatly onto the same page. When we have finished laying them out, we can save the new composite picture to the hard drive for future reference and finally print it out.

This method also allows us to get really clever and to 'paste' other images into the composite picture that may come from different sources. For example, you may choose to use another computer program to 'cut out' part of picture and to place the cut out bit onto the Clipboard. You can then 'paste' the contents of the Clipboard into the composite picture. One such computer program is Microsoft's Paint program that comes with every version of Windows. You can find it from the Start button by choosing '(All) Programs' and then 'Accessories'. The Paint program is also useful for touching up individual pixels.

Note – If you want to know more about the Paint program and the Clipboard, see section 6.3 of the companion guide *'Using a Computer for the First Time'*.

Begin the exercise with the computer switched on and showing the desktop. Start the **MGI Photosuite** program running and displayed full screen size.

Instead of opening a picture to start with, let us create a 'blank page' to work with and then paste other pictures on the top of it. From the opening screen, click first on the **Compose button** in the group at the top. Then click the **Collages button**. This time, the left-hand panel appears with the **Blank Canvas option** selected with a dot in its little circle. Click the **Next button**.

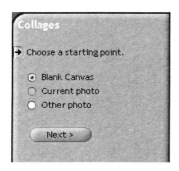

The New Project pop-up window will then appear in the middle of the screen. Here we specify the characteristics of the blank page. The top two boxes you see in this window are 'drop down list' boxes, and you click on the down-arrow on the right side of them to see their lists. The other three boxes are 'textboxes' and you can click on them to place a vertical cursor inside. Using the cursor and the keyboard, you can then rub out their existing values and type in a new one. Go ahead now and alter each box so that you change their values to those shown in the next picture...

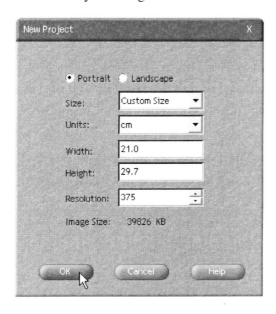

The height and width in this picture are those of European A4 page size. North American readers may want to choose Letter size (8½in x 11in). The resolution value I have chosen is such as to match the 'natural' resolution of the epsilon 1.3 digital camera. This means that when we place our digital pictures on the blank page, then we start with the full benefit of all pixels being present before resizing. When you are ready, click on the **OK button** and the blank page will appear in the working area.

Down the left-hand panel, you should now see the **Compose menu** set of buttons. Click on the **Add Photos button**. You then see the **Add Photos panel**. Click on the small **Computer button.**

This then pops up the **'Add Photo to Project' dialog box**, which is almost identical to the **Open dialog box** seen in our previous exercises. The first time that this appears, the entry in the **Look in: box** at the top will probably not be set for your picture's sub-folder. Consequently, you will have to navigate to it in the usual way. Click on the down arrow at the right side and choose 'My Documents' from the drop down list. Click on 'Epsilon Pictures' and then click the **Add button**. Click on your particular date sub-folder and click the **Add button** again. Eventually you see your picture files appear in the large white box. As we have done before, click to select a picture file that you would like to add to your composite picture. Finally, click the **Add button** when you have chosen one.

Your picture now appears in the middle of the blank page. You will also notice that it has the familiar side and corner 'handles' around it. Having these handles means that you can resize it. If you place your mouse point inside the dotted-line frame you will see the hand symbol, meaning that you can move it around on the blank page. There is something else that the 'handles' and dotted-line frame are telling you. They are effectively indicating that this is an 'object' much the same as we learnt about the 'word balloon object' in Exercise 27. One very important consequence of treating this picture as an object is that you can delete it from the picture. If either you made a mistake in selecting it or you have changed your mind for the composite picture, to remove it all you need do is to press the keyboard's **Delete key** (usually just to the right of the Enter key). This is true of any object that you place upon the blank page. As long as you can see the 'handles' and frame of an object, then it is at the focus of attention on your page, and actions you take with the keyboard or the mouse will affect that object rather than any other. To switch the focus of attention from one object to another, all you do is click upon the object you want and this will make the 'handles' and frame visible for that object.

Because this picture (the one now in the centre of the blank page) is treated by the MGI PhotoSuite program as an object, it means that we are not working on the picture file directly. We therefore don't have to worry about copying the picture back to the hard drive with a new filename (as we have done in previous exercises).

Let me demonstrate another consequence of the picture being an 'object'. Using you mouse pointer, click on **Edit** from the main menu bar and select **Copy**. This action places a complete copy of the 'object' onto the computer's internal Clipboard. Now go back to the picture in the centre of the blank page and perform a **drag action** (press and hold the left mouse button) to move the picture and relocate it in the top left-hand corner of the page. Leave yourself a small border on the left and top. Here comes the important point – click on **Edit** again from the main menu bar and now choose the **Paste** option. After a black progress bar momentarily appears, you will then see a new object appear in the centre of the blank page. It is a complete (but separate) copy of the first picture. You can even perform a drag action to place this object in another part of the page. Get the idea?

Okay, you may not want to keep the copy. In which case, make sure its handles and frame are visible (click on it if you have lost them) and then press the Delete key on the keyboard. The second object will vanish.

You are now at liberty to add as many additional digital pictures to your page as you care to. Go ahead and repeat the procedure of clicking the small **Computer button** in the left-hand panel and then choosing other pictures to add to the final composite one (by repeatedly selecting them with a click, and then clicking the **Add button**). Resize and locate them to suit. When you have finished, click the **Return button** in the left-hand panel to return to the **Compose menu.**

We should now save the composite picture to protect the work we have done. From the main menu bar, click on **Save As...** (or **Save**, it does not matter which) and click in the **File name: box** to add a number to the suggested name, so that it reads 'Project01'. Then click on the **Save** button. It will probably take a few moments to save the composite picture back to the hard drive.

If you want to print out your composite print, then you may do so. Remember when you go through the procedure of using the **Print button**, you need to adjust the **'Properties' option** to select the best quality print and correct paper type and size, in order to guarantee the best printing that your printer is capable of doing. Each time you close the MGI PhotoSuite program, it resets the printer properties settings and if you forget to reset them then you end up with a poorer quality print.

This concludes Exercise 28, and the chapter.

8

More About Photo-Quality Printing

8.1 General photo-quality printing

Printing good pictures for yourself is not difficult to do these days and can save you both time and money. It can also be a lot of good fun too, for there is a genuine feeling of excitement about seeing quality digital pictures slowly emerging line by line from the printer. They are something that you can rightly claim to have created yourself from start to finish, and you may naturally feel proud of your work.

To maintain high quality results, you only need follow simple guidelines. If you pay attention to these then you may be assured of consistently good photographs. If you don't however, then a few factors can lead to disappointment. My aim in this chapter is to spell out these simple guidelines so that your results are always in the first category and rarely in the second!

It goes without saying that your printer must be of a reputable standard to produce good quality work. The **HP Photosmart 7150** that we introduced in chapter 5 is certainly such a device, and assuming that you are using this or a comparable printer, then there four key issues to bear in mind for quality pictures. These are:

a)   the digital picture itself
b)   the quality that you are asking for
c)   the paper you print upon
d)   the ink that is squirted at the paper.

If your photographs are not up to scratch, then you must examine which of these issues is causing the problem. In the coming sections of this chapter, I will discuss these in turn, so that you have the general guidelines to follow.

8.2 The image and the quality you ask for

It seems a very obvious thing to say, but I will state it anyway. The quality of your printed digital pictures depends very much on how good the images are that you start with. It you have a poor image in the beginning, then you are not going to have a great image after you have printed it! I am not particularly referring here to the artistic content, although that will certainly affect how pleasing the prints are to your eye. I am referring to images that have good brightness, contrast and colour content. They must also have picture detail in the required sharpness of focus. The secret of brightness and colour is the amount of white light that you have available, and the secret of contrast is where is that light coming from. The secret of picture detail in focus is in keeping the camera still for the instant that you take the picture!

If we presume that your pictures possess good brightness, contrast and colour, and that the detail is sharp, are there any other factors that can affect them when they are finally printed? My answer is yes, there are two major points that I can identify and in a sense they both relate to the quality that you ask for. The first point is the quality that you ask for 'from the camera', and the second is the quality that you ask for 'from the printer'.

If you want to get the absolute maximum picture quality from the epsilon 1.3 camera, then you should adjust the 'Size' setting to '1600 x 1280' and make a change to the 'Quality' setting from 'Normal' to 'Fine'. These settings can be altered from the menu choices that we mentioned in section 6.1. The first change gives you the maximum number of pixels. The second one affects the level of fine detail transferred into the resultant digital picture file when it is stored in memory. You will end up with a bigger sized file after changing the settings and it takes up more space in the camera's memory, but you will also have a better reproduction in the final print of what it was that the camera lens actually captured in the original snapshot. To show you an example of using these settings, here is a picture from my own collection featuring York Minster taken just as the sun was setting...

When you want to return to taking ordinary everyday pictures, then you should change the settings back to Size equals '1280 x 1024' and Quality equals 'Normal'.

The quality that you ask for from the printer is normally defined by the **'Properties' button** settings that we mentioned in the description of 'Control No.1' within Exercise 16, section 5.3. I cannot stress enough that you must always check that you have actually asked your printer to give you the highest quality print that it is capable of doing, if that is what you want to achieve. All photo quality printers are normally capable of at least two or three different quality levels for the range of tasks you have in hand, and the current setting may not be the highest one. These levels range from 'Draft' at one extreme, where you get a very quick print but the quality level is 'rough and ready', through to 'Best' or 'Highest' where the printing speed is very much slower but the tiny drops of ink that it squirts at the paper are much more numerous.

To summarise our guidelines then on the image and the quality you ask for:

- Start with images made in good lighting to produce brightness and colour. Get the light coming at the right angle to give you good contrast. Keep the camera still at the critical moment.

- Make sure the camera picture is taken at the maximum pixel setting and the finest quality of file storage. These are both settings on the epsilon 1.3.

- Make sure that you set the printer to print the 'Best' quality of print in the printer's 'Properties' settings.

8.3 Types of paper and sizes

The type of paper that you use for printing digital photographs is very important. Because there is such a large range on sale these days, it will be helpful to understand what the differences are between the various types. One big factor, but not the only one, is weight and this is quoted in grammes per square metre, gm/sq m or commonly 'gsm'. Sometimes this is shortened to just gm (but implying per square metre).

Starting at the bottom of the scale, for most of the general work that you do with a computer, such as writing letters, printing documents and such like, you can get away with using cheap paper that you can buy in bulk. This paper is not suitable for photographs. You will see it marked on the box or wrapper as either 70gm or 80gm per square metre and you often see a further classification such as 'Laser' paper or 'Inkjet' paper. Some companies are marketing 'multi-function' paper meaning they consider it suitable for both types of printer. The reason why it is not suitable for photographs is two-fold. One, the surface has loosely bound fibres and ink dropped in one spot tends to run with the fibre. This may all right for printing text but is of no real use for a photograph. Two, it is a little thin and gets wet through with the amount of ink deposited for a photograph.

The next range of paper is either 90gm or 100gm. Now this normally has a better quality finish to it and the fibres are packed tighter together, consequently ink does not run as much along the fibre. You can print a reasonable picture upon it, but again not a high quality photograph. Manufacturers start to grade the 'whiteness' of paper in this range and you will see references to 'extra white' and 'ultra white'. I use paper in this range to produce a draft of my work and I set the Printer Properties (in the 'Print Preview' panel) to 'normal', 'plain' or sometimes '360 dpi paper' for the heavier grade.

At the top end of the range we begin to get the true 'photo' type papers weighing in at around 150gm per sq metre and going up to the real quality material at 240gm or 260gm. The surface finish is now specified as well as the weight and you will come across various surface descriptions such as 'glossy', 'satin' and 'matt'. This surface finish is the real difference why this type of paper is considered to be of photographic quality. It accepts a lot of ink without creating 'runs' or 'wetting' the paper. All three finishes are suitable for photographs but they will each have different presentational appearances, so much depends on the nature of your work that you want to do. I personally like both 'glossy' and 'satin' for my photographs and it is very easy with these finishes to know which side of the paper is the printing side!

When you are handling the top end range type of 'photo' papers, do so by their edges or their underside to avoid putting fingerprints on the printing surface (often the underside has the company's logo printed on it). Paper also absorbs moisture so only put enough paper for your immediate needs in the paper tray; keep the rest in the plastic wrapping or box and stored in a dry location.

When inkjet printers squirt their very tiny drops of ink, then the paper's surface will dramatically affect the way that the ink drop dries, how fast it dries and how it reflects light back to your eye when you look at it. Ultraviolet light will also have a fading effect over time. These are the kinds of factors that are taken into consideration in manufacturing paper, and a lot of research goes into the study of these properties by the big companies. They each try to optimise these factors for their own printers, so if you want to get the very best results then you should purchase both paper and ink to match the printer. For the **HP Photosmart 7150,** the paper known as '**HP premium plus photo paper'** will give you excellent results and long-term stability.

Earlier in the book, in chapter 5, we saw how a device like the **Dahle 507 Personal Trimmer** can cut out your photographs from larger sized paper, such as the European A4 size or North American Letter size. This is a great way to keep the costs down for both paper and inks are quite expensive. If you don't wish to bother with trimming then you may consider buying smaller purpose-sized paper such as 150mm x 100mm (6 in by 4in) with a perforated tab. This is also available as 240 gm 'HP premium plus photo paper' for the 7150 printer. You can print 'borderless' photographs with this paper. The tab is a small extension on its longest side, and it allows the printer to hold the paper when the very last part of the picture is being printed. You then detach the tab along the perforation to produce your 'borderless' photograph.

The **HP Photosmart 7150** printer has a special compartment for this smaller size paper in the top tray. You can leave the normal European A4 (or letter size for North America) in situ. Just slide the small light-grey knob lever (in the right side of the paper tray) towards you to (that is, away from the printer body) and flip up the little compartment lid built into the top tray. Place up to 20 sheets of your 150mm x 100mm paper in the compartment with its 'glossy' side down (hp logo side is facing upward) and ensure the perforated tab end is nearest to you. Make sure it is now lying completely flat and square in the compartment. Close the flip-up lid. When you are ready to print with it, slide the grey knob lever forwards, to engage the paper in the mechanism. Do this slowly but firmly until you meet some 'resistance' that prevents it going any further forward. This action tells the printer to select this compartment for the next print, rather than use the larger tray below it. If the printer's orange panel light starts flashing during the printing phase, then the paper has not correctly engaged. Pull the lever back and sort it out, then push it forward again to re-engage. Press the button at the side of the orange light to stop it flashing and get the printer to try printing again. Later, when you have finished and want to use the large tray once more, pull the grey knob lever fully towards you to disengage the smaller size paper. You can leave it in the compartment if you want to for the short term, but if you don't intend to use it for a while then it is better to place it back in the plastic wrapper or box for safe keeping and dry storage.

One little problem that often does arise with using smaller paper is getting the picture size to agree with the paper size, so that the aspect ratio (that is the ratio of the height to the width) is maintained in the correct proportions. The digital pictures that come out of the camera are not the same ratio as 150mm x 100mm paper and have to be 'cropped' to fit it, particularly if you want borderless printing. With **MGI Photosuite**, this is very easy to do. Use the 'Crop' facility as we did for Exercise 13 in section 4.2, but instead of dragging the handles about to define your **Selection Area**, choose the preset '15 x 10 (Landscape)' (the numbers are referring to cm here). This is an option from the drop down list that appears in Section 1 of the of the 'Crop' menu's left-hand panel. The new Selection Area will then be automatically defined for you, and you may drag it up or down a little to get the best appearance. You then crop the picture as normal to exactly the correct height/width ratio.

When you progress to the **Print** stage, you have a few changes to make with the **Print Preview** menu in the left-hand panel. In Section 1 of the panel, click the **'Properties...' button** (see the part about Control No.1 in Exercise 16). Not only do you set the quality to '**Best**', but you also click on the **'Layout' tab** and click the **'Borderless Printing' button** in the 'Paper Size' section. Select 'Borderless Photo 4 x 6in (with tab)' from the size list and also 'hp premium plus, glossy' from the type list. This then changes the paper size setting accordingly on the 'Layout' tab. Click the OK button when you have done. In Section 2 of the left-hand panel, the default orientation is likely to be wrong. Alter it from 'Portrait' to 'Landscape' (I'm assuming of course that you are going to print a traditional form of borderless photograph, which is more often than not a 'Landscape'). Finally, in Section 3, choose the 'Fit to page' and alter the measurement units to be 'cm'. You should then have a width showing of '15.23' and a height of '10.15' (which is exactly 6.00 inches by 4.00 inches) in the two boxes respectively. Now in the working area, your picture is displayed without any white border showing. This is just how the picture will appear on the smaller size paper after printing. Then click the **Print button** as normal.

There are other types of 'paper' available that you might want to consider using. These are types such as 'Greeting Card' paper for printing your own photos on cards, or 'Iron-on T-shirt Transfers'. You can be the envy of all your friends when you stroll into the pub with a custom made T-shirt having a photo and a speech bubble emblazoned upon it! Just be careful if you choose some of these unusual 'papers' to make sure they do not exceed the maximum permitted weight for your printer, which for the HP Photosmart 7150 is 300 gm/sq m.

To summarise our guidelines about paper for high quality photographs:

- Always use a heavy paper in the range 150gm/sq m and above for you final result. For the HP Photosmart 7150, 'Premium plus photo paper' at 240gm is a good choice.

- Make sure you have the correct paper type selected in the Printer Properties section to match the paper you are using. This is very important.

- Check that you put the paper into the paper tray the right way round. For the HP Photosmart 7150, this is with the glossy or printing side face down and the hp logos on the back of the paper facing upwards.

- You can use 90gm to 100gm for draft work but remember to set the Printer Properties accordingly.
- Manufacturers paper is specially developed to match their inks and gives the optimum combination of quick ink drying time, colour matching and long-term retention.
- If you want to print on smaller sized paper, the height/width ratio of your digital picture will need adjusting (using 'cropping') to match the paper size.
- Store your paper in the plastic wrapper or box in a dry location, to avoid moisture absorption.

8.4 Inks and inkjet cartridges

'First-timers' to digital photography often wonder what is the real difference between a standard inkjet printer and a 'photo quality' one? I think that the ink issue, probably more than most other aspects, defines the answer to this question. In the early days of colour inkjet printing, the ink colours were limited to just four if you include Black. The other colours were (and still are) Cyan, Magenta and Yellow. Now the quality of the colour photographs that you could print with these four colours was not bad. In fact, I remember that with my own first experiments I was surprised and amazed at the quality I could achieve. Towards the end of the 1990s, the 'photo' inkjet printers arrived on the market. These were six colour ink devices. The two additional colours are Light Cyan and Light Magenta and the reason why they are needed is to get better colour rendering on images where the human eye is sensitive to the lighter colour shades, such as the 'skin tones' in pictures of human faces.

Now you may wonder how these 'strange' colours of Cyan, Magenta and Yellow can reproduce the full range of colours that we see in our pictures. This puzzled me when I was first introduced to inkjet printers. Without going into a rigorous treatise on colour theory, a brief explanation goes something like this ...

When we look at a photograph, the image that we see is created by light reflecting from its surface into our eyes. The variations in colours are all formed from three basic 'pure' colours called the primary colours, and these are pure Red, Green or Blue. If we see equal amounts of Red, Green and Blue reflected light then they combine together to appear as White. This is a curious fact and a very important one, as we shall soon discover. When the primary colours combine in differing amounts, then they appear as the shades of colour that we see in the photograph.

You can observe for yourself how any colour can be formed from combining the primary colours. Have a look at a working colour TV screen at very close quarters and you can easily see the individual Red, Green and Blue dots of light. A TV set works on the additive colour principle of simply creating these primary colours for itself and 'adding' them together, side-by-side on the screen, to produce a colour 'dot' (which is the same thing that we refer to in the digital camera world as a pixel!).

Colour printing, on the other hand, works in a slightly different way using the 'subtractive' colour principle. It relies upon the fact that White light is a balanced combination of Red, Green and Blue. By subtracting one of the primary colours from White light then we get the secondary colours of Cyan, Magenta and Yellow. Take a look at these next two diagrams to see how this works ...

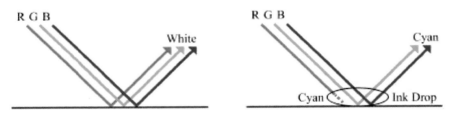

The diagram on the left shows white light reflecting from the surface of white paper. All three primary colours are reflected equally so the reflection appears to our eye as being White. The diagram on the right is similar, but there is now a drop of Cyan ink on the paper surface. This drop absorbs the Red light from the incoming White and only reflects Green and Blue. The paper below the surface of the ink drop now appears as the colour Cyan.

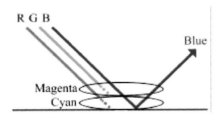

If we used a Magenta ink drop instead then we should see that Green is absorbed, reflecting only Red and Blue. If we used Yellow ink, then Blue is absorbed, reflecting only Red and Green. I think you can now appreciate that each ink colour (Cyan, Magenta and Yellow) subtracts one of the three

190

primary colours from the incoming light and allows the other two to continue onward in the reflection.

Now what happens if we squirt a Magenta ink drop on top of a Cyan one? Look at the third diagram on the opposite page. The Magenta drop absorbs the Green and the Cyan drop absorbs the Red. The only colour not subtracted is Blue, so the paper under both these dots appears pure Blue. We can also obtain the other primary colours by a similar combination of ink drops on top of each other.

From these 'strange' ink drop colours of Cyan, Magenta, and Yellow, together with pure Black, a colour inkjet printer is able to produce areas in a photo that appear Red, Yellow, Green, Cyan, Blue and Magenta and various shades in between. The intensity of the colour depends on the amount of light, and this in turn is controlled by the size of the dot. The dots produced by the inkjet printer have to be very small and very accurately positioned. This means that the nozzles in the printer's mechanics squirting out the dots have also to be very small (less than the thickness of a human hair), and there has to be quite a number of them. If for any reason the inkjet nozzles become clogged, then essential colours will be missing and this is very obvious in the final photograph. Most inkjet printers therefore have a method of cleaning the nozzles and we discuss this further in the next section.

Returning now to 'photo' quality inkjet printers, one major difference with standard inkjets is that they have two extra colour inks – Light Cyan and Light Magenta. This arose because manufacturers discovered that when combining the standard Cyan and Magenta in very tiny dots, it is quite tricky to control their sizes accurately to produce the lighter colour shades. A much better idea was to use a larger dot size from a lighter coloured ink, and hence the addition of the two new colours. Because Yellow is naturally a lighter colour, the need for a Lighter Yellow was not found to be as critical and the compromise was to leave it out.

The way that these five 'strange' colours plus Black are engineered into a printer differs with different manufacturers. Some put the five colours together into one cartridge and Black into a separate one. This means that if you run out of one particular colour, then you must throw away the whole cartridge. On the other hand, if you also use the printer for doing a lot of text work then the Black cartridge can be replaced on its own. With the HP Photosmart 7150, Hewlett Packard have devised a very ingenious arrangement whereby the standard colours of Cyan, Magenta and Yellow, are put into one cartridge (this is the hp57), and the Light-Cyan, Light-

Magenta and Black are put into another (the hp58). They also produce a third cartridge for just Black on its own (the hp56). If you want to do heavy text work, you can remove the hp58 cartridge and replace it with the hp56, thereby using up only the Black cartridge for text, but still having the standard colours available for diagrams if they are needed. When you want to do photographs, you can remove the hp56 and put the hp58 back again, so that you have all six colours available.

Another interesting difference between manufacturers is the way that they engineer the print heads. The print heads are where all the tiny ink nozzles are located. Some manufacturers have the print heads separate from the ink cartridges. This means that when you have replaced a cartridge, you have not changed the print head. If a blockage existed in a nozzle before you swapped a cartridge then it will still be there afterwards. Hewlett Packard, however, have designed their print heads into the ink cartridge as a combined assembly. When you replace the cartridges on the HP Photosmart 7150, you are effectively also putting in new print heads each time. This can be very useful for making sure that you don't get stuck with a blocked nozzle. If the nozzle cleaning process doesn't clear it, you can as a last resort replace the whole cartridge. Another point is that nozzles do wear over long periods of use, and this degrades the highest quality of prints. The small size of the nozzle makes it sensitive to changes as a result of wear. Installing new cartridges on the Hewlett Packard printer overcomes this problem entirely.

Another issue that can arise with inks from cartridges is the positioning and alignment of printing one ink in relation to another. Earlier, I talked about how the colour process worked by printing two coloured dots one on top of the other. The ink for these dots comes from different sets of nozzles. You may now appreciate for this to work properly then different coloured dots have to be accurately aligned in relation to each other. Most inkjet printers have another procedure that you can carry out in order to correct any misalignment that may exist, and we shall also cover this topic in the next section.

These days, you will see a number of third party companies selling printer cartridges that they claim to be compatible with the genuine ones made by the printer manufacturer. These are normally cheaper than the genuine ones and there is a natural tendency to think that they are better value. I recommend that you do not use these third party products for a number of reasons. First of all, you may invalidate your warranty for the printer by doing so. Many printer manufacturers expressly forbid the use of these third party products in their printers. Second, printer cartridges are prone to drying out which renders them useless. Such third party products are much more likely to be kept on the shelf for longer periods than the genuine article, purely as a result of marketing. If you do buy the cheaper alternative and end up throwing it away, then it becomes an expensive alternative. Third, we discussed before how the printer companies go to a lot of trouble to research the combinations of paper and ink in order to produce a fast drying, small drop size that retains its colour properties over a long time. If you want consistent high quality prints, then you should not consider using any cartridge other than that specified by the manufacturer.

Another feature of many modern inkjet cartridges is that they have some electronic circuitry built into them to monitor the amount of ink in the reservoirs. When the ink finally falls below a certain level, then this circuitry informs your computer that you need to replace the cartridge. You are given a warning in two ways. You may see a light illuminate on the printer itself and usually a warning message appears on your computer screen.

To summarise our guidelines for inks and ink cartridges:

- Photo quality printers use six colour inks to be able to create high quality photographic prints.
- The colouring process is very dependant on ink drop sizes and their positions being accurately controlled. If one of the nozzles is not performing, then the effect on the print can be very obvious.
- You can clean a clogged nozzle by a cleaning procedure (see section 8.5).
- You can adjust the alignment of different coloured nozzles with an alignment procedure (see section 8.5).
- Hewlett Packard's ink cartridges for the 7150 printer have new print heads and nozzles combined within the cartridge. You are therefore replacing the nozzles for new ones each time you change a cartridge. Some other manufacturers don't do this.
- Do not use third party 'compatible' cartridges if you want high quality printing. They are not likely to have the same rapid drying, colour quality and long-term stability as genuine ones. They may have been on the shelf longer. They can invalidate your printer warranty if you do use them.

8.5 Maintaining your inkjets

To maintain the inkjets of a printer in good order, manufacturers normally provide software 'utility' programs so that you can print test or diagnostic pages, clean out blocked nozzles if you need to, and align the print heads that contain the nozzles. It is difficult to generalise about such software for all types and makes of printer, but normally these utilities can be found in the pop-up menus that appear when you click on the **Printer Properties** button. This properties button is itself usually available somewhere in the Print menu for the photo editing software that you are using such as MGI PhotoSuite. You can also find the properties button in the print sections of any other programs that allow you to print, for example, a word processor.

With the HP Photosmart 7150 printer, all these maintenance utility programs are grouped together in a window known as the **Printer Toolbox**. The next exercise is a simple one to take you to this toolbox, and the subsequent exercises demonstrate each utility in turn.

Exercise 29 – How to access the printer toolbox

Begin the exercise with the computer switched on and showing the desktop. Start the MGI Photosuite program running. Use the Get button and the Computer button as we have done in previous exercises to open any convenient picture into the working area. It does not matter which picture you choose because we shall not be doing any work it; this is only to allow the Print facilities to become active.

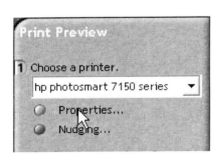

When the picture is visible, click on the Print button from the group of buttons above and then click on the Print button in the left-hand panel. You will then see the Print Preview menu. With the printer type displayed in the box, click on the **Properties button**, as shown here.

This will open the **Properties window**. Click on the tab labelled '**Services**'.

Then click on the **'Open the HP Toolbox' button** in the centre of the **Services tab...**

Open the HP Toolbox

You will now see the **Toolbox window** and the opening tab is called **'Device Services'**.

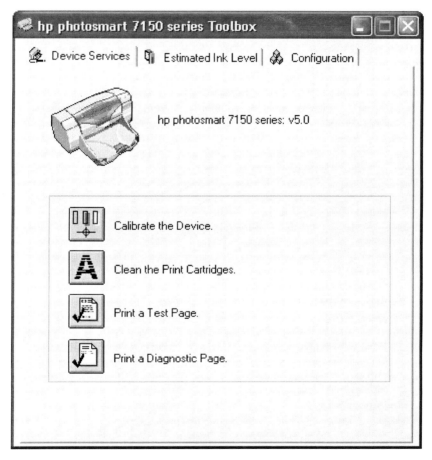

In this first 'Device Services' tab of the Printer Toolbox, we can see four buttons. The top two of these are the utility programs for aligning the print head and cleaning the nozzles, which we referred to in section 8.4. The bottom two are simple test prints to give you an idea of how the printer is performing. These four buttons will be discussed further in the following exercises.

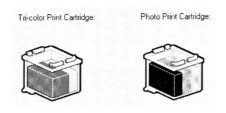

Tri-color Print Cartridge: Photo Print Cartridge:

Click now on the second tab labelled **'Estimated Ink Level'**. Here you see a pictorial representation of the ink levels in each cartridge. The one on the left represents the 'hp57' cartridge of standard colours. The one on the right represents the 'hp58' cartridge of the extra photo 'light' colours plus Black. If at any time you want to know the state of the ink levels, then you can open the Toolbox and click on this tab.

If you click on the third tab labelled 'Configuration', you will see some additional controls that are of a specialist nature. These are not of any particular interest for us in our exercises and are best left at their current settings.

Click back on the **'Device Services'** tab and you will then be ready for the next exercises.

This concludes Exercise 29.

Exercise 30 – Printing test and diagnostic pages

With the **Toolbox** window open and the **'Device Services' tab** showing, check that you have some paper in the large paper 'In' tray. To avoid wasting the expensive highest quality 'photo' paper, I recommend for this exercise that you use either 90gm or 100gm paper if you have it, or 70gm, or 80gm, if you don't. In future, if you need to check the true highest quality of print, then you must repeat the exercise with the heavier 'photo' type paper. Check also that the grey lever knob for engaging the smaller sized '150mm x 100mm' paper (6in x 4in) is pulled fully forward, that is furthest away from the mechanism.

Click on the third button down labelled **'Print a Test Page'**. You will then see a message confirming this task and giving you the option to cancel if you have made a mistake. Click on the **'Print'** button to proceed.

The printer mechanism will now start whirring away, and if you watch the printer's green indicator light, you will see it begin to flash. Very soon afterwards a small but very high quality image appears printed on a page in the 'Out' tray. The image is of the central part of a trumpet (showing the 'valves' used for playing different notes) and it should be flawless. When the printing is complete, the monitor screen will return to displaying the **'Device Services' tab** again.

Though a test print is a useful method of checking that your computer's connection to the printer is working OK and that a high quality image can be printed, if there is a problem with the image it doesn't tell you which colour specifically in which cartridge might be giving you a problem. To find out how individual inkjet nozzles are performing, you can print a 'Diagnostic' Page. Click now on the bottom button labelled **'Print a Diagnostic Page'**.

Again you will see a confirmation message appear giving you the option to cancel if you have selected this option by mistake. Click on the 'Print' button. The printer now prints a page containing a special pattern, like this one shown here...

This pattern has fine detail that is difficult to reproduce in this book, but if you examine your printed page you will see that it consists of six coloured columns, one for each colour of the printer. The left-hand three columns are from the 'hp58' cartridge and the right-hand three are from the 'hp57' cartridge. The fine structure of each column is itself divided into ten thin columns between the vertical bars, and there is a staggered horizontal line in each thin column. The key point to note from this diagnostic is if any of the tiny horizontal lines appears to be missing, then it is showing a clogged nozzle that cannot deliver its ink drop appropriately. The Yellow pattern is a particularly difficult one to see.

If you do experience a clogged nozzle, and you are keen to have the highest quality photographic print, then you can use the utility demonstrated in the next exercise in order to clean it. My experience is that sometimes this takes more than one attempt, but eventually you should be able to reproduce a perfect pattern where there are no missing horizontal lines.

This concludes Exercise 30.

Exercise 31 – Cleaning the inkjet nozzles

With the Toolbox window open and the **'Device Services' tab** showing, check that you have some paper in the large paper 'In' tray. To avoid wasting the expensive highest quality 'photo' paper, I recommend for this exercise that you use either 90gm or 100gm paper if you have it, or 70gm, or 80gm, if you don't. Check also that the grey lever knob for engaging the smaller sized '150mm x 100mm' paper (6in x 4in) is pulled fully forward, that is furthest away from the mechanism. Now click the third button down labelled **'Clean the Print Cartridges'**. You will see a confirmation message appear, giving you the option to cancel if you have made a mistake. Click the **'Clean' button** to proceed.

The cleaning process now begins. From the printer mechanism you will hear a variety of whirring noises. What is happening is that each nozzle in turn within the cartridge print heads is being flushed with a small amount of ink to clean it out, and the ink is collected in a waste reservoir. The process normally takes about one minute and at the end of it, the printer will print another form of test page, as shown here...

ABCDEFGHIJKLMNOPQRSTUVWXYZ

ABCDEFGHIJKLMNOPQRSTUVWXYZ1234567890!@#$%^&*()+-=[]{}/\?.,
ABCDEFGHIJKLMNOPQRSTUVWXYZ1234567890!@#$%^&*()+-=[]{}/\?.,
ABCDEFGHIJKLMNOPQRSTUVWXYZ1234567890!@#$%^&()+-=[]{}/\?.,*
ABCDEFGHIJKLMNOPQRSTUVWXYZ1234567890!@#$%^&*()+-=[]{}/

On your monitor screen, you will see the following message...

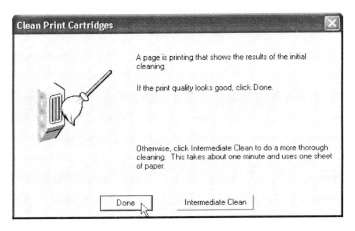

Clean Print Cartridges

A page is printing that shows the results of the initial cleaning.

If the print quality looks good, click Done.

Otherwise, click Intermediate Clean to do a more thorough cleaning. This takes about one minute and uses one sheet of paper.

Done | Intermediate Clean

If the test page just printed is still showing signs of misprinting, this message gives you the option of performing a more thorough cleaning. Click on the 'Done' button and the message is removed. You are now returned to viewing the 'Device Services' tab of the Toolbox.

Note – Whenever you perform the inkjet cleaning process, it uses up ink and inkjet cartridges are not cheap. It follows therefore that you should normally only use the program when necessary.

This concludes Exercise 31.

Exercise 32 – Aligning the print heads

With the **Toolbox** window open and the **'Device Services' tab** showing, check that you have some paper in the large paper 'In' tray. To avoid wasting the expensive highest quality 'photo' paper, I recommend for this exercise that you use either 90gm or 100gm paper if you have it, or 70gm, or 80gm, if you don't. Check also that the grey lever knob for engaging the smaller sized '150mm x 100mm' paper (6in x 4in) is pulled fully forward, that is furthest away from the mechanism. Now click the third button down labelled **'Calibrate the Device'**. You will see a confirmation message appear, giving you the option to cancel if you have made a mistake. Click the **'Calibrate' button** to proceed.

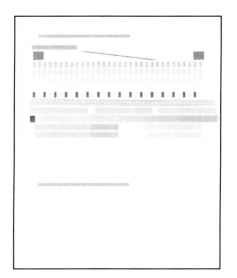

The calibration process now begins in order to align the print heads. From the printer mechanism you will hear a variety of whirring noises. Slowly, as the process runs through its stages, another form of test page will be printed. It emerges more gradually this time because the printer is using the page to check the print head alignment. After about a minute, a test page like the one shown here will appear in the out tray.

On your monitor screen, you will see the following message...

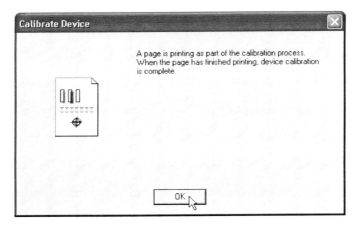

Click on the 'OK' button and the message is removed. You are now returned to viewing the 'Device Services' tab of the Toolbox.

This concludes Exercise 32.

8.6 Digital pictures and resolution

When a picture is taken with a digital camera, it is made up of a very large number of picture 'elements' – the so-called pixels. They are the smallest areas that exist within the picture and can be considered as tiny squares of solid colour. A good analogy is to think of a pixel as similar to a child's coloured building brick and by putting millions of different coloured bricks together, we finally arrive back at our total picture. The vast number of these pixels gives us the final quality of our printed photograph and because they are so small, sometimes we forget that they are there. The main point I want to examine in this section is how adjusting pictures in software affects the pixels, and how this ultimately affects the final quality of the print.

What happens to the pixels when we crop a picture? Well, cropping is simply a slicing action. It 'slices' pieces off the edges of the picture either as horizontal strips or vertical strips, or both at the same time. If you think about the analogy with children's building bricks, then all you are really doing when you crop a picture is remove a number of rows and maybe columns of these bricks from the outer edges. For any part of the image at the centre then the action of cropping the picture does not change the number of bricks that go to make up that centre. It simply remains the same. To illustrate the cropping action, consider these next two images...

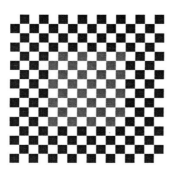

The image on the left represents a digital picture printed before it has been cropped, and the one on the right represents afterwards, when the blue and white checked area has been removed. If the only adjustment we make is to crop the picture and not to resize it, then the second image is naturally smaller than the second, but its fine detail (as compared with the same part of the first image) has not changed. We would therefore have to admit that the 'quality' of the image has also not changed.

The measurement of the 'fine detail' is called the resolution and its unit is in pixels per given length. For arguments sake, let us consider each square to be one pixel, and that both of the previous images has a resolution of 4 pixels per cm.

Okay, now resize the cropped image to make it print the same height and width as the original picture. What about the fine detail and the quality now?

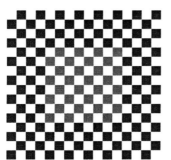

The act of resizing in the previous illustration has doubled the size of the second image compared with the first. This also means that all of the fine detail has been magnified by a factor of two. To pin this down numerically, the resolution of the original image is 4 pixels/cm but after cropping and resizing the resolution has changed to 2 pixels/cm. The image 'quality' has suffered accordingly.

My illustrations shown here have exaggerated the point, but the same effect is true with practical photographs where it is not quite so easy to pick out each individual pixel with the naked eye. This effect occurs not just with resizing, but with scaling as well. For example, if you use a large sheet of photo-quality A4 paper and re-scale a digital picture to take advantage of the available space, then the final picture quality will necessarily be affected.

This same effect also applies to the facility of a digital camera known as 'digital zoom'. When a camera magnifies a picture using digital zoom, it is doing exactly the same thing as we have discussed here. It is magnifying a selected part of the image, but not altering the number of pixels that make it up. Many experts suggest that using software programs to 'magnify' a digital picture is just as good (if not better) than using the 'digital zoom' facility found in the camera. The same is not true for 'optical zoom', for then the number of pixels in the magnified image is substantially greater.

Another interesting point when considering picture resolution is to consider how the printer handles things. Printer resolution is normally quoted in dots per inch (dpi). The 'photo-quality' printers are capable of printing a very high number of 'dots per inch', generally much higher than most digital cameras are capable of producing. This is why they often supply their own high quality images to show you what the printer is really capable of doing.

Finally, when considering the printer and its 'dots per inch', I think this issue is the biggest cause I have seen for poor quality photographic images being printed from digital cameras. When you are setting up the printer for a quality print, you must have the printer's properties set to use the highest or best quality setting if you want to see the finest photographic detail. It is this quality setting that dictates to the printer how many dots per inch to actually use in the print. Very often, this quality setting is adjusted automatically in conjunction with the 'type of paper' setting. If you forget to make these setting changes in the Printer Properties window then your resulting photograph will suffer.

8.7   Printer and computer communication

We will end this chapter about photo quality printing with a thought on the subject of communication between the computer and the printer.

To print a quality photograph of any appreciable size, there is a great deal of information that has to be transferred from the computer down the printer cable. This normally works by the computer transmitting it to the printer in batches. The printer has to be able to accept the information at the speed that the computer wants to send it – that is, as fast as it is electrically possible to do so. But when printing dots on the paper, it can only print them out at the mechanical speed of the mechanism. There is normally a difference between the electrical speed of information flow down the cable and the mechanical speed that the printer can operate at.

To iron out this difference, the printer has some electronic storage memory of its own. What it does therefore is to accept the computer's information and place it into the storage memory until needed. This is what the experts refer to as a 'buffer'. The printer often won't start printing until the buffer has filled to a certain level, and you can actually see this happening in practice. If you watch the green indicator light on the printer at the start of a print, you can see it flashing as information is being received from the computer, but it may be several seconds before the print head begins moving.

Now when you print out a high quality photograph, the ideal situation is where the printer is printing at a nice smooth continuous rate. To be continuous, the printer always needs information inside the buffer to be replenished in good time, and this in turn means that the computer's processor unit must keep up with sending batches as fast as the printer wants to receive them. There are however, several reasons why the computer processor unit may slow down and not keep up. If this happens, then the printer will start to pause for periods, and the smooth continuous motion is thereby interrupted.

The most common reason for the computer not to keep up with the rate of printing is when you ask it do other jobs. If you start other programs running while you are waiting for a large print to complete, then you can quite often witness the printer pausing, as the computer's processor unit becomes momentarily 'distracted'. You may even see the printer come to a complete halt. This can particularly happen when other mechanical devices such as CD-ROM drives or floppy-disk drives start to interrupt the processor unit.

The moral of the tale is that if you want to make a print of the highest quality, then it may pay you to wait awhile until it has finished before you give your computer another arduous task to fulfil. If you want to do something useful while you wait for the print, then normally typing at the keyboard into a document that is already open does not cause any significant problem, but if you set something running such as a graphics editing program that needs intensive communication with the hard drive (either writing back to the drive or reading from it) then don't be surprised if the printer comes to an unexpected and grinding halt. I don't think that there is anything more frustrating than to have a large quality picture almost finished and then to see the printer go into 'extreme slow mode' as though it was deliberately trying to provoke you!

9

Emailing Your Pictures

9.1 An overview of emailing pictures

One of the really useful characteristics of digital pictures is that it is so easy to share them with your family and friends using email over the Internet. The procedure for doing this is quite simple and straightforward...

❑ First, you write a standard text email in the normal way, making it as short or as long as you like.

❑ Second, before you send it, you attach your digital picture to it by clicking various items with your mouse.

This creates a two-part email of text and attachment. You then send this two-part email just as you would send an ordinary email.

When the email arrives at its destination, the person who reads it will see one of two things, depending on the method or program that they are using on their computer. If they are using a program called **Outlook Express**, which is the standard email program that comes as part of the Windows system, they will see your text message first and immediately following it they will see a copy of your picture. Usually they have to scroll a bit further down the screen to see its full extent. If on the other hand they are using **webmail**, which is email using a 'browser' program such as **Internet Explorer**, then they may have to click some more buttons to see the picture attachment. In either case, they can 'detach' the attachment from the email and save it as a separate digital picture file into one of their own folders, or they may be able to print it out.

The above method of sending a picture is in itself straightforward and it works fine as a procedure. The only problem with it is that people often complain that the picture appears very big on the screen. In fact much too big! Scrolling horizontally and vertically with the mouse pointer can reveal all the individual parts of it, but they are unable to see the whole picture in one single view. This problem can be dealt with in one of two ways:

❑ Either, you can ask them to detach the picture from the email and then use another program (such as MGI PhotoSuite) to view the picture as a whole.

❑ Or, you can resize your picture to make it smaller before you send it.

The first solution requires the person receiving your picture to have a copy of **MGI PhotoSuite** or another similar program, and more often than not they won't have one. If their computer uses a later version of Windows such as Windows XP, then there is a built-in picture viewer (a new part of the Windows system) that they can use. Unfortunately, this viewer is not built-in to Windows 98.

The second solution is a much 'friendlier' way to send you pictures, but it requires you to do some extra work before you send it. In the next section we will explore how you go about doing this with a practical exercise.

One aspect of digital pictures that often confuses the 'first timer' is the fact that there are several different picture 'types' in the computing world. Today, the type most commonly used for emailing to other people is one known as '.jpg' (that is pronounced 'dot jay peg' or simply 'jaypeg'). Fortunately for those readers using the epsilon 1.3, the '.jpg' type is the natural picture type for this camera. It is with many other cameras also. Because it is so very common, it is perhaps worth making a few comments about it. Here they are:

1) The **.jpg** picture type actually refers to the file that contains the picture, rather than anything to do with the picture content itself. It is a method of taking a picture – any picture – and 'folding it up' to put it inside the file. If you would like an everyday comparison, think of the way that you fold a blanket to put it inside a blanket box. The box represents the file and the blanket is the picture. The .jpg method of 'folding' is a special way of folding, not just an ordinary way.

2) The special way of 'folding up the picture' squeezes it into a very tight bundle! We call it a 'compressed' file type. This compression leads to a much smaller size of containing file than you would get if you did not compress it. If we simply folded up a picture in an ordinary way then it

206

would not be compressed. We measure file size in **bytes**, or **kilobytes** (thousands of them), or **megabytes** (millions of them). The ordinary way of folding a picture into a file is called a 'bitmap' and has a file type of '**.bmp**'. The size of the compressed .jpg file is normally at least twenty times fewer bytes than the corresponding .bmp file for the same picture.

3) The fact that compressed .jpg files are generally very much smaller than corresponding un-compressed files is the key reason why we tend to use them for email attachments. They travel a lot faster via email over the Internet because there are fewer bytes of information to send. However, this big advantage of smaller size does not come without a few penalty points.

4) The first penalty point is that you need to have a program that can 'un-compress' a .jpg file, in order to get access to the picture inside it. It isn't so much of a penalty these days because Windows computers possess several standard built-in programs that can do this – **Outlook Express**, **Internet Explorer**, and even **MS Paint**.

5) A second penalty point is that some very fine detail can be lost from the picture using a .jpg file, and some detail can even be added to it that wasn't there in the original! This is caused by the compression process itself and is particularly noticeable if objects in the picture's content have sharp corners or if you add text to it. When there is a need to preserve the true picture content, for example, if you are involved in sending graphics art work to a third party, then you should consider using an alternative file type such as '.tif' (sometimes also known as '.tiff') instead of '.jpg'.

With these points about .jpg files in mind, let us now proceed to some practical exercises, starting with how to create a smaller digital picture.

9.2 Resizing the pictures again

As explained in the last section, many people complain that when they receive digital pictures via email, they appear too big on the screen for them to be able to see the picture as a whole. This is not a problem for everybody. If the person receiving the picture can detach it and use another program to view or print it then, fine, you will not need to be concerned about it. However, it is a problem for a significant number of people, so in this section we will follow through an exercise that allows you to resize the picture appropriately and make it much easier for the recipient to enjoy looking at it.

Before I begin the exercise, I would like to explain why this size problem happens, so that you understand what the root cause of the issue is. Our discussion will necessarily get a little technical and if you are not particularly interested in such detail then you are at liberty to skip forward over the next few paragraphs to begin the exercise straight away.

Monitor screens for use with your computer are available in different sizes. Many these days have a 17in. screen (this measurement is along the diagonal of the tube face itself). The screen display for Windows is commonly set up to use a screen area of 800 dots of display horizontally by 600 dots vertically. We refer to a display of 800 x 600 screen dots as 'Super VGA' or simply 'SVGA' (VGA means 'video graphics adapter' to give it its full title). These dots on the screen are effectively the same as the pixels for a digital picture. When a picture is displayed on such a screen without any change of magnification, then one dot of the screen will be used to display one pixel. Now if you consider the Image Size of your digital pictures, this can vary with the epsilon 1.3 between Small, Medium and Large, depending on the setting in the camera. Let us imagine that we have taken a picture on the Large setting. This setting represents a pixel size of 1600 x 1280 and is shown by the large rectangle in the following diagram...

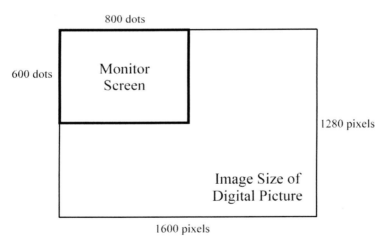

You can easily see from this diagram that if each dot of the monitor screen displays a single pixel of the digital picture, then there is only enough area on the screen to see about one quarter of the total picture. This is the basic issue that the person receiving your picture is face with. If they are reading your email with Outlook Express or using webmail via Internet Explorer, then these programs don't adjust the magnification in any way so you are only going to be able to see a fraction of the picture on the screen at any one time.

When using **Outlook Express**, the person receiving your email won't even be able to use the full width of the monitor screen. If you are familiar with this program then you may recall that there is often a column down the left-hand side of the screen that displays email folders such as the **Inbox** and **Outbox**. For this reason, I work on a ratio of about 3 to 1 to make sure that the picture fits in the available width. That is to say, I reduce the digital picture to one third of its original size, and then 3 pixels of the picture will be represented by 1 dot on the screen. This is normally ample to see the full picture width without horizontal scrolling.

The idea of reducing the digital picture size before you send it has both a good point and a bad point to it. The good point is that by cutting it down, the final size of the file containing the picture will also be reduced and it will be much faster to send down the telephone line from your computer into the Internet. This is over and above the file size reduction from the .jpg file compression principle. The bad point is that you lose a bit of the detail in the picture and if the person at the far end wants to print it out, then the quality of their print won't be as good as the original. However, for casual viewing on the monitor screen, this loss of detail is normally quite acceptable.

Okay, with the root cause of the problem understood, let us now commence with another exercise to perform the resizing.

Exercise 33 – Resizing a picture before attaching it

Begin with the **MGI PhotoSuite** program running and maximised on the screen.

Click on the **Get button** at the top of the screen and then click the **Computer button** at the top of the left-hand panel. The **Open dialog box** will pop up and you will see the last folder that you used showing in the '**Look in: box**'. Its contents will be displayed in the large white box below it.

Our task now is to find a digital picture that we wish to resize. To select the desired digital picture, you may wish to change folders. If you look along the top of the **Open dialog box** and to the right of the **Look in: box**, you will see a small icon of a yellow folder with a 'bent arrow' on it, as shown in the next picture.

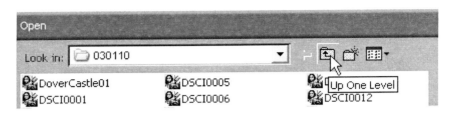

This icon is a button to quickly take you up one level in the folder structure, so that you can see the 'parent' folder that holds the sub-folder currently showing in the **Look in: box**. The parent folder for my sub-folder named '030110' is the one named 'Epsilon Pictures', and after clicking the 'bent arrow' icon button to go up one level, I then see the parent folder appear in the Look in: box, as illustrated in this following picture.

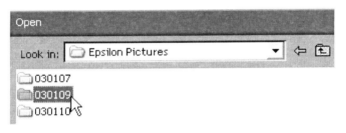

To go down a level inside a different sub-folder, all I then have to do is click on it to highlight it blue, and then click the **Open button** in the usual way.

Using this technique to navigate around the folder structure, select for yourself a suitable digital picture to use in this resizing exercise. It does not really matter which one you choose. Click the chosen filename in the large white box to highlight it blue, and then click the **Open button** to open up the picture into the working area of the program.

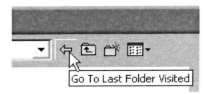

By the way, the little light blue arrow is another button to quickly take you back to the folder you have just come from, if you should ever need to use it.

With the picture now open, we should save it with a new filename. This is in keeping with the philosophy of not working on original copies of our digital pictures. From the main menu bar, click on **File** and select the **Save As...** option.

The **Save Photo dialog box** will now pop up. You will notice when it appears that the name inside the **File name: box** is highlighted blue. This means that the very first letter that you type at the keyboard will cause the existing letters in the box to vanish. Go ahead and type a new name for your picture. If for any reason you get into difficulties, then simply click with your mouse inside the **File name: box** to put a vertical line 'cursor' there, then use the Delete or the Backspace keys to remove the old letters and allow you to type in your new ones. In my example shown in the next picture, I am naming it 'Sunset01'. I don't need to bother putting '.jpg' at the end of the name (as the original name would have appeared) because the 'Save as type:' box is showing 'JPEG Image etc.' and the program will automatically save it as this type.

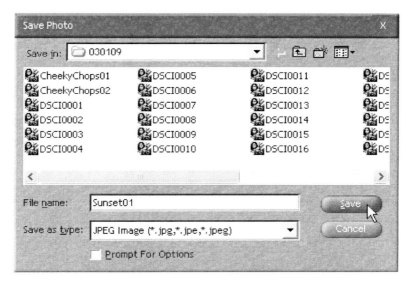

When you have the new filename showing in the box, press the **Save button** and your picture will be saved back to the **hard drive** as a new file. The picture in the working area will also be the new copy of the file, not the original one.

Okay, with the new copy in the working area, click on **Adjust** from the main menu bar at the top of the screen and then select the **Resize...** option.

This will pop up the **Resize dialog box**, as shown in the next picture...

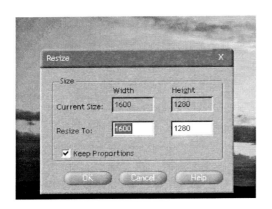

The numbers displayed here are quite interesting. The fact that we see my picture sized at 1600 pixels wide and 1280 pixels high corresponds to the 'Large' image size for the epsilon 1.3 camera. If I had taken this picture with the camera's image size set to 'Medium' then this would show 1280 wide and 1024 high, and for the 'Small' setting it would be '640' by '480'.

Applying my rule of thumb of approximately 3 to 1, I need to reduce the size by about one third. The actual value is not critical and for an easy round figure, I am going to choose '500' for the new width (three times this would obviously be '1500'). You can do the same if you have selected a 'Large' picture, or I would suggest '400' for a 'Medium' one (three times this would be '1200', which is near enough a 'Medium' width of '1280'). There is generally no need to resize a 'Small' picture.

Notice in the previous picture that the **'Resize To:'** width value is highlighted blue when the box opens. This means that I can type immediately at the keyboard and the very first number that I type will caused the existing figures in the box to vanish. Again, if you get into difficulties, click inside the box to put a vertical line 'cursor' there and use the Delete or the Backspace keys to remove the old figures. Go ahead and type in the new figures for your own picture, similar to that shown here...

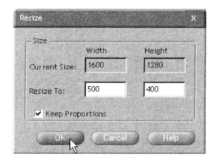

When you do so, the height value changes automatically. This is because the **'Keep Proportions'** checkbox is ticked. When you are ready, click the **OK button** and the picture is then resized.

All that now remains to do is to save the changes back to the file on the hard drive. From the main menu bar, click on **File** and select the **Save option**.

There is a short pause while information is written back to the hard drive, during which time the mouse pointer changes to an 'hourglass' symbol. When it returns to being shown as an arrow pointer, then the save is complete.

Close the **MGI PhotoSuite** program with the **Close button** ('X') in the top right-hand corner of the screen.

This concludes Exercise 33.

9.3 Attaching and detaching pictures – conventional email

There are two different ways that you may be using email. One way is using an email reader program such as **Outlook Express**. I call this the 'conventional way' because you are receiving your email messages down the telephone line and they are stored on your own computer's hard drive. This was the way that email originally developed. The other way is using a browser program such as **Internet Explorer** and I call this **webmail** because you are reading your email as a 'web page'. Such emails are not normally stored on your computer's hard drive. A good example of webmail is the way that you read email in an Internet Café.

Note – If you are interested in learning more about the details of these differing methods then you may like to read section 10.3 of the companion guide *'Using Email for the First Time'*.

Although the two methods use different programs and have some other features that distinguish them, essentially they produce the same end result. If you should ever be the recipient of two separate emails, one produced by the conventional method and the other by webmail, you would have difficulty recognising any difference between them.

In this section, I am going to demonstrate how to attach and send a digital picture using conventional email. Exercise 34 will show you the method for attaching and sending it, and Exercise 35 will show you the method for receiving and detaching it. If you are more interested in the webmail equivalent of these exercises, then jump ahead to section 9.4. The email program I shall be using is **Outlook Express**. If yours is different then you may have some interpretation to do for your own situation.

Exercise 34 – Attaching and sending a picture with conventional email

Begin from the desktop with all other programs closed down. Start the Outlook Express program running. If it does not appear full screen then maximise it with the Maximise button (the middle one of the three in the top right-hand corner).

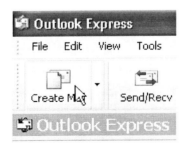

Our first task is to create an ordinary mail message. Click on the **Create Mail** button from the toolbar.

This brings up the **New Message** window. In the **To: box** put your own email address and fill out the rest of the email in a similar manner to that shown in this next picture.

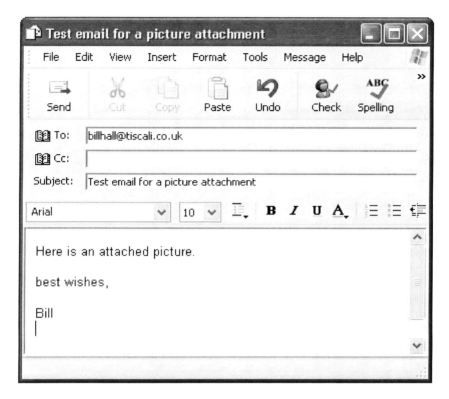

You have now created a standard email message and the only unusual thing is that you are going to send this to yourself (so that you can receive it in Exercise 35). When you have finished writing the message, from the main menu bar at the top of the window, click on the **Insert button**, and select the **File Attachment...** option as shown in the following picture ...

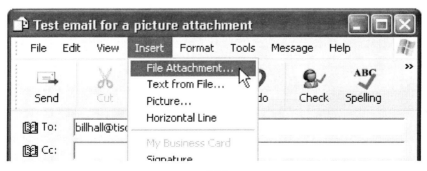

This will display the **Insert Attachment dialog box**.

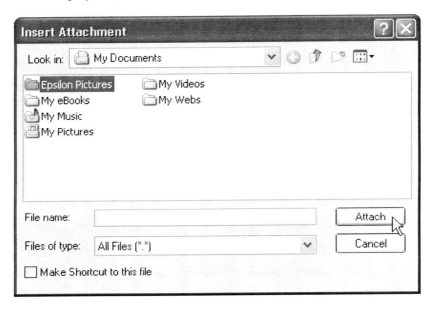

This dialog box works just the same as the **Open box** that we met in the last exercise. We now need to use it to navigate to the sub-folder containing the resized digital picture in order to attach it.

Start your navigation with 'My Documents' in the **Look in: box** at the top of the window. If it is not currently showing, click the down-pointing arrow on the right of the box and select it from the drop-down list. In the large white box below it, click to highlight the 'Epsilon Pictures' sub-folder and then click the **Attach button**.

This puts 'Epsilon Pictures' in top **Look in: box** and you should see the date sub-folders in the large white box. Now click to highlight the date sub-folder where your resized picture is held ('030109' in my own example) and click the **Attach button** again.

Your date sub-folder name should now be in the **Look in: box** and below it you should see all your picture files in the large white box. Finally, click on the file that we resized in the last exercise in order to highlight it ('Sunset01' in my own example), and then click the **Attach button** one last time. This last action is the one that does the actual attaching of the picture file to the email text body and is illustrated in the next picture...

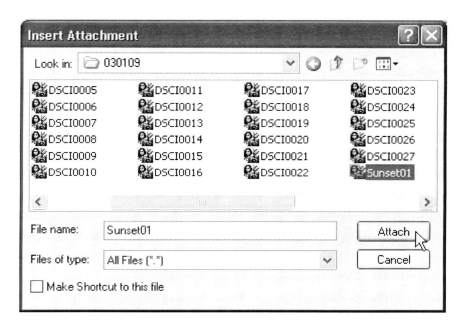

After you have pressed the button, the **Insert Attachment dialog box** window disappears and you will then see that the original email window has changed slightly. Just below the **Subject: box** a new box has appeared with the label 'Attach:'. This is shown in the next picture.

Inside this **Attach: box,** you will see the name of your resized file and in brackets its size will be shown. The size is a very useful measure to indicate how long it will take you to send this file down the telephone line into the Internet. I work on a general figure of about 3 Kilobytes per second for the higher speed modems (56Kbits/sec).

We now have the final two-part email completed with its resized picture attachment. Click on the Send button to send it. This puts it into the Outbox.

If you are currently on-line to the Internet, then your email will be sent in the normal way. If you are not on-line, then press the **Send/Receive button** to force an attempt to make an Internet connection, and login in the normal way. Your email will then be sent as soon as the on-line connection is established.

Finally, to check that the email has actually been sent, click on the Outbox folder as shown in the following picture. In the right-hand upper section of the Outlook Express screen, you should see that it is empty.

You can also click on the Sent Items folder (see just below the Outbox) and the last entry in the right-hand upper section should be the email that you have sent.

 TIP – The content of the Sent Items folder shows you how your email will appear at the receiving end, if they are also using Outlook Express and have their monitor screen display set up the same as yours. This is a good way to check that they can in fact see the whole picture as a result of your resizing.

 Note – If the sub-window showing the list of folders is not visible on your own computer screen, then Appendix V of 'Using Email for the First Time' Note has some simple instructions of how to change your settings to make it so.)

This concludes Exercise 34.

Exercise 35 – Receiving and detaching a picture with conventional email

Begin the exercise with the **Outlook Express** program running and maximised on your monitor screen. You should also be connected on-line to the Internet. If you are not currently connected then follow your normal procedure to become so.

Press the **Send/Receive button** on the toolbar at the top of the screen and wait for any email to arrive that may currently be held for you with the Internet Service Provider.

Now click on the **Inbox Folder...** You should then see the contents of the Inbox folder. Click in the upper section on the email that you sent to yourself, it should look something similar to this...

Notice with **Outlook Express** that when you receive an email with a picture attachment, the program shows you the picture immediately following the text part. There are circumstances where this may not happen, but the normal case is that you will see it. The benefit of this feature is that the recipient does not have to go through the full action of detaching the picture in order to see it.

Okay, now we shall see how to detach it. The action of detaching is really a bit of a misnomer. It really means to create a separate copy of the picture as an independent file.

If you look at the 'header' part of the lower section just above the text of the email, you can see a **'Paper Clip'** symbol. This is a button for you to click on with your mouse pointer. Click on it and you will then see two options, as shown in this next picture...

Now you have a choice here. You can save your picture attachment using either the first option, which is the name of the attached picture ('Sunset01.jpg' for my own example) or you can use second option, the 'Save Attachments...' option. I personally think of the two choices, the first one proves to be easier in the long run, so we will use it in this exercise. Select the first choice with a click, which should be the name of your own digital picture file. This then usually brings up the warning message.

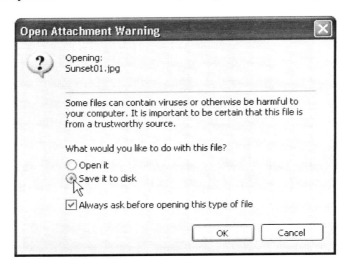

Quite rightly, the message here is advising you to watch out. Attachments to emails are the biggest cause of 'computer viruses' being transmitted around the world. If you want to avoid the possibility of a computer virus being clandestinely dumped onto your computer system, then you should be using special virus protection software. This software automatically scans your incoming emails to make sure that they don't contain a known virus.

Note – Chapter 9 of the companion guide *'Using Email for the First Time'* covers the topics of viruses, hackers and 'Spam' in much more detail.

Because we made and sent this attachment ourselves then I think we should be able to trust it! By the way, it is good sense to leave the checkbox 'Always ask before opening this type of file' in the ticked state. If you decide to clear this tick mark, then you won't see this warning on the next time that you click the **'Paper Clip' button**.

Looking now at the warning message, it has two optional actions that it will perform in respect of the attached file. Make sure that the 'Save it to disk' option has the dot inside its circle (click within the circle if you need to put it there). Then click the **OK button**.

The next item to pop up on your monitor screen is the **'Save Attachment As...' dialog box...**

Here again you have a choice. The dialog box is allowing you to decide whereabouts in the whole folder structure you would like to place the copy of the digital picture that it is about to make. As you can see from this last illustration, it also pops a copy of the filename into the **'File name:' box** automatically for you. You may decide to change the name here if you really wish.

For the purpose of this exercise, we will simply keep the original name and place the picture file in the **'My Documents'** folder. If your dialog box does not have 'My Documents' showing in the 'Save in:' box at the top then click the down-pointing arrow at the right side of it, and select 'My Documents' from the list that then appears. With the box showing 'My Documents', go ahead now and click on the **Save button**, and the picture copy is finally made. That is it finished.

In future, if you want to store it elsewhere, then you have to navigate to the different folder before you press the Save button, and remember that you can always click on this button to create a new folder of your own...

If you do make a new folder, then you should also change the new folder name to something that is meaningful. New folders can also be made inside any other folder as a sub-folder. This is using the classic folder structure to save information in the way that you want to do, not just accepting what the computer is offering you.

Our picture attachment has been 'detached'. This concludes Exercise 35.

9.4 Attaching and detaching pictures – webmail

The exercises in this section perform the same tasks as those of the last one, but now using **webmail** rather than conventional email.

For this section, I shall be using the **Internet Explorer** program. Should you be using a different web browser there may be differences in these exercises that you will have to interpret for your own situation. I shall also be using an Internet account from the Internet Service provider company – Tiscali (UK) Ltd.

Exercise 36 – Attaching and sending a picture with webmail

We begin at the stage where you are logged into your Internet account and looking at the web page where you normally create your email. Here with my Tiscali account it is at the Inbox page.

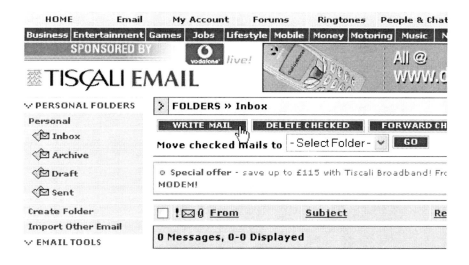

To create the basic email text message, press the **Write Mail button**, as shown in the centre of above picture. Notice how the mouse pointer changes to the 'hand' symbol whenever you are over a button or some other item that you can click upon. Pressing the Write Mail button then takes us to the next page displaying a blank email form. In the To: box write your own email address, then fill out the Subject: box and the message part as shown in the following picture.

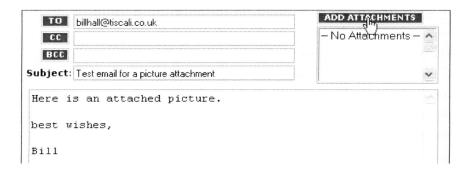

Now if you look carefully at the last picture, over in the top right-hand corner there is an **Add Attachments button**. Press the button and a new window pops up, like this next one...

You can see here that the process of attaching a file to the basic text message part of the email has four possible steps. First, you must locate your digital picture file using the **Browse button**. Second, you click the Attach button to actually attach it to the email. Third, if you wanted to attach any other files then you can repeat the first two steps again. We shall have no need to do this in our exercise. Finally, you click the Done button to close this window and return you to the text message part. Go ahead now and click on the Browse button. This will pop up a dialog box much like the ones we have seen before.

Using the dialog box controls, navigate your way to the folder where your resized digital picture is stored. Start by making sure that 'My Documents' is shown in the Look in: box at the top of the window. If it not currently showing then click the down-pointing arrow at the right side of the box to get a drop down list, and then select 'My Documents' from the list. Then click on the 'Epsilon Pictures' folder to highlight it blue and click the

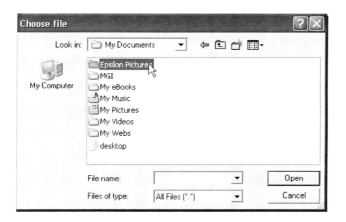

Open   button.
This puts 'Epsilon
Pictures' into the
Look in: box and
you can then see
all the sub-folders
holding your digi-
tal picture files.
Choose the one
where your resized
digital picture is
stored from Exer-
cise 33, using the
same technique of highlight it and click on the **Open button**. Eventually,
you will see all the individual picture files in the large white area of the
window. You may remember that my example was called 'Sunset01'.

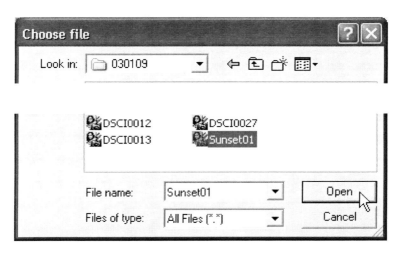

Finally, click on the picture file to highlight it, and click the Open button one
last time. The window disappears, and you are returned to the one showing
you the four steps.

Now take the action of step two and click on the Attach button...

225

This action will show you that your digital picture file has been attached by listing it in the list box at the top of the window. An illustration of it for my own example is demonstrated in this next picture...

The last action is to click the Done button, which closes the window.

You are now back looking at the form showing the basic text part of the email. However, there is one very important difference that you should be able to see – the **Add Attachments list box** over on the right-hand side is showing the name of the digital picture file. This is proof that you have made the attachment correctly.

The final action is to actually send the email and its attachment to the Internet for delivery. Click on the **Send button** as shown in the top left-hand corner of the above picture. There may be a short pause now while the email is transmitted down the telephone line. You then receive confirmation that the email has been sent...

Click the Close button. This concludes Exercise 36.

Exercise 37 – Receiving and detaching a picture with webmail

We begin at the stage where you are logged into your Internet account and looking at the web page where you normally read your email. Here is my Tiscali account at the **Inbox page**. If you have followed on immediately from the last exercise, you may need to click on the **Check For New Mail button** (shown centre right in this next picture). This will refresh the Inbox page and you can then receive the email sent in Exercise 36.

You should now be able to see the email in your Inbox. Click on it as shown in the following picture in order to read it in the normal way...

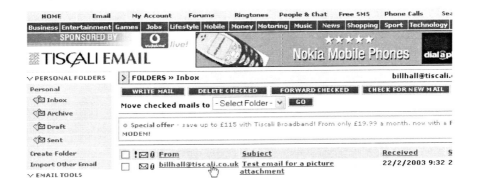

When the email opens to display the basic text message, you should be able to see a Paper Clip symbol indicating that there is an attachment to it. In this next picture it is shown at the bottom of the page. Click on name of the attachment...

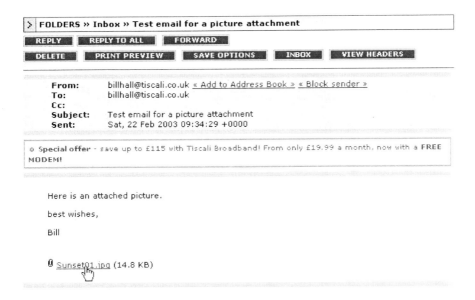

This will then display the digital picture in its full glory...

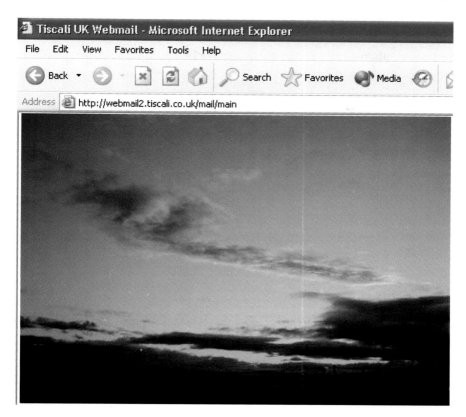

There are two very important points to understand now! You have to appreciate that:

❑ First, even though you can see the picture now in your web browser, it is not yet saved on your computer. What you are looking at is a web page image created by the Internet Company made from the attachment. Both the email's basic message and its attachment are still located at the remote end of the telephone line on the Internet Company's computer (section 10.3 of the companion guide *'Using Email for the First Time'* has a good diagram and explanation of what is actually going on now).

❑ Second, if you want to manipulate the picture or save it for the longer term, you must 'detach' the picture from the basic email. The action of detaching it will make an independent copy of it and you can then save this copy on your own computer's hard drive. Once you have this copy on your hard drive, then you can manipulate it, such as scaling it for printing out on a printer.

Many is the time that I have had people say to me 'Yes, I have received the email and its attachment, but I cannot find the picture anywhere on my computer's hard drive so that I can print it out!' The reason they cannot find it is simple. It was never stored on their computer in the first place, only on the Internet Company's computer. This is what webmail really means! You can certainly see the email – both its text message and its attachment – but you are not really looking at the email proper. You are looking at web pages that your Internet Company has kindly created for you from the email proper. This is a very important and key difference between webmail and conventional email.

Okay, now we understand things, how do we go about detaching it?

Using your mouse pointer, position it anywhere over the picture itself on the screen and make a click with the **right mouse button** (not the left one). This is called a 'right-click', and it normally brings up a small menu of its own, depending on where your mouse happens to be when you make this right-click. In the circumstance now, it will bring up a menu like the one shown in this next illustration…

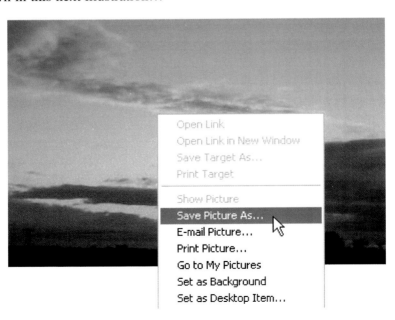

Select the **'Save Picture As...'** option from the menu. This then pops up a **'Save Picture' dialog box...**

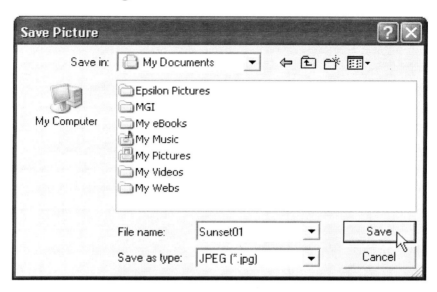

You are now at liberty if you wish to navigate to any folder that you care to, in order to save the picture attachment inside a specific folder. For this exercise, I suggest that you simply choose 'My Documents'. If this folder is not showing in the **'Save in:' box** at the top of the window, then click on the down-pointing arrow at the right side of it and select 'My Documents' from the drop down list. Be aware also that you can change the name if you want to before you save it, if you would rather give it a different name to that as sent inside the received email.

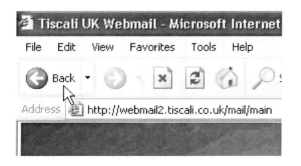

When you are ready, click on the **Save button**. There may now be a short pause while the picture is being stored on your hard drive. Then click on the **Back button** as shown in this illustration, to return to the basic text message screen.

And finally, click on the **Inbox button** to return to the starting point of the exercise.

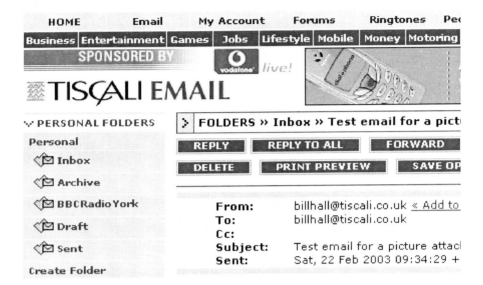

This concludes Exercise 37.

9.5 Printing emailed pictures

Whether you have followed the two exercises in section 9.3 for conventional email, or the two exercises in section 9.4 for webmail, the end result is the same. You now have a copy of the picture saved to your own hard drive. This copy is no longer an email 'attachment' but is saved on the hard drive as a file in its own right. In a real life situation, the person receiving the email may wish to manipulate the picture and print it out locally on his or her own printer. This is where special programs for manipulating graphics, such as **MGI PhotoSuite** or other such programs come in handy. Chances are though that they may not have such programs installed on their computer.

The earlier versions of Windows don't have the more advanced capabilities for graphics built in as standard, as for example Windows XP has. Nevertheless, there is one good old trusty program that every Windows computer has called **'Paint'**. This can normally be found in the **'Accessories' folder**, which is reached by clicking the **'Start button'** and selecting

'**Programs**'. One of the big advantages of sending someone a picture that has already been 'resized' to a smaller version is that they will be able to see it whole if they use the Paint program. You can also print from Paint.

If they are fortunate enough to be using Windows XP system, then there is a very easy way to both view and print pictures. To do this, they simply need to open the 'My Documents' folder from the Desktop (or open the appropriate sub-folder if they have stored it somewhere else) and either double-click on the file's name or icon, or right-click on it and select 'Open'. This will then automatically start up the 'Windows Picture and Fax Viewer' program, as shown in the following picture. This program has some good print facilities using the Photo Printing Wizard.

10

Having Fun on the Internet

10.1 Preparing the camera as a webcam

In this final chapter, we are going to explore a new way of using your digital camera. It is very different from anything that you could do with a conventional film camera, and the first time I had it working I was completely taken by surprise. What we will achieve by the end of Exercise 40 is one of the most impressive demonstrations of the power of the Internet that you could ever wish to see. It is incredibly exciting and unbelievably good fun. We are going to investigate how to use the camera as part of a video and sound link-up with your family or friends. Our final exercise will let you talk to people face to face and literally see what they are doing. If you haven't met up with them for some time then you will be able to see what they look like these days. My word, are you in for a treat!

When the camera is used in this way, it is commonly referred to as a **'webcam'** (a buzz-word for 'world-wide-web camera'). Is it difficult to do? Not in the least. If you follow my guidance in the exercises that follow, then you will have it up and running in no time at all.

Now this idea of making a video link with another person is quite new at the time of writing. To encourage you to have a go, even if you cannot think of a friend or family member to link up with, I am going to provide details of a scheme whereby you will be able to try it out. Please see my personal website for further information about the scheme, under the section titled 'Video Linkups'. Who knows – one day you might even find yourself chatting with me directly! You can find my website at…

www.billhall.me.uk

I will also be posting regular updates about digital cameras on this site in the future so do give it a visit if you can. There is also further information listed there about my books and myself in general.

The preparation work for using the camera as a webcam is two-fold:

- first we check that the camera is connected properly to the computer
- then we install the video link software to connect it up to the Internet.

When these two actions have been completed then we will be ready to make an Internet video call.

Exercise 38 – Checking that the computer recognises the camera

The purpose of this exercise is to prove that the computer can recognise the camera operating in the 'webcam' mode. It is very quick and straightforward. We begin at the desktop with all other programs closed down, and with the camera <u>not</u> connected to the computer by its cable. Also check that the camera is switched off.

Without switching the camera on, turn the camera's Function Switch to the 6th position labelled **'PC Cam'**, as shown here.

Now insert the camera's cable into the miniature USB 'B' type connector at the side of the camera. Then insert the other end of the cable into a USB 'A' type socket on the rear of the computer processor unit.

The first thing you should notice is that the small monitor screen at the rear of the camera lights up blue with a message saying 'PC CAM mode', and its indicator light illuminates first red then finally green. This is despite the fact that you did not switch the camera power button to 'on'. If you are using Windows XP, then you should also hear the familiar two-note ('dum-ding') sound to signify the computer has spotted a new piece of hardware attached to it. With Windows 98, you may see the 'New Hardware Found' message, but this disappears automatically after a few seconds when it finds the 'driver' software installed earlier in the book.

Note – With Windows 98, if you see the 'Add New Hardware' wizard message appear at this point, then you don't have a recognised 'Camera Driver' software program installed (we did this installation for the epsilon 1.3 camera in Exercise 8, section. 3.1).

Now there is a simple check that you can do to test that the camera and computer have correctly linked up with each other. For Windows XP, click on the **Start button** and select **Control Panel** from the menu. For Windows 98, you click on the **Start button** and the select **Settings** from the menu, and then **Control Panel**. The Control panel window opens and you should be able to see an icon labelled 'Scanners and Cameras'...

Scanners and Cameras

Double-click on this icon (or right-click and select 'Open') and you should then see the 'Scanners and Cameras' window open. Now there may be icons shown in this window for other devices besides the camera, but you should see something that has a label for '1.3M DigitalCAM' (the next picture illustrates Windows XP), or an alternative for the camera you are using.

1.3M
DigitalCAM

The fact that you can see this item labelled '1.3M Digital CAM' (or whatever, if you have a different camera) means that your computer and camera have connected together properly in the 'PC CAM' mode of operation. This is a very different mode of operation from that of 'Mass Storage', which we have come across previously.

Note – Some cameras also allow a diagnostic test to be performed from this item (but not the epsilon 1.3 camera). If you have a camera that does, then it will be available from a button in the 'Properties' section for the item (to see 'Properties' with Windows XP perform a right-click on the icon, with Windows 98 it is a button).

Close both the 'Scanners and Cameras' window and the 'Control Panel' window.

This concludes Exercise 38. Leave your camera connected by its cable to the computer in the 'PC CAM' mode of operation ready for the second action of configuring the NetMeeting program.

Exercise 39 – Installing and configuring the NetMeeting program

'NetMeeting' is the name of the program that allows us to do the video linkup. In this exercise we will install and configure the program, and then test that it is working with the camera.

You may remember that back in Exercise 8 (section 3.1), I advised you not to install NetMeeting at that time. The reason is that there is a significant difference between those readers who have Windows XP and those that don't...

- If you have Windows XP, then the NetMeeting program software is already installed on your computer – you just need to configure it.
- If you don't have Windows XP on your computer then you will install NetMeeting from the Digital Dream CD-ROM that came with the camera.

To bring users of both versions to the same point, I will now quickly run through installing the program from the CD-ROM. Users of Win XP should jump forward to Stage B.

Stage A – Installing from CD-ROM...

Follow the instructions given at the start of Exercise 8 and continue until you reach the stage where you can see the main Digital Dream menu of seven buttons (the menu buttons are labelled 'Camera Driver', 'MGI PhotoSuite' etc.).

From the menu, use your mouse pointer to press the **'NetMeeting' button** (the fifth one down). A message then pops up on screen to ask you if you want to continue. Click **'Yes'**. Next you will see the 'software license' screen. Click on **'Yes'** to accept the conditions. A few things then happen automatically and come to a halt with a message asking you which directory (it means which folder) you want to install the NetMeeting files into. Click on the **OK button** to accept the suggested one.

The installation procedure then automatically copies files from the CD to your hard drive. This only takes a minute or two and a progress bar appears on the screen throughout. Finally, you see a message saying, 'NetMeeting has been installed successfully'. Click the **OK button**. Then click the **Exit button** on the Digital Dream menu to close it. Remove the CD-ROM from the drive and close the drive tray.

Stage B – Configuring the program...

All users should now be looking at the desktop on the monitor screen with all other programs closed.

For those users of Windows XP only, begin the configuration procedure by clicking on the **Start button** on the task bar in the bottom left-hand corner of the monitor screen. Then select the option labelled **'Run...'**. A window pops up like the one in the next picture. Type the four letters - conf - and click the **OK button** ('conf' by the way stands for 'conference', as in 'video conference')...

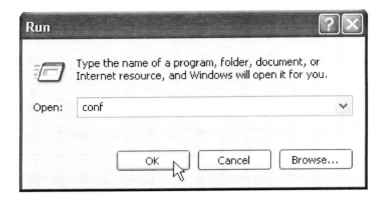

For those readers not using Windows XP, begin the configuration procedure by clicking on the **Start button** on the task bar in the bottom left-hand corner of the monitor screen. Select **Programs**, and from the next sub menu click on a new option labelled '**NetMeeting**'.

Whether you are using Windows XP or not, at this stage you have now set the NetMeeting program running. The very first time that it runs, and only the first time that it runs, it will go through a configuration routine. If you want to re-configure in the future, then you will need to use the menus and options from the program itself to change things. You won't be able to go backwards and re-run the configuration routine for a second time. However, don't be too worried about this because the menus and options can do all of the things that the configuration program achieves.

All users should now be looking at the pop-up window, as shown in the following picture on the left. Click the **Next button** and you will then see the picture on the right.

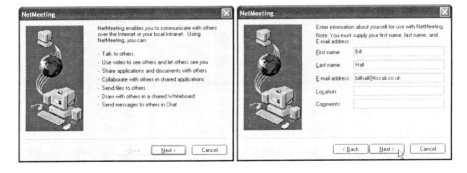

238

This screen on the right is asking you to enter information about your 'First name', your 'Last name' and your email address. These three boxes must have an entry made in them. The last two boxes labelled 'Location' and 'Comments' are optional and you can leave them blank if you want to. When you have completed the boxes then press the Next button. You will subsequently see the next picture on the left.

In this window, you will notice that the checkbox labelled 'Log on to a directory server when NetMeeting starts' is already ticked. It refers to the fact that every time you start up the NetMeeting program, it will try to connect through the Internet to a list of directories. This list is located on a computer permanently connected to the Internet called the 'directory server' and the particular one shown here is owned by Microsoft and called the 'Microsoft Internet Directory'. The principal of using these directories is to find someone else on-line that you can connect to if you so wish. Now it is because you may be a bit shy and not be keen to connect up with a complete stranger that I am setting up the scheme I referred to earlier in the beginning of this section (the one that you can read about on my own personal website titled 'Video Linkups'). Leave this option ticked for the moment. You can always clear it later via the menus if you want to. Click the **Next button**.

The next screen that you see is shown in the former picture on the right. Here you are telling the program what the method is by which you normally connect to the Internet. Most people these days will be using the '28800 bps or faster modem' Click the Next button. This brings up the message shown in the following picture on the left.

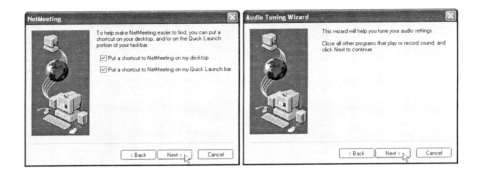

The picture shows two simple options that you can change if you wish. I suggest you leave them checked. Click the **Next button** when you are ready, and you will see the picture on the right.

Now here we begin what is known as the '**Audio Tuning Wizard**' and it makes three assumptions that you need to be aware of. The first assumption is that you have facilities for sound available on your computer. This can be either a sound card fitted into one of the card slots at the rear of the processor box, or it can be a 'built-in' sound capability on the computer's 'motherboard' itself. Either way, you should see a group of three (sometimes four) miniature-jack sockets, located somewhere on the rear panel of the processor box (see next picture on the left). The second assumption is that you have a pair of audio speakers attached. The third assumption is that you have a microphone attached. Although you can operate NetMeeting without sound, it is much, much better with it. How is it that you can operate a video linkup without sound? Well, there is a '**Chat**' facility built into the NetMeeting program that allows you to exchange text messages with whoever is at the other end of your linkup.

If you have speakers and a microphone but they are not plugged in, you can easily plug them in yourself and get them working. This next picture on the right shows you how to do it. Here a speaker jack plug is being inserted into the speaker socket, which is the one usually identified with a Light Green collar and a symbol with an outbound arrow. Speakers often require a separate power source from a mains power unit. When the speakers are attached they need to be switched on and the volume adjusted.

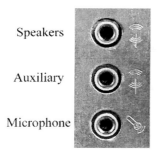

Speakers

Auxiliary

Microphone

The microphone's jackplug socket is also shown in the previous left-hand picture. It is usually identified with a Pink coloured collar and a symbol of a microphone.

Okay, your speakers and microphone are now set up – or perhaps you don't have one of them (or both) available. Whichever is the case, you need to continue with the 'Audio Tuning Wizard' in order that the configuration procedure is fully completed. Click the **Next button** now showing on screen.

The next picture shown on the left below may or may not appear on your computer. It usually shows itself when there is the possibility of selecting from more than one sound source. A complication is the fact that, as strange as it may seem, your modem can be considered a sound source by the computer, in addition to a microphone. This could be the reason why this picture appears.

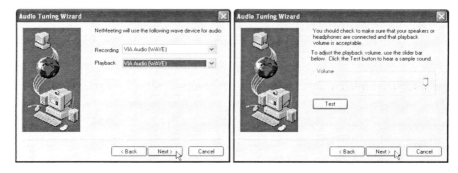

If you don't see this screen, then it will move on to the one above on the right and you can continue from there onwards. If you do see the screen, then it is very important that you select the correct '**Recording**' and '**Playback**' devices from the drop down lists. Make a note of what the settings are before changing them, and then click on the down pointing arrow at the right-hand side of these boxes to see the other devices that you may be able to choose from. My own computer displays two devices in my lists. These are displayed to me as:

VIA Audio (WAVE)
Modem #0 Line Record (or Playback)

Yours may be similar, but probably with different wording. 'VIA' is the name of my motherboard and it has a built-in sound card system, hence it is showing me 'VIA Audio (WAVE)' as one option. Your sound card system may have a different name such as 'Creative Labs SoundBlaster' for instance. It is difficult to guide you precisely here (I obviously don't know what sound system you have!) but my general advice is to select an option that does not refer to a modem. If there is only one other alternative, then this will be the one to select. Should you make the wrong choice then fear not, for you will soon know from the 'sound tests' that are conducted in the subsequent screens. You can then backtrack and try a different one. When you believe that you have set the 'Recording' and 'Playback' options correctly, click the **Next button**.

This leads us to start the first of these sound tests as shown in the previous picture on the right. This test will check that your speaker system is functioning correctly. Click the **Test button** and you should hear some sounds coming from your speakers. If the volume is too loud then either adjust the slider control (shown in the middle of the picture) towards the left using a drag action with the mouse, or alternatively you can adjust the rotary volume control on the speakers units themselves. If everything is fine and you can hear the sounds satisfactorily then press the **Stop button**.

If you cannot hear the sounds and the speakers are definitely plugged in correctly, then there are three reasons I can think of that may be causing your problem:

- The first could be the speakers themselves. Are they powered up and is the volume control set to an adequate level?
- The second is that you may have selected the wrong device in the last screen in the 'Playback' option. You can backtrack by pressing the Back button and choose an alternative if there is one.
- The third is that the 'driver' software for the sound card system may not be set up properly for the computer.

You must decide yourself which of these options is giving you trouble. If you cannot resolve the issue, then you can still use the NetMeeting program but you obviously won't be able to hear the person that you link up with. Do try and get help from someone more expert to fix it in the future, for having sound is well worth the effort of solving the problem.

Click now on the **Next button**. The window that you then see is shown on the left below. This will only be of interest if you have a microphone available and it is plugged in (skip to the next stage by pressing Next if you don't have one). We will assume that you have one available and we can now test if it is working properly.

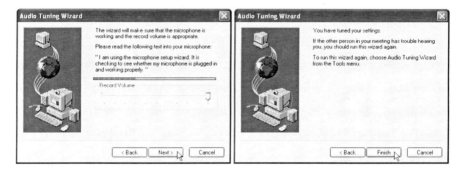

Read through the wording on this window. It is asking you to speak into your microphone to create some output signals from it. When you talk into the microphone, you should see a green horizontal line appear jiggling about in the centre of the screen, as shown in the picture. Its length will vary with your voice. This line indicates the strength of the signals being received. Much depends on the microphone sensitivity but you should see the green line reaching to at least a quarter of the full line length. If you reach the accepted limit of sound volume, the line will have some yellow bits shown on the end of the green part. If you completely 'overdrive' it, then red bits appear after the yellow ones! During this procedure, the record volume level may adjust itself automatically, and the pointer on the scale starts to 'back off' to reduce the sound input (thereby preventing it from overdriving the system). When you are confident that your mike is functioning okay, then press the **Next button**.

If you have a microphone plugged in, but talking into it doesn't give you any jiggling green line, then there is a problem that needs solving. You may try shouting just to see if it gives any response at all. Also check that it is plugged into the correct jack socket at the rear of the computer's processor unit. If the connection is correct but you still get no response, then I can think of three reasons that may be at the root cause of the problem:

- The first may be that the microphone itself (or its lead) is faulty.
- The second may be the wrong choice of 'Recording' device selected earlier in the procedure. You can backtrack if you wish to choose an alternative option if there is one.
- The third may be that the 'driver' software for the sound card system is not set up properly for the computer.

Again, you must decide yourself which of these options is giving trouble. If you cannot resolve the issue, then you can still use the program but you obviously won't be able to speak to the person that you link up with. Try getting help from someone more expert if you can, to fix this in the future. Your friend being able to hear your voice at the distant end of a video linkup is well worth the effort of sorting it out.

After the microphone test, you should now see the final screen, as illustrated in the last picture on the right. If by chance you see an error message at this stage instead, then this is confirming that something is not right with either the mike or your sound card system. The error message will tell you what it believes to be at fault and you can come back and fix this later when you have had time to think about it. For those that do get an error message, press the **Next button** to remove it and move on to the final screen.

The last part of the procedure is simply to click on the **Finish button**. This ends the 'Audio Tuning Wizard' and starts the main part of **NetMeeting program** running. You should now be able to see the main window for the program as shown in the following picture.

Okay, we now have the program configured and running. We should also still have the camera connected to the computer by its cable and operating in the 'PC CAM' mode. Position the camera on a good level surface and make sure its lens is pointing at you as you sit facing your computer. Here comes the true test to see if it is all working!

In the very centre of the program window there are three buttons. The left-hand one is the **Play/Pause button** and it has 'Play/Pause' symbols upon it just like a normal TV video recorder. Press this button now and wait for about three or four seconds...

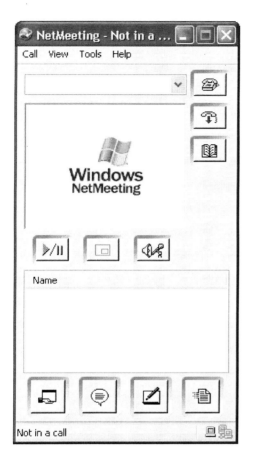

You should now see a picture of yourself in the program's little video section (where it says 'Windows NetMeeting' here). Wave at the camera and you should see yourself waving back!

If by any chance the camera appears not to be working, the reason more than likely will be because you did not have the camera plugged in to the computer before you started the program running. This is bit of a silly feature with NetMeeting but you have to have the camera connected first - you cannot plug it in once the program has begun. If this is your situation, simply close the program down using the Close button ('X') in the top right-hand corner, and then start it running again (there should now be an icon for the program on the desktop).

This concludes Exercise 39.

10.2 Making a video phone-call

In the next exercise (Exercise 40) I am going to show you how you can make a real video linkup with someone else (lets say a friend) over the Internet. This will be a true video phone-call using sight and sound. How exciting! Some thirty years ago, I once worked on a project called 'videophone' for a large telecommunications company. We could only dream back in those days that such a video phone-call would ever become a practical reality. Now anyone can do it!

For this exercise to work, it goes without saying that both you and your friend each need to be using the NetMeeting program and a camera, and ideally both have a microphone and speakers. You must also both have independently completed Exercises 38 and 39. The cameras that you use do not have to be the same model, as long as the appropriate 'driver' software for each camera has been properly installed. Exercise 38 will confirm for you whether this has been done or not. If either party does not have a microphone or speakers then you can still make the video linkup, but you will have to type messages to each other, rather than talk and listen. It is not quite as good as using sound, but it can work. I will mention later on how you do this.

Before we proceed, I first want to touch upon some key principles of operation. If you appreciate these principles then it makes it much easier to understand and resolve any minor problems that may arise in the coming exercise.

The principles of how it works

Every computer connected to the Internet is given a different number known as its **IP Address** (pronounced 'eye-pee' address). This number – the IP Address – works just like a telephone number. It is a unique number throughout the world by which any particular computer can be identified and contacted. To make a video linkup with another person all we need to know is what their IP Address is, and then we can 'dial' this number (using our own computer) and make the link.

Note: 'IP' is an abbreviation for 'Internet Protocol', and the jargon word 'Protocol' simply means the rules by which it all works, that is to say, the nitty-gritty details of the numbering scheme and the way that information is exchanged etc.

The comparison with using a telephone is a very close one, and you know that international telephone numbers are composed of three separate parts joined together to make a person's complete and unique phone number. These parts are first the 'International Code', followed by the 'Area Code' and finally the 'Exchange Number' (sometimes called the 'Central Number'). Well so it is with an IP Address. In fact there are four separate parts that need to be joined together to make a complete IP Address. Such addresses are always thought of as being international and unique throughout the world. The four parts are each joined together by a dot symbol ('.'), so when you see an IP Address written down then it looks like this example -

80.225.178.51

Just so that you understand this correctly, in words this is spoken as 'eighty **dot** two hundred and twenty five **dot** one hundred and seventy eight **dot** fifty one'. By the way, the separate part numbers are always restricted to the range between zero and two hundred and fifty five (0 to 255).

In the early days of the Internet, there were always plenty of spare numbers to give to new 'subscribers' who wanted to join the network. However, somewhere about twelve to fifteen years ago, they started to run out. The explosion in the use and growth of the Internet meant that if somebody didn't do something about it pretty quickly, they would run out completely. The solution dreamt up has worked well enough up until today, but it makes understanding it a little more complicated, especially for 'first-timers' new into the business of computers.

The solution works like this. The number of people actually connected to the Internet at any given moment is only a small fraction of the total number who could possibly be connected. As with the phone system, the number of people engaged on a phone call this instant is only a small fraction of the total number of telephones in existence. Consequently, unlike phone numbers, they decided not to give everybody an IP Address that they could keep forever as their own. Instead, they would only give people an IP Address to use for the duration that they are actually on-line. So, when you start dialling your Internet Company and <u>before</u> you are connected, *your computer does not have an IP Address.* When you are finally connected 'on-line', *then your computer is given an IP Address.* Only those computers actually connected are using an IP Address.

This solution doesn't cause any difficulty if you only want to read web pages or send emails, but it does raise a few problems if you want to link up with someone else's computer. The main problem is that you cannot know in advance what their IP Address is going to be. And even when you find out once they are connected, it will change completely the next time that they log in.

Note - Once you disconnect from the Internet (or even get thrown off, as sometimes happens) then the IP Address is taken back from you by the Internet Company and given to someone else who has just connected. By sharing the numbers this way, they solved the problem of not having enough.

It would be wonderful if the IP Address numbering scheme could be expanded. Then everybody (and their dogs and their cats) could each have their own individual addresses to keep. In fact, steps are now being taken with a new IP Addressing system to do precisely that. Unfortunately today we are stuck with old IP Addressing system and it is going to be a little while before we are all moved over onto the new one.

Once you have understood the peculiarities of this IP Address numbering scheme, then it is relatively simple to get to grips with how a video linkup actually works. The first part of the procedure is that both you and your friend must connect to the Internet and consequently both be given a unique IP Address. This is done invisibly, but when we start the exercise I will show you how you can use the NetMeeting program to quickly see what it is. Let us now go through the process of making a call step by step. Assume that you both have the NetMeeting program running and that you will be the person originating the video phone-call...

❑ The process begins with your friend connecting on-line to the Internet (they are the '**called party**', you are the '**calling party**'). Your friend must look up her or his own IP Address at that particular moment. They then send you an email five minutes before the scheduled linkup time, telling you what their IP Address currently is (by writing '80.225.178.51' for example in the email). They must also remain on-line for the duration, until your call is received.

❑ You connect on-line to the Internet and look out for an email from them five minutes before the scheduled linkup time. When you have received it, you can then make a video phone-call to them by clicking the '**Place Call' button**. The program will respond with a little pop-up window, asking you to enter the IP Address for your friend. You enter the number and then click the **Call button.**

❑ The program now automatically sends information over the Internet and it is delivered directly to your friend's computer system. They already have NetMeeting running; consequently an **Incoming Call window** suddenly pops up telling them that a call is coming in from you.

❑ They answer the call by clicking an '**Accept' button**, and a few seconds later you are both connected to each other. You will then see a live video screen of each other respectively, and be able to talk to each other using your sound systems.

This is Absolute Magic! There can be no other way to describe it. Here you are, making a video phone-call to possibly the other side of the world, and it is costing you both at most the cost of a local telephone call. You might even be doing it for no extra cost at all, if you have one of the 'Anytime' type of Internet packages. Truly unbelievable!

10.3 - A quick word about Firewalls

Before we begin the next exercise, I quickly want to mention something else that may be important for your success. If either your computer, or that of the remote party, is using what is termed 'Firewall' software to protect it (see section 9.2 of *'Using Email for the First Time'* for more information about 'Firewalls'), then the Firewall may block any incoming communication from the other party and the video linkup will not work.

For the purpose of the exercise you should temporarily disable any such Firewall software so that you can initially get things working satisfactorily. When you know that everything is working fine, then you can re-introduce the Firewall software. It will need adjusting to allow the NetMeeting program to function properly, and some Firewall software can do this automatically. However, it is difficult to generalise about this in all cases. To try assist you, I shall be putting further information about this issue on my personal website (see next paragraph for the web address).

Now enough of all the rhetoric and promises! Let's go do this for real and introduce Exercise 40. Remember, if you don't have a friend or family member to try this with between yourselves, please read about the scheme on my web site at the web address www.billhall.me.uk, in the section titled 'Video Linkups'.

Exercise 40 – Making a video linkup

This exercise is to be performed jointly between you and a friend. Naturally, they too must have the correct equipment and have already performed Exercises 38 and 39 to install and configure the NetMeeting program. The first step is to make arrangements with your friend to be available for the video linkup at a particular date and time. We call this part of the process 'making a sked' (sked is a new buzz-word for 'scheduled meeting'). You can agree your sked date and time by email, a phone call or even writing a postal letter.

In making your arrangements, tell your friend that they need to be connected on-line to the Internet at least five minutes before the appointed date and time. They should have their NetMeeting program opened and running, and they will also need to have their email program opened and ready for use. Furthermore, ask them to press the **Play/Pause button** (see next picture) so that they can see their own camera image within the NetMeeting program window, as soon as they have it running. This proves that everything is working ahead of the sked and can save precious time. It also means that the moment you make the video linkup, you will see a picture of them on your screen.

For your part, we begin the exercise at the desktop at least five minutes before the sked time on the agreed date. Connect to the Internet in your normal way. When you are connected on-line, start up your own email program and minimise it using the **Minimise button** (the left-hand button of the group of three in the topmost right-hand corner). Now start the NetMeeting program running and click on the **Play/Pause button**, which is this one...

You should now see your own video image from your own camera. As an example of what you may be looking at, here is a picture of myself while using my own system. Your NetMeeting program should show you something similar (well maybe without the beard!) ...

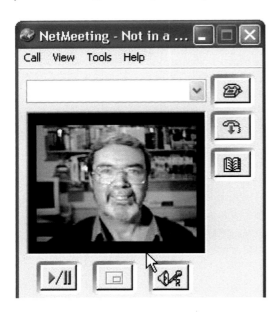

On a small point, notice how the Play/Pause button slightly changes the colouring of its symbols once it begins playing video (compare it with the last little picture, and you can see what I mean).

Returning to the actions for your friend, five minutes before the sked time, they need to click on the **Help button** from the main menu of the NetMeeting program. They should then select the **'About Windows NetMeeting'** option, as shown in the following picture.

250

This action pops up a message window that looks like the next picture...

At the very bottom of this picture we can see that the IP Address for your friend is '81.135.64.92'.

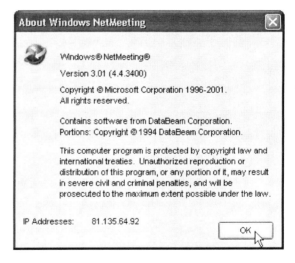

Your friend should now now send you an email with this IP Address number in the message contents. It should be short and look something like...

'Dear Bill, I am currently on-line and my IP Address is 81.135.64.92. Local time in Perth, Western Australia, is now 7.55pm. Best wishes from your friend down-under, Bruce'

You on the other hand have been watching the clock. In the UK, it will be 8 hours behind, which is 11.55am (Greenwich Mean Time). You receive your friend's email a minute or two after it was sent. From it, you now know your friend's IP Address and that they are waiting to link up with you.

You must click now on the **'Place Call' button**, as shown in the following picture.

This action pops up a window similar to the picture below. There you will see a vertical cursor flashing inside the To: box. If it should stop flashing for any reason, just click with your mouse pointer anywhere inside it to put it back again. Now type in the IP Address that your friend has just emailed to you. Be careful to check that there are four individual number parts separated by only three dots (full stops '.').

The individual number parts are always somewhere in the range 0 to 255. Now click on the **Call button** at the bottom of the window.

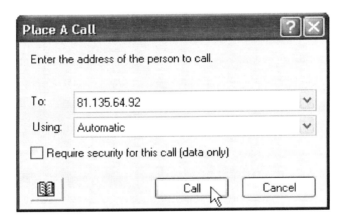

This last action is the critical one that sets the linkup mechanism in motion. What happens next is that your computer system will issue a **'Calling' message** across the Internet, duty-bound for the computer who's IP Address matches that which you have typed into the **To: box**. This message is an urgent one, and is treated by the Internet with a degree of urgency. It is not like an email message that can take much longer to travel across the Internet. Within seconds of sending the 'Calling' message, it should arrive at its destination, even at the other side of the world.

When it does arrive at the far end, it activates a **'Ringing' procedure** within the NetMeeting program that is running on your friend's computer. Your friend will hear a telephone ringing sound from her or his speakers, and will see a little message pop up on their monitor screen like that shown in this following picture.

They simply press the **'Accept' button** and the link will be made automatically.

Normally, there is a delay of a few seconds between information being transmitted from one computer across the Internet to the other (it varies obviously and will be slightly longer across continents). When the link is finally made, there should be a video picture in the NetMeeting program window and you should be able to talk face to face...

Isn't this just fantastic! Surely one of the marvels of our modern age!

You both may need to adjust the microphone position, so that it is picking up sound satisfactorily and you can hear each other loud enough, or you may need to adjust the volume control of your speakers. You may also need to adjust the position of your cameras and the lighting arrangements, so that your image is square within the video screen part of the program window and is adequately illuminated.

253

The picture quality that you receive is not going to win 'Arts, Film & Television Academy' awards, but nevertheless it is a stunning achievement.

There are many other features within the NetMeeting program that you can share with your friend during a video linkup besides the essential video and sound capability. We don't have the time or space to explore them all here in this exercise, but I will list them at the end of the section. In particular, I will give you details of using the **'Chat' facility**, which allows you to type messages to each other. This will be of interest to those who are lacking sound capability.

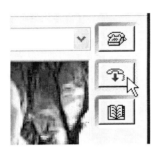

When you have thoroughly enjoyed the video linkup with your friend and you are ready to end the call, click on the **'End Call' button**, the middle one of the three shown in the following picture...

You will then hear an 'exclamation' sound in the speakers and you will lose the sight and sound from the remote location. You should now see your own picture again in the video square coming from your own camera. The video linkup has now been disconnected.

This concludes Exercise 40.

NetMeeting's additional facilities

Here are the additional feature buttons that you can activate as part of the video linkup using the NetMeeting program. You can see these along the bottom of the program window. They are not difficult to operate and I'm sure that you can have hours of fun with your friends and family on the Internet, exploring and experimenting with them ...

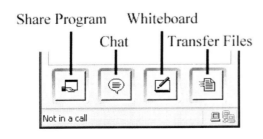

Share Program Whiteboard

Chat Transfer Files

When you use these features, new windows not only pop up on your computer screen, but they also pop up on your friend's computer screen too! Sometimes there is a slight delay before they show up at the far end, but they will show nevertheless.

The SHARE PROGRAM button

This button is used to share another program between the two of you during the video linkup. Take, for example, a word processing program. Just imagine the situation where you may want to work jointly on a particular document and to discuss some important changes to it. Not only will you be able to see the document on your own screen, but your friend will be able to see a copy of it as well. You can then argue about the changes you want to make, and debate the merits or otherwise of your proposed modifications! This is true even if your friend does not have a copy of the word processing program.

The CHAT button

This button allows you to type messages to each other that appear in a pop-up window of the screen. If you don't have sound capability available for some reason, then this is a good way to still communicate. Here is a typical example of its use...

To create the text, you need to type into the Message: box and then click on the button at the right-hand side to actually send it (you can also send it by pressing the Enter key on the keyboard instead, which is a much faster way of working). As you can see from the previous picture, each person's text appears in chronological order in the display box in the top half of the window. A vertical scroll bar appears once the 'conversation' becomes too big to all fit within the display area.

When you have finished using the Chat window, you will see a message asking you if you would like to save the text 'conversation'. You can then save the text to a file for future reference if you would like to.

The WHITEBOARD button

This button activates a 'whiteboard' for you both to draw upon. Again, the whiteboard is visible on both screens simultaneously, and you can both draw upon it together. It is very similar (but not quite identical) to the 'Paint' program that we have discussed before in the companion guide 'Using a Computer for the First Time'.

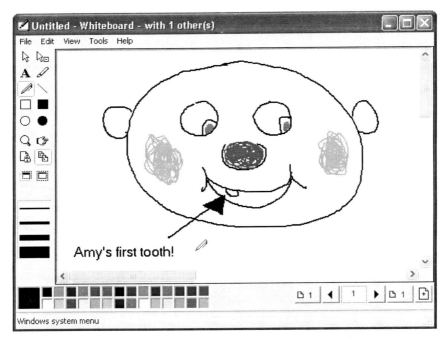

When you have finished with your drawing, you can save it as a new file to your computer's hard drive.

The TRANSFER FILES button

This button allows you to transmit any file (or group of files) that you specify to the remote end, during the linkup. The person receiving them can then save these files to their own hard drive. However, you have to be a little careful when using this facility to remember that the video link can only transmit information as fast as your Internet connection will allow it. If you are both using broadband then this will be very quick, but if you are using dial-up modems then it is going to be a lot slower. If you try to send a large file, or group of files, don't be surprised when the video and sound of the link become temporarily interrupted!

Okay, that covers the additional feature buttons of the NetMeeting program. There is a lot more that I could tell you, but space does not permit. Perhaps I shall return to this amazing program in a future book. Keep a check on my website for future information.

10.3 Closing remarks

This last section is the hardest part of any book to write. I would much prefer that I was embarking on a new exercise and introducing a new aspect of the subject, but sadly, time and space have both run out and I must bring things to a close. In these last few paragraphs, are there any words of wisdom about digital cameras that I can pass on to you from my personal experience? Let me have a think.

I can tell you that I bought my first digital camera in 1998. It was a very expensive device setting me back £450. The hours of pleasure I have had from it since though have amply repaid its cost and I would do it over again. Fortunately today, you don't have to spend the same amount of money because you can buy a much better camera for a lot less. But that is technical progress.

In this book I have introduced a specific camera and a specific printer, that is, the **epsilon 1.3 from Digital Dream**, and the **HP Photosmart 7150 from Hewlett Packard**, respectively. These are both current models that you can go out today and purchase. My reason for using specific models is that I am a firm believer in passing knowledge on by worked example. If I had made the book more general, and talked about cameras and printers in very general terms, then I could not have written quite as much detail as I have done and you the reader would not have had the practical benefit of worked exercises that you can copy. With computers and other electronic gadgets today, it is essential that you know the detail, or you can become frustrated very quickly. The choice of both devices has been fortunate, for they have many general characteristics that most other cameras and printers will also exhibit.

One such characteristic of the epsilon 1.3 camera is the way that it becomes a 'removable disk' when attached to a computer. My first digital camera did not do this, and I had to use special program software in order to get the digital pictures out of the camera and onto the computer's hard drive.

One bit of experience I can pass on to you is about Memory Cards. Don't limit yourself to having just one card. They are cheap enough to carry at least two around with you (one in the camera, one spare in a bag). The good thing about having a spare card is that when you fill up the one inside the camera with pictures (and it is very easy to do that when you are taking video clips) then you don't miss out on that next special 'photo opportunity' by trying to decide which old ones can be deleted, in order to make room for taking more. If you carry a spare Memory Card, then just pull out the full one and pop the spare empty one in. You can transfer all of your pictures on to the computer when you get back home, and free up both cards.

The same piece of advice goes for batteries. Don't just have enough for fitting one set in the camera. I always have four sets. I know from bitter experience that the worst thing is for your batteries to go flat on you at a family gathering or other important event. By having three spare sets, I can continue for a few days snapping away all day long, before I have to return to base and recharge them. By the way, rechargeable batteries are a must for digital cameras!

When I first bought my digital camera, I quickly realised that there are many bits and pieces that you also need to keep handy. I bought a medium sized zip bag with many pockets in it and a shoulder strap for carrying. This has proven itself to be a very good idea. In the pockets I keep my spare sets of batteries and Memory Card. I also have enough room in it to keep the USB cable. By keeping all these bits together in the one bag, if I am in a rush to go somewhere, I just grab the bag and dash. That way I don't forget and leave essential bits and pieces behind.

The personal trimmer device from **Dahle (UK) Ltd** is also a good investment and well worth buying. It gives your digital pictures a professional look and you can also make them any size you want up to the full paper size.

If for any reason you have difficulty getting hold of any products seen in this book, please feel free to write to me at P.O. Box 521, YORK, YO19 6XZ, England.

Sadly, we have now reached the end of our journey, and the end of this third book in the 'First Time' series. I am sure you will get many hours of fun from your digital camera. I have really enjoyed writing this book for you. Perhaps we may meet one day on the Internet, using our cameras for a video linkup!

Appendix

Registering your products and programs

In Chapter 3, we demonstrated how to install software from the Digital Dream CD-ROM, and in Chapter 5 we did the same for the Hewlett Packard software. At the time of installation, we were engaged in the middle of various procedures and it would have been problematic to break off to connect to the Internet to fulfil the registration requirements. Registration of your products and software is a good idea, for it allows you to get the full benefit of product warranties and it also allows you to get help from support staff, if you run into difficulties. Consequently, this appendix is provided to give you information about how you can now register your products and programs using the 'on-line' facilities over the Internet.

1 – Registering the epsilon 1.3 camera

To register your camera, connect to the Internet and visit the Digital Dream website at www.digitaldreamco.com. The first web page that you see invites you to choose your language. On the page that follows, click on the **'Users' button**. Then click on the 'Register your product and Members area' and follow this with a click on 'Register here'. You will then see a form to fill out with your details. All the boxes on the form marked with an asterisk ('*') are ones that must have information put into them. When you are ready, click the **Register button**.

2 – Registering the HP Photosmart printer

From the desktop, click on the **Start button** and select '(All) Programs'. From the next pop-up menu select 'Hewlett Packard', then 'Photosmart etc.' and finally 'Product Registration'. This shows you the 'HP Product

Registration' screen. Click on the **Register button**. If you are not connected to the Internet at this point, then your system will prompt for a connection. When you are 'on-line' click the **OK button** for the 'Secure Connection' message. You are then shown the first web page for registration. Follow the on-screen instructions and again you will eventually be presented with a form to fill out with your details.

3 – Registering MGI programs

Every time that you run any of the three MGI programs before you have registered, you will be presented with 'Online Registration' message. Click the **Continue button** when you see it. In a change from the other registration procedures outlined in 1 and 2, the MGI software presents you with a form before you have connected to the Internet. Complete the form appropriately and the click the **Register button**. This then prompts for an Internet connection. When you are 'on-line' it automatically attempts to send an email message, containing the details from the form.

An alternative method of registration is to click on ' Help' from the main menu of the program itself. Then select the Contents tab and select 'Product Registration'. Follow the on-screen instructions. When you are 'on-line' to the Internet, you will see an MGI form to complete, similar to the ones before.

Index

THE DIGITAL CAMERA COMPANY

epsilon 1.3

The epsilon 1.3 is featured in this book and comes with a host of extraordinary features. It is one of the cleverest and most compact digital cameras in the world. The brilliant programs that accompany it allow you to create beautiful and memory-ful photographic images to keep and cherish.

DIGITAL dream

Digital Dream Company Europe Ltd
Maybrook House, Dover, Kent, CT17 9AH, UK

hp photosmart 7150

www.hp.com/uk/create

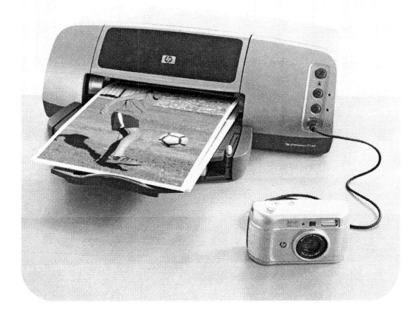

The HP Photosmart 7150 prints spectacular
photos using up to six inks. The easy
access front USB port allows quick
connection to an HP digital camera with
direct printing capability and direct photo
printing without a PC/Mac.

Consultancy
Writing & Lectures
Special Projects
MS Access Databases
Visual Basic Programs

Voice & Data Technology Ltd
P.O. Box 521
YORK   YO19 6XZ
United Kingdom

www.billhall.me.uk